# BRITISH QUAKER THEOLOGY SINCE 1895

# BRITISH QUAKER THEOLOGY SINCE 1895

Martin Davie

The Edwin Mellen Press
Lewiston•Queenston•Lampeter

**Library of Congress Cataloging-in-Publication Data**

This book has been registered with the Library of Congress

ISBN 0-7734-8611-9   (hard)

A CIP catalog record for this book is available from the British Library.

The Edwin Mellen Press
Box 450
Lewiston, New York
USA 14092-0450

The Edwin Mellen Press
Box 67
Queenston, Ontario
CANADA L0S 1L0

The Edwin Mellen Press, Ltd.
Lampeter, Ceredigion, Wales
UNITED KINGDOM SA48 8LT

Printed in the United States of America

*TO*
*ALYSON*

# CONTENTS

# PREFACE

One of the most fascinating (and arguably one of the most important) questions arising from the study of religious thought in the modern era is the way in which religious ideas are reformulated in the light of shifting understandings in the fields of the natural and social sciences. To what extent are religious ideas 'fixed'? And to what degree can they be restated without losing sight of their fundamental points of reference? Many observers of modern theology have suggested that some recent writers and schools of thought have been too ready to cut their links with the past and have become little more than pale and derivative reflections of trends within society as a whole.

In this important and highly relevant study, Dr Davie documents the loss of confidence within British Quakerism concerning its distinctive ideas. He shows not only how many modern Quakers felt the pressure of 'modern thought forms', but also how they were willing to accommodate their thinking in response - even when that led to the deliberate and systematic loss of Quaker identity.

Dr Davie's book is an important study in its own right, and must take its place as one of the most seminal works dealing with modern Quakerism. What gives it an even wider appeal, however, is its clear documentation of what happens to a religious grouping that loses sight of, or confidence in, its distinctive ideas. As Dr Davie shows so clearly, the inevitable result is a loss of identity, purpose and vision. What was once a well-focused group, with a clear sense of its identity and mission, becomes amorphous and derivative, seeking definition in terms of norms and ideas which are borrowed from others, and will be discarded once their utility has been expended. Rarely have we seen such a powerful account of the inevitable results of the liberal trends which dominated theology until recently. Dr Davie's important book is both a milestone in Quaker scholarship and a challenge to those who champion the cause of cultural accommodations.

Alister McGrath   Wycliffe Hall, Oxford

# ACKNOWLEDGEMENTS

No piece of scholarship or research is an entirely solitary effort, and this study, which was originally an Oxford University D.Phil. thesis, is no exception. I therefore have to thank a number of people for their assistance with this work.

First of all, many thanks to my supervisors, The Revd Dr Jan Womer and the Revd Dr Alister McGrath and to Mr John Punshon of Woodbrooke College Birmingham for their invaluable advice at various stages of its production. My thanks also go to the Librarians at the Bodleian Library, Friends House London, Mansfield College Oxford and Woodbrooke for helping me to obtain the source materials I have needed.

I am grateful to the following for permission to quote from copyright material:

Friends United Press for permission to quote from Joseph John Gurney *A Peculiar People* Richmond, Indiana: Friends United Press 1979.

Mary Philipson for permission to quote from the article 'Newcastle Upon Tyne Friends and Scientific Truth' written by her father Lawrence Richardson and published in the *Journal of the Friends Historical Society* vol XLV 1953

Oxford University Press for permission to quote from F L Cross and E A Livingstone (eds) *The Oxford Dictionary of the Christian Church* 2ed Oxford: OUP 1974

Quaker Home Service for permission to quote from a large number of books and pamphlets published by them and by their predecessor the Friends Home Service Committee and from the journal *Quaker Monthly*.

SPCK for permission to quote from Keith W Clements *Lovers of Discord* London: SPCK 1988

The Friend Publishers for permission to quote from material published in *The Friend* and *Friends Quarterly*

The New Foundation Fellowship for permission to quote from Lewis Benson's essay 'George Fox's Message is Relevant Today' published in *The Quaker Vision - New Foundation Publications* No.4 Gloucester: George Fox Fund 1979

The Quaker Universalist Group for permission to quote from Tim Miles *Towards Universalism* Leicester: Quaker Universalist Group N.D.

Finally, I wish to acknowledge the support and encouragement given to me by my wife, Alyson, and my parents John and Brenda Davie, without which this work would never have been completed, and to express particular thanks to my mother for her help in getting my thesis ready for publication.

Martin Davie                                                    London  January 1997

# Introduction

This study examines the nature and development of modern British Quaker theology during a period of uncertainty and transition, as Quakerism has sought to align itself with contemporary thought forms and to re-evaluate its relationship with its past. As will be shown, the 1895 Manchester conference of the Society of Friends gave a new direction to the movement as the views traditionally held within the Society were gradually relinquished and more liberal ones were adopted. The extent to which liberal views have since gained the ascendancy within the movement will be shown by an examination of Janet Scott's 1980 Swarthmore lecture.

These major changes within British Quaker thought have never been the subject of extended scholarly analysis. The factors which gave rise to them, and their consequences for modern Quakerism in Britain, have remained unexamined within the modern scholarly world. Even Adrian Hastings' magisterial *A History of English Christianity 1920-1985* [1] does not refer to Quaker theology, let alone explore the major developments within the movement to be documented in this work.

The very idea of a 'Quaker theology' requires explanation. Many Quakers, on learning that this study was being written, responded by observing that 'Quakers do not have any theology'. This reaction is understandable. Quakers do not place much emphasis upon the importance of theology; this leads outsiders, and even some Quakers, to draw the conclusion that Quakers do not have any theological opinions. However, it can readily be shown that Quakers do engage in theology. John Macquarrie defines theology as:

> ... the study which, through participation in and reflection upon a
> religious faith, seeks to express the content of this faith in the
> clearest and most coherent language available.[2]

---

[1] Adrian Hastings, *A History of English Christianity 1920-1985* London: William Collins 1986

[2] John Macquarrie, *Principles of Christian Theology* London: SCM revd.ed.1977 p.6

As will become clear in this study, Quakers have been, and still are, constantly engaged in trying to express their faith in the most clear and coherent language available.

Because Quaker theology worldwide is too large and complicated a subject to be covered in a single book , I shall limit myself to consideration of the theology of British Quakerism.  In order to understand what is meant by 'British Quakerism' it is necessary to know a little about the organisation of the Religious Society of Friends in the British Isles.  In the Quaker form of Church government, each separate branch of Quakerism in the world constitutes a separate Yearly Meeting. In the British Isles there are two such Yearly Meetings.  Quakers in England, Wales and Scotland, belong to London Yearly Meeting, those in Northern Ireland and the Irish Republic belong to Ireland Yearly Meeting.[3]  These two Yearly Meetings are as separate and distinct as branches of Quakerism as the Church of England and the Church of Ireland are as branches of the Anglican Communion, and in this thesis 'British Quakerism' refers to that branch which constitutes London Yearly Meeting.  Therefore I shall be primarily concerned with the theology produced by those Quakers from England, Wales, or Scotland who belong, or have belonged, to London Yearly Meeting.  For the sake of convenience I shall hereafter refer to this theology as 'British Quaker Theology'. Theology produced by other Quakers will only be studied in so far as it impinges on this area of primary concern.

This study focusses on British Quaker theology since 1895.  The development of that theology prior to that date has been examined in detail, whereas its development since then has been neglected.  The only writer to cover the whole of the period since 1895 is John Punshon in his book *Portrait in Grey*, and for reasons of space he is unable to deal with the major events of this period in detail.[4]  Why 1895?  As this study will demonstrate, this date represents a point of transition.  It marks the beginning of a shift within British Quakerism away from the then predominant Evangelical theology towards the Liberal and Radical theologies favoured in the years since.

---

[3] For details of Quaker organisation see Barry Wilsher *Quaker Organisation* London: Quaker Home Service 1986.

[4]  John Punshon *Portrait in Grey* London: Quaker Home Service 1984 Chapters 9 & 10

My starting point for the study of British Quaker theology since 1895 will be the 1980 Swarthmore Lecture *What canst thou say? Towards a Quaker Theology*[5] which was delivered by Janet Scott, a lecturer in Religious Education at Avery Hill College in London.

In order to understand why I have chosen this lecture as my starting point it is necessary to know something about the importance of the Swarthmore Lectures within British Quakerism.

In Churches which have ordained Ministers it is the role of these Ministers to teach and interpret the beliefs of their Churches to Church members and to those outside. As British Quakerism has no ordained Ministry this role is performed instead by a number of influential Quakers whose knowledge and spiritual maturity carry especial weight with their fellow Quakers.

These 'seasoned' or 'weighty' Friends, as they are technically called, carry out this role in a variety of ways. One of these is the delivery of the annual Swarthmore Lecture. This lecture, which is normally delivered to the yearly assembly of British Quakers and then published, was established in 1907 as part of an attempt to heighten theological awareness amongst Quakers in this country. In the words of the rubric printed in the front of the published version of every lecture, the lecture's function is to:

> ... interpret further to the members of the Society of Friends their message and mission: and secondly to bring before the public the spirit, the aims and fundamental principles of Friends.

Every year some seasoned Friend (the one exception to the tradition of a single Quaker delivering the lecture came in 1986 when it was delivered jointly by several members of the Quaker Women's Group) is invited by the Committee responsible for the Swarthmore Lecture to perform this function by lecturing on some matter which is of interest or concern to British Quakers. Thus in 1975 Ralph Hetherington, visiting Professor in Clinical Psychology in the University of Liverpool, lectured on the psychological interpretation of religious experience. In 1982 Gerald Priestland, former religious affairs correspondent of the BBC,

---

[5] Janet Scott *What canst thou say?* London: Quaker Home Service 1980.

lectured on a Quaker View of Christian Doctrine. In 1988 Harvey Gillman, Extension Secretary of Quaker Home Service (the Quaker Home Mission Committee), lectured on the experience of being a member of a minority culture. As the Lectures are given by influential Quakers on topics of interest or concern to Quakers in general they are reliable indicators of the development of British Quaker thinking. This can be verified by comparing the ideas expressed in the successive lectures since 1907 with what is known of the development of British Quaker thought from other sources.[6] Because this is so, Scott's lecture, which is about the nature of Quaker theology, can be seen to indicate the point reached by the development of British Quaker theology in 1980 and, since it has not altered significantly in the intervening decade, where it stands today.

Her lecture takes the form of a miniature Quaker systematic theology, a short but comprehensive account of what Scott sees as the essentials of Quaker belief. In her lecture Scott does two things. Firstly, she considers the five topics of Revelation, God, Christ, Man and Salvation which lie at the heart of all Christian theology. These headings are mine rather than hers but I believe they correctly summarise the subjects dealt with in her lecture. Secondly, she endeavours to produce a view of these topics which will both encompass the great diversity of thought to be found in modern Quakerism and also reflect the insights of feminism and the need to promote dialogue and unity betwen the world's religions.

The theology which Scott puts forward in her lecture likewise has two aspects.

Positively, she argues that God is revealed to us in a potentially infinite number of different ways and all of these have to be taken equally seriously and seen as complementary, even when they appear to contradict each other. She also maintains that God is seeking to bring everyone to salvation and that he will eventually succeed in doing so.

Negatively, in her consideration of Revelation, God, Christ, Man and Salvation she rejects the traditional Christian beliefs that Christ and the Bible give us a uniquely important revelation of God, that God is Triune, that Christ was God

---

[6] A fair comparison is the way in which successive Bampton lectures can be used to trace the development of Anglican thought.

incarnate, that humanity is afflicted by original sin, that Christ's death was necessary for our salvation and that in the end some people may be damned.

**Argument and Structure of this Study**

In examining the developments in British Quaker Theology since 1895 I shall show:

(1) The internal and external factors that have shaped these developments and how they are reflected in Scott's lecture.

(2) That these developments have led British Quaker theology to move progressively away from the mainstream theological tradition. I shall explain what I mean by the mainstream Christian theological tradition at the end of this chapter.

(3) Furthermore, that these developments have also caused British Quaker theology to move progressively away from the theology produced by the first Quakers in the seventeenth century.

In order to consider these three points my thesis will be divided into the following seven chapters.

CHAPTER ONE will give the background to the development of modern British Quaker theology by outlining the history of British Quakerism before 1895. It will also show that although Quaker theology did not conform completely to the mainstream Christian theological tradition it was nevertheless in general agreement with it.

CHAPTER TWO will show how the beginnings of modern British Quaker theology were influenced by developments in late nineteenth century English religious thought. It will show how these influences contributed to the replacement of Evangelical Quakerism by Liberal Quakerism as the dominant form of theology within the Society of Friends after a conference held in Manchester in 1895.

CHAPTER THREE will consider the theology of Liberal Quakerism as exemplified in the works of five prominent Liberal writers. It will demonstrate that in attempting both to re-affirm and re-interpret the Quaker theological tradition these writers in fact departed from it and moved further away from the mainstream Christian theological tradition than had their Quaker predecessors. This chapter will show how Liberal theology remained dominant in British Quakerism until the end of the 1950's and how a minority tradition of Evangelical Quakerism persisted until at least the 1940's.

CHAPTER FOUR will examine how developments in mainstream Christian theology contributed to the divisions which have arisen in British Quakerism since the 1960's. It will show how the Society of Friends has become split between a radical wing, that has departed further from Quaker tradition than did Liberal Quakerism, and a conservative wing which has remained closer to them, and how these two wings are themselves theologically divided.

CHAPTER FIVE will explore what a representative selection of British Quaker writers since the 1960's have had to say about the subjects of Revelation, God, Christ, Man and Salvation, addressed by Scott in her Swarthmore Lecture. It will argue that what they have said about these subjects indicates that contemporary British Quaker theology is now characterised by extreme diversity and, in general, by a marked divergence from the beliefs contained in both the mainstream Christian theological tradition and the Quaker tradition. It will also explain the reasons for this diversity and divergence.

CHAPTER SIX will show how Scott's theology faithfully reflects both the diversity and the departure from the mainstream Christian theological tradition and the Quaker tradition which mark contemporary Quaker thought.

CHAPTER SEVEN will summarise the findings of the previous six chapters and suggest a number of questions which these findings raise for contemporary British Quakerism.

It should be noted that, in accordance with Quaker usage, the words 'Quaker', 'Friend' and their derivatives will be used interchangeably throughout this thesis. The official title for the Quakers is 'The Religious Society of Friends', and individual Quakers are properly referred to by the title 'Friend', but the terms 'Quakers' and 'Quaker', which were originally nicknames, are now in equally common use.

### The Mainstream Christian Theological Tradition.

Earlier in this introduction I referred to the mainstream Christian theological tradition. I shall now explain what I mean by this term.

In his book *The Identity of Christianity* Stephen Sykes declares:

> ....it would not be unreasonable to suppose that conflict in
> Christianity is not accidental and occasional, but intrinsic and
> chronic and that Diversity...is the norm for Christianity.[7]

Sykes is surely correct. As can be seen from histories of the Church such as
Edwyn Bevan's *Christianity*[8] or Stephen Neill's *The Christian Society*,[9]conflict and
diversity have been part of Christianity from the beginning of its history to the
present day.

Christian theology too has not been exempt from conflict and diversity.
Works such as *A History of Christian Doctrine* edited by Hubert Cunliffe-Jones
and Benjamin Drewery[10] or Jaroslav Pelikan's *The Christian Tradition*[11] clearly
show that throughout the Church's history theologians have disagreed about the
meaning of Christian belief and have interpreted it in a wide variety of ways.

However, looking again at these works, or at collections of works by
Christian writers such as the *Library of Christian Classics*[12] or at collections of
Church Creeds and Confessions of Faith such as John Leith's *Creeds of the
Churches*[13]it can also be seen that, alongside all the arguments and variety, there
has also existed a continuous mainstream theological tradition which has agreed on
what Gabriel Fackre calls a "core of conviction" about the basics of Christian
belief.[14] That is to say, during the history of the Christian Church there have been a
number of basic Christian beliefs which have been accepted by the majority of
Christian theologians irrespective of the particular branch of the Church to which
they belonged. The clearest example of this is perhaps the way in which the beliefs
contained in the Apostles' Creed, the original form of the Nicene Constantinoplian

---

[7] Stephen Sykes *The Identity of Christianity* London: SPCK 1984.

[8] Edwyn Bevan *Christianity* London: O.U.P. 1963.

[9] Stephen Neill *The Christian Society* London: Collins 1964.

[10] *A History of Christian Doctrine* Hubert Cunliffe-Jones and Benjamin Drewery (eds.)
Edinburgh: T & T Clark 1980.

[11] Jaroslav Pelikan *The Christian Tradition* Chicago: University of Chicago Press Vols. 1-5
1971-89.

[12] *The Library of Christian Classics* London: S.C.M. Vols 1-26 1954-64.

[13] John Leith *Creeds of the Churches* Oxford: Basil Blackwell 1973.

[14] Gabriel Fackre *The Christian Story* Grand Rapids: Eerdmans 1978 p.15.

Creed of 381, and the Chalcedonian definition have been accepted over the centuries by Catholic, Protestant and Orthodox theologians alike.[15] To use an image coined by C.S.Lewis, such basic beliefs resemble a central hallway and the works of individual theologians are like rooms opening off it[16], or, to change the metaphor, they are like a theme upon which the works of individual theologians are variations. For instance, despite the wide differences between the theologies put forward by the Council of Trent and the Westminster Assembly, underlying both these theologies there is an acceptance of the beliefs found in the Nicene Constantinoplian Creed.[17] It is these basic beliefs which C.S.Lewis described as constituting "agreed, or common, or central, or 'mere' Christianity"[18]which I have in mind when I refer to the 'mainstream Christian theological tradition' and for the sake of clarity and brevity I shall use the term 'core of conviction' for this tradition during the remainder of this work.

It is true that there has been a minority of theologians who have dissented from the beliefs of the core of conviction. For example, theologians within the Unitarian tradition in Protestant Christianity have rejected the Nicene belief in the Trinity, while theologians within the Monophysite tradition in Eastern Christianity have rejected the Christology of the Chalcedonian definition. However this minority is the exception which proves the rule, since the fact that it has been a minority of theologians who have dissented from the core of conviction serves to underline the fact that the majority of theologians have adhered to it.

In seeking to establish that British Quaker theology has moved away from the core of conviction I shall be concerned with an issue of fact rather than of value. That is to say, I shall not be examining whether Quaker theology should have departed from the core of conviction but simply whether it has actually done so.

---

[15] Although the Apostles' Creed is a Western Creed the beliefs which it contains have also been accepted by Eastern Orthodox theologians, see, for example, Kallistos Ware *The Orthodox Way* London and Oxford: Mowbrays 1979 and Vladimir Lossky *The Mystical Theology of the Eastern Church* London and Cambridge: James Clarke 1957.

[16] C.S.Lewis *Mere Christianity* London: Geoffrey Bles 1952 pp.XI-XII.

[17] See the texts of the *Westminster Confession* and the *Decrees of the Council of Trent* in Leith op.cit. pp.192-230 and 399-439.

[18] Lewis op.cit. p.VIII.

# Chapter One
# The Rise and Development of Quakerism

Although this study will concentrate on developments since 1895, I shall begin by examining the development of British Quakerism and Quaker theology in the two and a half centuries prior to that date. I shall do this for two reasons. Firstly, because the development of British Quakerism since 1895 has been partly determined by its previous history and some knowledge of this history is necessary for a proper understanding of this development. Secondly, an examination of British Quaker history before 1895 will enable me to demonstrate the relationship between Quaker theology and the core of conviction before that date.

## The Early Period

The Dutch Quaker historian William Sewel begins his standard 1717 *History of the rise, increase, and progress of the Society of Friends* by giving an account of the background to the emergence of Quakerism from 1652 onwards. In this he states that Quakerism arose in England in the mid-seventeenth century because, as a result of the Continental and English Reformations:

> ...the stem of human traditions and institutions had been shaken strongly, yet much of the root was left. Therefore it pleased God, who is used to enlighten Men gradually, to make yet a clearer discovery of his truth, which in some places already darted forth its beams to mankind, in a time when many godly people were zealously seeking after a further manifestation of the will of God from a sense that notwithstanding all their outward observations of

religious performances there still stood a partition wall, whereby the
soul was hindered from living at peace with its Creator.[1]

Omitting Sewel's theological interpretation, he is saying that Quakerism
arose in England in the mid-seventeenth century as a development of the
Reformation at a time when many pious people were looking for a further
manifestation of God's will, because, in spite of their religious activities, they still
did not feel at peace with God. Just as the Reformation took place ultimately
because people did not feel they had attained peace with God through late
Mediaeval Catholicism, so also Quakerism emerged because people did not feel
that they had attained it through 17th century English Protestantism. This
understanding of the background to the rise of Quakerism reflects that put forward
by the earliest writers on the subject such as William Penn in his works *The rise
and progress of the people called Quakers* published in 1694, and *Primitive
Christianity revived in the Faith and Practice of the people called Quakers*
published in 1696.[2] It is also the explanation of the background to the rise of
Quakerism generally accepted by historians of the period.[3]

The reasons for the widespread religious dissatisfaction to which Sewel
refers are well summarized by Punshon in Portrait in Grey. He contends that in the
middle of the seventeenth century the failings of the Church and its clergy,
together with the emphasis on sin in the prevailing theology, meant that:

> the generality of Christians were clear that they were living at a
> time of grave crisis. Most were content to let others worry for
> them, but for those who felt a personal responsibility there was a
> heavy burden as they contemplated a church that fell so far short of
> what they felt it should be. There was disunity and a persecuting
> spirit, a clergy which often displayed worldly ambition rather than

---

[1] William Sewel *History of the rise increase and progress of the Society of Friends* Lindfield:
Friends Library vol.5 1833 pp.14-15

[2] William Penn *The rise and success of the people called Quakers* London 1694 and *Primitive
Christianity revived in the Faith and Practice of the people called Quakers* London: 1696

[3] See, for instance, Robert Barclay *The inner life of the Religious Societies of the Commonwealth*
London: Hodder and Stoughton 1879, Hugh Barbour *The Quakers in Puritan England*, New
Haven and London: Yale U.P. 1964 chs. 1-3, William C. Braithwaite *The beginnings of
Quakerism* London: Macmillan 1912 ch.1, Punshon op.cit. chs. 1-2 and Michael Watts *The
Dissenters* Oxford: OUP 1978 pp.186-208

religious achievement, and a prevailing theology that all too often confirmed and worsened the sense of sin and inadequacy from which such people desperately sought relief. They suffered from a deep spiritual disturbance. They had mostly been through an experience of conversion, sometimes sudden, sometimes slow, but the joyous freedom of which the Bible spoke was denied them. They felt chained to the letter, but they also knew that somewhere there was the life. The Christ they were offered was too small. He was in the Book and not in the world, and too many clergy wished to keep him there. So at a deep level many thousands of people were in despair in their heart of hearts many people knew that the Reformation, indeed religion had reached a dead end. Restoration, true redemption would come, but not yet.[4]

The following quotation from the early Quaker writer Isaac Penington gives an example of what these people were looking for. Writing in a tract entitled *A brief account concerning the People called Quakers* and looking back to the time before he became a Quaker he states:

We wanted the presence and power of his (God's) Spirit to be inwardly manifested in our spirits. We had (as I may say) what we could gather from the letter, and endeavoured to practise what we could read in the letter, but we wanted the power from on high, we wanted life, we wanted the presence and fellowship of our beloved; we wanted the knowledge of the heavenly feast and kingdom, and an entrance into it, and the holy dominion and reign of the lord of life over the flesh, over sin, and over death in us.[5]

The catalyst which caused Quakerism to emerge as the answer that people like Penington were seeking, was the preaching of George Fox. Fox was born in 1624 to a Puritan family in what is now Fenny Drayton in Leicestershire. As Watts writes in *The Dissenters*,[6] in 1643:

when he was nearly nineteen and apprenticed to a shoemaker he was embarrassed by being in the company of two Puritans who, when visiting a fair, asked him to join with them in what turned out to be a drinking bout. This revelation of disparity between religious profession and moral behaviour came as a profound shock to the

---

[4] Punshon op.cit. p.35

[5] Isaac Penington *Collected Works* Vol 3 London: James Phillips 1784 3rd ed p.419

[6] Watts op.cit. p.186

young apprentice and led him to embark on a spiritual pilgrimage in search of perfection.[7]

Fox's spiritual pilgrimage lasted some four years. At the end of it, not having found what he was looking for from any of the clergy or from any of the dissenting religious groups such as the General Baptists he reached a point of religious despair.

In this despair he felt he heard the voice of God telling him that Jesus Christ Himself could provide that for which he was looking. He was later to record this experience in his *Journal*:

> ....as I had forsaken all the priests so I left all the separate preachers also, and those called the most experienced people; for I saw that there was none among them all that could speak to my condition. And when my hopes in them and in all men were gone, so that I had nothing outwardly to help me nor could tell what to do, then, o then, I heard a voice which said, 'There is one, even Christ Jesus, that can speak to thy condition', and when I heard it my heart did leap for joy. Then the Lord did let me see why there was none upon the earth that could speak to my condition, namely, that I might give him all the glory; for all are concluded under sin , and shut up in unbelief as I had been, that Jesus Christ might have the pre-eminence, who enlightens, and gives grace, and faith, and power.[8]

In the next year, 1648, Fox felt that, following this revelation, he was commissioned by God to go as a missionary to bring people to Christ through the Spirit, and that bringing people to Christ meant bringing them out of the existing churches. To quote again from his *Journal*:

> I was sent to turn people from darkness to the light, that they might receive Christ Jesus, for to as many as should receive him in his light, I saw that he would give power to become the sons of God, which power I had obtained by receiving Christ. And I was to direct people to the Spirit that gave forth the Scriptures, by which they might be led into all truth, and so up to Christ and God, as they had been who gave them forth. And I was to turn them to the grace of God, and to the Truth in the heart, which came by Jesus, that by

---

[7] For details see John W.Nickalls (ed.) *The Journal of George Fox* London: Religious Society of Friends 1975 pp.2-3

[8] ibid p.11

this grace they might be taught, which would bring them into salvation, that their hearts might be established by it, and their words might be seasoned, and all might come to know their salvation nigh. For I saw that Christ had died for all Men, and was a propitiation for all, and had enlightened all men and women with his divine and saving light, and that none could be a true believer but who believed in it. I saw that the grace of God, which brings salvation, had appeared to all men, and that the manifestation of the Spirit of God was given to every man to profit withal.

I was to bring people off from all their own ways to Christ, the new and living way, and from their own Churches, which men had made and gathered, to the Church in God, the general assembly written in heaven, which Christ is the head of, and off from the world's teachers made by men, to learn of Christ, who is the way, the truth, and the life, of whom the Father said,'This is my beloved son, hear ye him'; and off from all the world's worships, to know the spirit of Truth in the inward parts, and to be led thereby, that in it they might worship him, which spirit that that worshipped not in knew not what they worshipped.[9]

In response to this commission Fox spent the next four years or so ( the chronology at this point in the *Journal* is imprecise) in an itinerant evangelistic ministry in the North Midlands and Yorkshire, interrupted by two long imprisonments in Nottingham and Derby on account of his preaching.[10] During this period Fox began to convince people of the truth of his message, and gathered together the first Quaker meetings. In 1652, a breakthrough occurred which led to the emergence of Quakerism as a mass religious movement.

This breakthrough took place in the fell country of North Lancashire, North West Yorkshire, and South Westmorland. In his book *The Quakers in Puritan England*,[11] Barbour shows that in the middle of the seventeenth century this was a backward and neglected area of England, one that had not been strongly affected by orthodox Calvinist Puritanism, and one in which the parochial clergy appear to have exercised little effective pastoral care. The result was the sort of religious dissatisfaction to which I referred earlier, and the existence of a network of separatist congregations independent of their local parish churches.

---

[9] ibid pp.34+35

[10] ibid pp.39-103

[11] Barbour op.cit. ch.3

At Whitsuntide in 1652 Fox began to preach to these separatist congregations[12]and as a result a revival began similar to the 'Evangelical Revival' in Britain, and the 'Great Awakening' in America, in the following century.[13] During the first couple of years this revival was confined to the North of England, but from the summer of 1654 Quaker missionaries fanned out over the rest of England. Subsequently the Quaker message was spread to the rest of the British Isles, to the English colonies in North America, to Europe, and as far afield as Alexandria in North Africa.[14]

As Barbour indicates in *The Quakers in Puritan England*,[15] the message proclaimed by the early Quaker missionaries was about what they called the 'Lamb's War'. A clear example is the 1657 tract *The Lamb's war against the Man of Sin*, which was written by the early Quaker leader James Nayler. In this "compact summary of Friends' understanding of the basic conflict of good and evil"[16] Nayler makes use of the imagery of Rev.17:14 to make three basic points.

Firstly, Nayler declares how God has manifested Himself through Christ (the Lamb) in order to make war on the Devil:

> And now his appearance in the Lamb (as ever it was when iniquity was full) is to make war with the god of this world.[17]

Secondly, God's purpose in this warfare is to redeem out of their captivity of the Devil:

> ...all who will but believe in the Lamb and are weary of this service and bondage to his enemy, and who will but come forth and give

---

[12] Fox op.cit. pp.106ff

[13] For this comparison see Hugh Barbour and Arthur Roberts (eds.) *Early Quaker Writings* Grand Rapids: Eerdmans 1973 P.22

[14] For details of this missionary activity see Braithwaite op.cit.chs.8-10, 14, and 16

[15] Barbour op.cit. p.40

[16] Barbour and Roberts op.cit. p.104

[17] James Naylor *The Lamb's War against the Man of Sin* London: 1657 p.2

their names and hearts to join with him and bear his image and testimony openly before all men[18]

and to reverse the results of the Fall by restoring  "all things new as they were in the beginning, that God alone may rule in his own work".[19]

Thirdly, God's method in this war is to give His light into the hearts of all people so that they may learn:

> ...what he is displeased with, what is with him and what is against him;  what he owns and what he disowns, that so all may know what is for destruction, to come out of it, that so he may save and receive all that are not wilfully disobedient and hardened in the pleasure of this world against him.[20]

Those who respond to the revelation of God's will which His light brings are accepted by God and given the power to share, according to their human measure, in His moral perfection "as many as turn at his reproof he doth receive and gives them power in spirit and life to be as he is in their measure".[21]

Becoming a Quaker meant participating in the 'Lamb's War' by allowing God's light in your heart to reveal the evil in you, being willing to foresake this evil, and receiving God's power to live a life of moral perfection through obedience to the light's direction. This process of spiritual warfare is described repeatedly in early  Quaker journals.[22] As part of their participation in the 'Lamb's War' those who became Quakers altered their manner of life and adopted distinctive forms of speech and behaviour, known as 'Testimonies'.  These were intended to be a witness to those as yet unconvinced of the truth of the Quaker message, unresponsive to God's light in their hearts, and acting in a way which the Quakers believed to be evil. In the words of Fox in his 1661 tract *A line of righteousness stretched forth*, the Quakers' ideal was that it could be said of them:

---

[18] ibid p.2

[19] ibid p.2

[20] ibid p.3

[21] ibid p.3

[22] For examples see Barbour and Roberts op.cit. Part B. 'Journals of lives led by the light'.

> Your life and your words are a Terrour to all that speak not Truth;
> in your dealings and to all that act not truly and righteously in their
> doings, your lives do judge them; and through your Constancy,
> Faithfulness and life, which is Everlasting, you bring many to
> Amendment: For both life, Actions, Words, and Conversation
> preach....to the unrighteous world.[23]

Examples of such 'Testimonies' to the unconcerned were the Quakers' use of "thee" and "thou", and their refusal to take oaths. In seventeenth century England people would use "thee" and "thou" when addressing their social inferiors and their peers, but "you" when addressing their social superiors. Quakers felt that this custom served merely to encourage un-Godly pride in those addressed as "you". Therefore they addressed everyone, regardless of rank, as "thee" or "thou" in order to witness against this pride. Similarly, although Quakers justified their refusal to take oaths on Biblical grounds citing Matthew 5:33-37, and James 5:12, their fundamental reason was to testify against the fallenness of a world which required oaths to make sure that the truth was told or a promise kept.[24]

The well known Quaker belief in pacifism also had its origins in the Quaker belief in the 'Lamb's War'. Quakers believed that the 'Lamb's War' could not be fought with earthly weapons and that therefore human warfare was wrong. In an undated *Paper to Friends to Keep out of Wars and Fights* Fox writes:

> Christ's kingdom is not of this world, it is peaceable; and all that be
> in strifes are not of his kingdom, and all such as pretends to fight
> for the Gospel (the Gospel is the power of God, before the devil or
> fall of man was), which are ignorant of the Gospel, and all that talk
> of fighting for Sion are in darkness; for Sion needs no such helpers.
> And all such as profess themselves to be ministers of Christ and
> Christians, and go beat down the whore with outward carnal
> weapons, the flesh and the whore are got up in themselves in a blind
> zeal. That which beats down the whore, which got up by inward
> ravening from the spirit of God, the beating down of the whore
> must be by the inward rising of the sword of the spirit within.[25]

---

[23] George Fox *A line of righteousness stretched forth* London: 1661 p.8

[24] See Barbour op.cit. ch.6 for more details of the origin and significance of the Quaker testimonies.

[25] George Fox Swarthmore Manuscript 7:47 text in Barbour and Roberts op.cit. p.407

Becoming a Quaker did not only mean participation in the 'Lamb's War', and the adoption of the 'Testimonies'. It also meant becoming a member of the Quaker community. This was because the Quaker proclamation was concerned not only with individual conversions, but also with the restoration of the Christian Church. The first Quakers believed that, as Francis Howgill puts it in his 1661 tract *The Glory of the True Church discovered*,[26] at the end of the Apostolic era "the true Church fled into the wilderness", and " the false Church came into visibility _ to sit as Queen upon the waters"[27] with the result that:

> ...things are brought in and invented, which were not constitutions of Christ or the Primitive Churches; and these the world hath wandered after, in the dark night of Apostasy. And the worship hath been made up, and compacted partly from the Jews worship, partly from the Heathen, and partly from themselves, being corrupted, and the Scriptures perverted every way to prove all this deceit.[28]

They also believed, however, (like some of today's 'House Churches') that in their day the true church had emerged out of the wilderness and that they were this true church. As Barbour writes in *The Quakers in Puritan England*:[29]

> The Friends regarded themselves as 'primitive Christianity revived' in the 'last days'. They spoke and thought of themselves as the 'true church'. They rejected the sacraments and ordinances of all other churches throughout history, not simply because the forms were unbiblical or contrary to the "gospel order" but because these groups were not true churches". The Quaker community was the one true Church, and consequently those converted by Quaker preaching were expected to join it.[30]

---

[26] Francis Howgill The Glory of the True Church discovered London: 1661 p.30

[27] See Rev. 12 & 13

[28] For a detailed explanation of early Quaker belief about the apostasy of the Church see Isaac Pennington *Some positions concerning the Apostacy from the Christian Spirit and Life* London: 1680

[29] Barbour op. cit. p.189

[30] See also on this point Punshon op.cit. p.50

The form of worship of this one true church was based on two ideas which had been anticipated in some of the Baptist and Separatist circles from which many of the first Quaker converts came[31] – the idea of silent worship, and the idea of what we would now call charismatic ministry.  The one true church was to worship God in silence, and vocal ministry was to arise out of this silence only when God should raise it up through the power of the Holy Spirit.  In the words of Penington in *A brief account concerning silent meetings*:[32]

> And this is the manner of their (the Quakers) worship. They are to wait upon the  Lord, to meet in the silence of flesh, and to watch for the stirrings of his life, and the breaking forth of his power amongst them. And in the breakings forth of that power they may pray, speak, exhort, sing or mourn etc. according as the Spirit teaches, requires, and gives utterance_ God is to be worshipped in spirit, in his own power and life, and this is at his own dispose. His church is a gathering in the Spirit. If any Man speak there, he must speak as the oracle of God, as the vessel out of which God speaks, as the trumpet out of which God gives the sound. Therefore there is to be a waiting in silence, till the Spirit of the Lord moves to speak and also gives words to speak.

This silent worship and charismatic ministry left no place for liturgy nor for an ordained ministry.  There was also no place in it for the sacraments of Baptism and Communion because the Quakers believed that true Baptism and Communion were inward and purely spiritual rather than outward and sacramental.  For example, Edward Burrough declares in his 1654 tract *Truth defended or certain false accusations answered:*

> Baptism we own and witness, which is, with one spirit, into one Body, into the Death of Christ: And we deny all Baptisms which are imagined and imitated, by conforming the outward Man to the outward letter, which is but a likeness of the true Baptism"_ "Communion we live in, which is, in the light by the Spirit, which will endure eternally; and we deny the world's imitation, which is in

---

[31] See Watts op. cit. pp.191-2  and Punshon op.cit. p.61

[32] Penington *Collected Works* vol.4  London: James Phillips 1784 pp.58-6

word and declaration and visible carnal things which will pass
away.[33]


## Early Quakerism and the Core of Conviction

Having described the emergence and original message of Quakerism, I shall
now examine what the first Quakers had to say about Revelation, God, Christ,
Man, and Salvation, the topics dealt with by Scott in her Swarthmore Lecture.
This will enable me to determine how far their treatment of these subjects agreed
with the core of conviction. It will also establish a basis for comparison so that I
shall later be able to show to what extent the treatment of these topics by Scott
and other recent Quaker writers agrees with the teaching of the early Quakers.

On the subject of *Revelation* the first Quakers believed that, in the words
of Penn in *Primitive Christianity revived* "God through Christ hath placed a
principle in every Man to inform him of his duty and to enable him to do it".[34]

They believed that, through Christ, God gives a revelation of Himself to all
human beings in the form of an internal monitor, what Penn calls a "principle", in
order that they may know what God requires and be enabled to do it. This is the
same idea we have already encountered in Fox's description of his call to turn
people to the Spirit and to the light of Christ, and in Nayler's declaration that God
has put His light into the hearts of all Men.

As Penn goes on to state, the first Quakers further believed that this
internal monitor is "something that is Divine, and though in Man, YET NOT OF
MAN, but of God; that comes from him, and leads to him all those that will be led
by it".[35]

Although believing the monitor was divine, they did not agree on the use of
any one theological term to describe it. To quote Penn again "There are divers
ways of speaking they (the Quakers) have been led to use by which they declare

---

[33] Edward Burrough *The Memorable Works of a son of Thunder and Consolation* London: 1672
p.12

[34] Penn *Primitive Christianity revived* pp.1-2

[35] ibid p.2

and express what this principle is".[36]   For instance, the first Quakers sometimes spoke of their monitor as Christ, and at other times as the Light, or as the Light of Christ, or as the Spirit.[37]   As Barbour notes "Friends spoke of Light, the Spirit, and Christ within so interchangeably that no uniform distinction can be made clear".[38]

The first Quakers also believed that God has revealed Himself through the Bible, but held that revelation through the Bible was subordinate to that through the inward monitor. The early Quaker apologist Robert Barclay,[39] writing in his 1676 *Apology for the true Christian Divinity*, and describing  the internal monitor as the Spirit, states:

> From the revelations of the Spirit of God to the faithful have come the scriptures of Truth, which contain: (1) a faithful historical account of the actings of God's people in divers ages and with many singular and remarkable acts of God which they experienced, (2) a Prophetical account of several things, whereof some are already past, and some are yet to come, (3) a full and ample account of all the chief Principles of the Doctrine of Christ held forth in divers precious declarations, exhortations and sentences, which, by the movings of God's Spirit, were at several times, and upon sundry occasions spoken and written unto some Churches and their Pastors.
> Nevertheless, because they are only a declaration of the Fountain, and not the Fountain itself, therefore they are not to be esteemed the principal ground of all truth and knowledge, nor yet the adequate primary rule of Faith and Manners. Nevertheless, as that which giveth a true and faithful testimony of the first foundation, they are and may be regarded a Secondary Rule, subordinate to the Spirit, from which they have all their excellency and certainty.[40]

This understanding of revelation partly agreed and partly disagreed with the core of conviction.

---

[36] ibid p.2

[37] See Fox's *Journal* throughout for the use of all four descriptions.

[38] Barbour op.cit. p.110

[39] An ancestor of the later historian Robert Barclay.

[40] Barclay *Apology* London: 1678 The Third Proposition 'Concerning the Scriptures'.

It agreed in seeing the definitive revelation of God as given to us through Christ. Over the centuries there has been debate between Christian theologians on the subject of revelation. They have argued about the place of reason, creation and tradition in revealing God[41]. Nevertheless, the core of conviction has consistently held that the definitive revelation of God comes to us through Jesus Christ[42] and the early Quakers accepted this idea as well. For them, revelation through the internal monitor was not an alternative to revelation through Christ. It was, rather, the mode in which revelation through Christ became real in the life of an individual.

This understanding disagreed with the core of conviction in seeing God's revelation through Christ as being mediated to us primarily through the inward monitor and only secondarily through Scripture. The core of conviction has held that the revelation of God in Christ is made known to us primarily through the witness of the Bible, and that the Bible is therefore the primary source of our knowledge of God and the primary authority for Christian faith and practice.[43]

The early Quakers held that the internal monitor and not the Bible is the primary source of our knowledge of God, and the primary authority for Christian faith and practice.

However, it should be noted that while in theory the Bible held only a secondary place in the theology of the early Quakers, in practice it had the status

---

[41] See Alan Richardson *Christian Apologetics* London: SCM 1949 and the essays on 'Scripture and Tradition' by Oscar Cullmann and Joseph Geiselmann in Hans Kung, Karl Barth, Oscar Cullmann et al *Christianity Divided* London and New York: Sheed and Ward 1962 pp.3-72

[42] See, for example, *Epistle to Diognetus* Pt 1:7 in Maxwell Staniforth (ed.) *Early Christian Writings* Harmondsworth Penguin 1978 p.178. Heinrich Bullinger *The Fourth Decade* Parker Society edition Cambridge: CUP 1851 pp.149-50 and Macquarrie op.cit. p.270.

[43] See St.Augustine *The City of God* BkXI Ch.3 Tr. Henry Bettenson, Harmondsworth: Penguin 1972 p.431. The Edwardine Homily of 1547 *A fruitful exhortation to the reading and knowledge of Holy Scripture* in Leith op.cit. pp.231-9 and Kallistos Ware *The Orthodox Way* London: Mowbrays 1979pp.146-7. The concept of the primary authority of Scripture is often thought of as a specifically Protestant idea. Such is not the case. For example, as James Atkinson points out in chapter eight of his book *Martin Luther Prophet to the Church Catholic* [Exeter: Paternoster Press 1983] at the Reformation the authority of the Scriptures was axiomatic for both Rome and the Reformers alike. The difference between Protestantism on the one hand and Roman Catholicism and Orthodoxy on the other has not been about whether the Bible is the primary authority for Christian faith, but about how its teaching is to be understood, and the place of tradition in its interpretation.

of a primary authority. This was for two reasons. Firstly, the early Quakers held
that any doctrine or action which was contrary to the Scriptures was to be
rejected. In the words of Barclay, they believed:

> Whatever doctrine is contrary to their testimony may properly be
> rejected as false. We are very willing for all of our doctrines and
> practices to be tried by them. We have never refused to honour
> them as the judge and test for any disputes we have had on matters
> of doctrine. We are even willing to allow this to be stated as a
> positive maxim. Anything which anyone may do while claiming to
> be led by the Spirit, which is contrary to the Scriptures, may be
> considered as a delusion of the devil.[44]

Secondly, as Punshon notes, the early Quakers "refused to engage in theological
speculation that went beyond the concepts and vocabulary of Scripture"[45] and as a
result their statements of belief consisted almost entirely of the citation and
exposition of Biblical texts.

On the subject of *God*, the first Quakers agreed with the core of conviction
in seeing God in Trinitarian terms. During continuous debate about the doctrine of
God, the core of conviction has insisted on maintaining a Trinitarian concept of
God, even though the precise nature of the Trinity has been understood in a variety
of different ways.[46]

Although the first Quakers objected to the Patristic doctrine of the Trinity,
classically summarised in the 'Nicene' creed, because they held it was non-Biblical
and its language about the 'persons' of the Trinity imperilled God's unity,[47] they
too took a Trinitarian view of God because they believed that this accorded with
both the witness of the Bible and their own experience. Thus Penington writes in a
tract of 1660 that:

---

[44] Barclay op.cit. Prop.3 Section VI

[45] Punshon op.cit. pp.95-6

[46] See Christopher B.Kaiser *The Doctrine of God* London: Marshall Morgan and Scott 1982 and
also the *Nicene Creed* text in Henry Bettenson (ed.) *Documents of the Christian Church* 2ed.
Oxford: OUP 1979 p.26. Article 1 of the *Augsburg Confession* of 1530 text in Leith op.cit.
pp.67-8 and T.F.Torrance *Reality and Scientific Theology* Edinburgh: Scottish Academic Press
1985 p.186.

[47] See Donald S. Nesti *Grace and Faith: the means to salvation* Pittsburgh: Catholic and Quaker
Studies No.3 1975 pp.152-5

concerning the Sacred Trinity. They (the Quakers) generally, both
in their speakings and their writings, set their seal to the truth of
that Scripture, 1 John 5:7. That 'there are Three that bear record in
heaven, the Father, the Word, and the Holy Spirit'. That these
Three are distinct, as three several beings, or persons; this they read
not; but in the same place, they read, that 'they are One'. And thus
they believe, their being to be One, their life One, their light One,
their wisdom One, their power One; and he that knoweth and seeth
any One of them, knoweth and seeth them all, according to that
saying of Christ's to Philip: 'He that hath seen Me, hath seen the
Father', John 14:9. Three there are, and yet One; thus they have
read in the Scriptures, and this, they testify, they have had truly
opened to them by that very Spirit which gave forth the Scripture,
insomuch that they certainly know it to be true, and own the thing
from their very hearts.[48]

In 1668 William Penn was committed to the Tower of London after writing
a tract entitled *The Sandy Foundation Shaken* in which he attacked the idea of a:
"Trinity of Distinct and Separate Persons in the Unity of Essence"[49] on the
grounds that it was contrary to the Biblical teaching of the unity of God. However,
the fact that Penn published this tract does not mean that he rejected belief in the
Trinity, as can be seen from his later work *A key opening the way to every
common understanding* in which he declares that the Quakers:

....believe in the Holy Three, or Trinity of Father, Word and Spirit,
according to Scripture. And that these Three are truly and properly
one: of ONE NATURE as well as will.[50]

On the subject of *Christ*. The first Quakers agreed with the core of
conviction in accepting the Biblical witness to His nature and activity. The identity
and significance of Jesus Christ has been understood and interpreted in many ways
in the course of the development of Christian doctrine.[51] However, the generally
agreed starting point for Christology has been an acceptance of the testimony to

---

[48] Isaac Penington *An examination of the Grounds and causes etc.* London: 1660 pp.9-10.

[49] William Penn *The Sandy Foundation Shaken* London: 1668 p.12.

[50] William Penn *A key opening the way to every common understanding* London: 1694 p.14.

[51] See H.R.Mackintosh *The Doctrine of the Person of Christ* Edinburgh: T & T Clark 1912 and
Klaus Runia *The present-day Christological debate* Leicester: IVP 1984.

Christ borne by the Bible[52] and the first Quakers shared this starting point as can be seen in the following extract from Burrough's 1657 *Declaration to all the World of Our Faith*:

> Concerning Christ we believe that he is one with the Father, and was with him before the world was; and what the Father worketh it is by the Son; for he is the arm of God's salvation, and the very power and wisdom of the creator; and was, is, and is to come, without beginning or end. And we believe that all the prophets gave testimony of him, and that he was made manifest in Judea and Jerusalem, and did the work of the Father, and was persecuted of the Jews, and was crucified by his enemies; and that he was buried, and rose again, according to the Scriptures. And we believe he is now ascended on high, and exalted at the right hand of the Father for evermore; and that he is glorified with the same glory that he had before the world was; and that even the same that came down from heaven, is ascended up to heaven, and the same that descended is he that ascended. And we believe that he that was dead is alive, and lives for evermore; and that he cometh, and shall come again, to judge the whole world with righteousness, and all people with equity and shall give to every man according to his deeds at the day of Judgment.... [53]

On the basis of its acceptance of the testimony of the Bible the core of conviction has also consistently held to a belief in the Divinity of Christ[54] and the first Quakers subscribed to this belief also. Thus in his 1673 *Catechism* Barclay responds to the question "...what Scriptures prove the divinity of Christ against such as falsely deny the same?"[55] by citing John 1:1, Romans 9:5, Philippians 2:6 and I John 5:20 as texts which prove Christ's Deity.

---

[52] See Gregory of Nazianzus *The Theological Orations* 3 and 4 in *Christology of the Later Fathers* Edward R.Hardy (ed.) Philadelphia: Westminster Press 1954 pp.160-193. John Calvin *Institutes of the Christian Religion* Bk II Chapters X11-XV1 Tr.Henry Beveridge, Grand Rapids: Eerdmans 1975. H.P.Liddon *The Divinity of Our Lord and Saviour Jesus Christ* 14ed. London: Longmans Green and Co. 1900.

[53] Edward Burrough *Declaration to all the World of Our Faith* London: 1657pp.2-3

[54] See the *Chalcedonian Definition* text in Bettenson *Documents of the Christian Church* pp.51-2. *The Westminster Confession* Ch.VIII: II text in Leith op.cit.pp.203-4. Karl Barth *Church Dogmatics* 1:2 Pt.II: 15:2 Tr. G.T. Thomson and Harold Knight, Edinburgh: T & T Clark 1980.

[55] Robert Barclay *Catechism* London: 1673 Chap. III Question 9

However the first Quakers departed from the core of conviction when they tried to express what they thought the Biblical witness to Christ's Divinity actually meant.

As Howard Brinton notes in his book *Friends for 300 years*, the early Quakers saw Christ as a Man who was completely filled with the Spirit:

> They knew by experience how the divine light was related to their own human consciousness. They conceived of the relation between the divine Spirit and the human mind in Jesus as following the same principle, except for this important difference: 'God giveth not the Spirit by measure unto Him' (John 3:34)... This was as near as the early Quakers came to an explicit theory regarding the difference in nature between Christ and themselves. It was a simple Christology based on experience. Because they had themselves experienced a measure of the Spirit they realised what it might be to experience the Spirit without measure, that is completely.[56]

The core of conviction, on the other hand, summarised on this issue by the 'Definition of Chalcedon', held that Christ was not just a Spirit filled Man, but was, uniquely, someone who was both fully God and fully Man at one and the same time.[57]

On the subject of *Man*, the first Quakers followed the core of conviction in asserting Mankind's fallenness and depravity. Although Man's nature and situation has been understood in many different ways by Christian thinkers[58], the core of conviction has consistently held that Mankind is fallen and so tainted and depraved

---

[56] Howard Brinton *Friends for 300 years* London: George Allen and Unwin 1953 pp.39-40. For justification of Brinton's statement see Nesti op.cit. pp.191-3 and for further details of early Quaker Christology see Edward Grubb *The Historic and Inward Christ* London: Headley Bros. 1914 and Maurice Creasey *Early Quaker Christology* Manasquan New Jersey: Catholic and Quaker Studies No.2 1975

[57] For details on the 'Definition of Chalcedon see R.V.Sellers *The Council of Chalcedon* London: SPCK 1952.48. See Leith op.cit. pp.34-6

[58] See the entry 'Man, Doctrine of' by William Horden in Alan Richardson (ed.) *A Dictionary of Christian Theology* London: SCM 1967.49. Grubb *Authority and the Light Within* p.80

by original sin[59] and the early Quakers thought likewise.Edward Grubb points out in his book *Authority and the Light within*, that:

> For them, as for the most rigid Calvinist, Man was absolutely ruined and lost by the Fall. No spark of a higher nature remained in him; his whole being was, just so far as human, totally and hopelessly corrupt and evil.[60]

Barclay sums up this Quaker understanding of the human predicament in Proposition Four of his *Apology*, 'The condition of Man in the Fall'

> All Adam's Posterity (or Mankind) both Jews and Gentiles, as to the first Adam (or earthly man) is fallen, degenerated, and dead, deprived of the sensation (or feeling) of this inward Testimony or seed of God, and is subject unto the power, nature, and seed of the Serpent; which he sows in mens' hearts, while they abide in this natural and corrupted state, from which it comes that not their words and deeds only, but all their imaginations are evil perpetually in the sight of God, as proceeding from this depraved and wicked seed.[61]

It should, however, be noted that Barclay also argues that "Nevertheless this seed is not imputed to infants, until by transgression they actually join themselves therewith".[62]

On the subject of *Salvation* the first Quakers conformed to the core of conviction in three ways.

Firstly, they insisted that we are saved by Christ. Although there has never been an authoritative ecumenical statement concerning precisely how we are saved,[63] the core of conviction has always held that in whatever way it was achieved our salvation was brought about through Christ. However, the core of

---

[59] See Canon two of the Council of Orange text in Leith op.cit. p.38. *The Augsburg Confession* text in Leith op.cit. p.68 and E.L.Mascall, *Man: His origin and Destiny* Westminster: Dacre Press 1940 p.93

[60] Edward Grubb *Authority and the Light Within* London: James Clarke 1909 p.80.

[61] Barclay *Apology* Proposition 4 'Concerning the condition of Man in the Fall'

[62] ibid Proposition 4.

[63] See Sydney Cave *The Doctrine of the Work of Christ* London: Hodder and Stoughton 1947 and J.K. Mozley *The Doctrine of the Atonement* London: Duckworth and Co. 1915.

conviction has always held that in whatever way it was achieved our salvation was brought about through Christ.[64] The first Quakers also shared this belief. In the words of Burrough:

> ....we believe that salvation, justification and sanctification is only in Him, wrought by Him and no other: for there is no other name given under heaven but Him alone, by which salvation is.[65]

Secondly, they used the concept of sacrifice to explain how we are saved through Christ's death on the Cross. For example, Elizabeth Bathurst argues in a defence of the Society published in 1679 that the Quakers understood Christ's death:

> ....as an acceptable and most satisfactory sacrifice to God for the sins of all, and (that is) of blessed advantage to all, that shall receive faith in his blood; which agrees to Rom. 3:25. Eph. 5:2: whom God hath set forth to be a propitiation through faith in His blood, to declare his righteousness for the remission of sins that are past, through the forbearance of God: and He hath given Himself for us, an offering and sacrifice to God for a sweet smelling savour.[66]

This use of the concept of sacrifice to explain the significance of the cross is in accordance with the core of conviction and has been one of the main ways in which the core of conviction has understood the meaning of Christ's death.[67]

Thirdly, the early Quakers accepted the possibility that in the end some individuals might miss out on salvation and end up going to Hell. For instance, William Dewsbury declared in his 'True Prophecy of the Mighty Day of the Lord'

---

[64] See St.Athanasius *On the Incarnation of the Word* text in Hardy op.cit.pp.55-110, *The Westminster Confession* Chapter VIII text in Leith op.cit. pp.203-5 and O.C. Quick *Doctrines of the Creed* London and Glasgow: Fontana 1963 Part III.

[65] Burrough *Declaration to all the world of our Faith* p.2

[66] Elizabeth Bathurst 'Truth's Vindication' p.14 in Elizabeth Bathurst *Truth Vindicated* London: 1691.

[67] See St.Athanasius op.cit. Section 20, Thomas Vincent *The Shorter Catechism Explained from Scripture* London>P: 1679 Question 25, Frances Young *Sacrifice and the Death of Christ* London: SPCK 1975.

> ...the mighty day of the Lord is coming that shall burn as an oven,
> and all you that are proud, and all you that do wickedly shall be
> stubble, and the day that cometh shall burn you up, saith the Lord
> of Hosts, and it shall leave of you neither root nor branch.[68]

This agrees with the core of conviction which held that Hell is a reality and that, in the end, some people may not be saved.[69]

Although the early Quakers' understanding of Salvation agreed with the core of conviction in these three ways, there were also three areas in which their understanding of salvation was distinctive, not because it disagreed with the core of

conviction (which does not, in fact, cover these areas), but because it disagreed with contemporary Protestant theology.

Firstly, they denied the traditional Protestant belief that we are justified on account of Christ's death on the cross.[70] They took instead a two stage view of salvation, similar to that held by Medieval Catholicism[71], and contended that while the reconciliation between Man and God achieved by the cross made justification possible, it becomes actual through the sanctifying work of Christ in our souls. Thus in his *Apology* Barclay argues for this two stage view of salvation on the grounds that it is:

> ....that order and method of Salvation held forth by the Apostle in
> that Divine saying, Rom. 5:10, For, if, when we were enemies, we
> were reconciled to God, by the death of his Son, much more being
> reconciled, we shall be saved by his life. For the Apostle first
> holding forth the reconciliation  wrought by the death of Christ,
> wherein God is near to receive and redeem Man, holds forth his
> salvation and justification to be by the life of Jesus. Now... this life
> is an inward Spiritual thing revealed in the soul, whereby it is

---

[68] William Dewsbury *A True Prophecy of the Mighty Day of the Lord* London: 1655 p.12 echoing Malachi 4:1.

[69] See St.Augustine *Enchiridion on Faith, Hope and Love* Tr. J.F.Shaw, Chicago: Regnery Gateway 1961 p.129. *The Dordrecht Confession* Article XVIII text in Leith op.cit. p.308 and C.S.Lewis *The Problem of Pain* Glasgow: Collins 1978 p.106.

[70] For this see Calvin op.cit. Bk III ch XI.

[71] See A.E.McGrath *Iustitia Dei* Vol.I. Cambridge: CUP 1986 pp.40-51

renewed and brought forth out of death, where it naturally has
been, by the fall; and so quickened and made alive to God.[72]

Secondly, they did not accept the conventional Protestant idea that
freedom from sin is impossible in this life.[73]  In the words of Burrough they
maintained instead that even in this life we "...may be perfectly free from the body
of sin and death, and in Christ may be perfect and without sin, and may have
victory over all temptations by faith in Christ Jesus".[74]

Thirdly, they rejected the notion, inherited by the Protestant Reformers
from Augustine, that God had restricted the possibility of salvation to a limited
number of the elect.[75]  They held instead that God had placed the Light of Christ
in the hearts of all men, so that all might have the opportunity for salvation.  In the
words of Barclay:

> God, out of his infinite love, 'who delighteth not in the death of a
> sinner, but that all should live and be saved, hath so loved the world
> that he hath given his only son a light, that whosoever believeth in
> him should be saved; who enlighteneth every man that cometh into
> the world, and maketh manifest all things that are reprovable and
> teacheth all temperance, righteousness, and godliness': and this light
> lighteneth the hearts of all in a day, in order to salvation, if not
> resisted:  nor is it less universal than the seed of sin, being the
> purchase of his death, who tasted death for every man;' for as in
> Adam all die, so in Christ shall all be made alive.[76]

As a corollary to their belief in God's will to save all men everywhere they
also took the view that even those who had never heard of the Christian faith, if
they were obedient to the light of Christ in their hearts:

> ...may become partakers of the mystery of his death, even though
> they have not heard of it.  In this light, which Christ himself affirms
> is available to all, communion is enjoyed with the Father and with
> the Son.  Wicked men can become holy and lovers of that power by

---

[72] Barclay *Apology* pp.155+156.

[73] For this idea see Article XVI of the *Thirty Nine Articles* in Leith op.cit. p.271

[74] Burrough Declaration to all the world of our faith p.4

[75] For this notion see Calvin op.cit. Bk II chs XXI-XXIV

[76] Barclay *Apology* The Fifth Proposition 'Concerning the Universal redemption by Christ'

whose inward and hidden touches they feel themselves turned from
evil to good.[77]

In summary, there were a number of issues on which the theology of the
early Quakers diverged either from the core of conviction or from the conventional
Protestant thought of their day.    However, as a whole their theology was in
general agreement with the core of conviction because:

1.    They believed that the definitive revelation of God is that given to us
through Christ, and in practice they accepted the Bible as a primary theological
authority.

2.    They took a Trinitarian view of God.

3.    They accepted the Biblical witness to Christ and held that He is to be seen
as Divine.

4.    They agreed that Man is fallen and as a result depraved by sin.

5.    They held that it is through Christ that we are saved, and they followed the
core of conviction in the way they described the meaning of Christ's death.
Furthermore they also accepted the possibility that in the end some people may be
damned.

## The Rise of Quietism

After the initial burst of vigorous missionary activity and rapid expansion,
the Quakers in this country, in common with Dissenters in general, suffered a
prolonged period of state persecution following the restoration of Charles II in
1660 and the consequent imposition of Anglican religious supremacy. This period
of persecution lasted, with times of intermission such as that resulting from Charles
II's Declaration of Indulgence of 1672, until the passing of the Toleration Act
under William and Mary in 1689 gave legality to Protestant Dissent.[78]

---

[77] Barclay *Apology* p.7

[78] For details of this era of persecution see J. Besse *An abstract of the sufferings of the people
called Quakers* London: J.Sowle 3 vols. 1735- 1738 and William C. Braithwaite *The Second
Period of Quakerism* London: Macmillan 1919 chs II-VI

In the words of John Wilhelm Rowntree, after the passing of the Toleration Act, the Quakers in this country: 'like a rowing crew after a fierce race rested on their oars'.[79]

British Quakerism never recovered its original vigour, and by the end of the 17th century had started to move into what is known as the 'Quietist' period of its history. In this Quietist era British Quakerism changed its perception of itself. It ceased to see itself as a missionary movement called to proclaim the 'Lamb's War' to a fallen world, and to bring all people into the one, true, restored church. Instead it came to see itself as a remnant saved by grace whose duty it was to protect its own religious and ethical purity by keeping itself unspotted from the world. As Rufus Jones puts it in *The Later periods of Quakerism*, early Quakerism "is apostolic and catholic, strong in the faith that its discovery is to be proclaimed from the housetop and that all the world is to share its message" whereas Quakerism of the Quietist period "is timid and exclusive and is content with the cultivation of a remnant and with the making of a peculiar people".[80]

In order to keep itself pure and unspotted, Quietist Quakerism tended to withdraw from contact with the world as much as possible. Whereas the first Quakers believed the world was to be challenged and converted, Quakers of the Quietist period tended to see it as a source of potential spiritual pollution which was to be avoided if possible. To quote Loukes in *The Quaker contribution:*[81]

> ...they (Quietist Quakers) settled to the enjoyment and perfection of their peculiarity seeking to make a place in which they could live at peace with their sensitive conscience. They were like a new monastic order, living within walls thrown up for the protection of their devotion, their life revolving round their own centre, their service to the world valuable and unselfish but stopping short of full involvement.

Or, as the contemporary Anglican observer Thomas Clarkson puts it in his 1806 *Portraiture of Quakerism*:

---

[79] John Wilhelm Rowntree *Essays and Addresses* Joshua Rowntree (ed.) London: Headley Bros. 1905 p.65

[80] Rufus M Jones *The Later periods of Quakerism* Vol.1 London: Macmillan 1921 p.33

[81] Harold Loukes *The Quaker Contribution* London: SCM 1965 pp.52-3

> They consider themselves bound to give up such of the customs or
> fashions of men, however general or generally approved, as militate
> against the letter or the spirit of the Gospel. Hence, they mix but
> little with the world, that they may be less liable to imbibe its
> spirit.[82]

It is true that, as A Neave Brayshaw notes in *The Quakers their Story and Message*,[83] during the eighteenth century  Quakers in Britain did engage in a certain amount of evangelistic activity in the form of itinerant preaching, public meetings, and the publication of Quaker literature. It is also true that they took part in philanthropic activities such as the campaign against the slave trade. However it nevertheless remains the case that, on the whole, they tended towards seclusion. As Punshon writes: "In the eighteenth century, Friends created a religious culture of great refinement. Unhappily it stood apart from the world".[84]

Many reasons have been suggested for the development of Quietist Quakerism. For example, John Stephenson Rowntree argues in an 1859 essay entitled *Quakerism, Past and Present* that the causes of the decline of British Quakerism between 1690 and 1760 were a lesser presence of the Holy Spirit, commercial success among Quakers leading to religious indifference, a lack of proper education for Quaker children, a decline in the amount of preaching at Quaker meetings caused by the custom of acknowledging some Quakers as having a call to preach resulting  in those not so acknowledged being unwilling to do so, and the growth of a large number of nominal Quakers due to the registering of the children of Quakers as Quakers themselves.[85]  For another example, Brayshaw suggests in *The Quakers their story and message* that the causes of the move to Quietism were increasing prosperity, internal controversy, the emigration of thousands of Quakers to America, the untimely death of many of the early Quaker leaders, and the fear of renewed persecution causing Quakers to wish not to draw

---

[82] Thomas Clarkson *A Portraiture of Quakerism* London: Longman 1806 p.4

[83] A. Neave Brayshaw  *The Quakers their Story and Message* London: The Swarthmore Press 1927 p.167

[84] Punshon  op.cit. p.103. For details of Quakerism in the Quietist period see Clarkson op.cit. passim, Jones op.cit. chs 1-8 and Punshon op.cit. chs 5-6

[85] John Stephenson Rowntree *Quakerism, Past and Present* London: Smith, Elder & Co. 1859, ch 5

attention to themselves.[86]   For a third example, Loukes states in *The Quaker contribution* that what happened to Quakerism is typical of what happens in the second generation of any "movement for religious revival" in which "the fire dies down" as "a generation grows up to whom the 'new' ideas are familiar".[87]

All these suggested causes may have contributed to the emergence of Quietism. However, as Punshon points out:

> The halting of the forward movement of Quakerism...was a complex phenomenon and did not spring mainly from weakness or defection in Friends themselves, as some are inclined to suggest. Underlying all apparently consistent theological positions, there is a world-view which their authors do not fully appreciate. Such was the case with Quakerism. The whole system of ideas surrounding the apostasy and the millenium was beginning to creak. The issue of pluralism or uniformity had been settled. The contrast between spiritual and formal religion in Quaker terms was no longer the issue it had been. It was not yet clear what the issues of the future would be, but there was no doubt that Quakerism needed to be expressed in a different way, and a period of re-adjustment was undoubtedly necessary.[88]

The early Quaker message of the 'Lamb's War' and the restoration of the true Church had made sense when it was first proclaimed in the 1650s because it had fitted into a prevailing concern with personal holiness and a widespread sense of millennial expectation. However, by the end of the seventeenth and the beginning of the eighteenth centuries the religious atmosphere had changed, and Quakerism needed to be re-interpreted for a new age. This re-interpretation took the form of the Quietist spirituality which has given its name to the second era of British Quaker history, and which was the fundamental reason for the difference between early and Quietist Quakerism.

This Quietist spirituality has been so called because of an alleged resemblance to the teaching known as 'Quietism' espoused by the Catholic writers Miguel de Molinos, Madame Guyon, and Archbishop Francois Fenelon. The *Oxford Dictionary of the Christian Church* notes in its entry on Quietism:

---

[86] Brayshaw op.cit. pp.148-151

[87] Loukes op.cit. p.52

[88] Punshon op.cit. pp.102-103

The fundamental principle of Quietism is its condemnation of all human effort. According to the Quietists, in order to be perfect a man must attain complete passivity and annihilation of will, abandoning himself to God to such an extent that he ceases to care even about his own salvation. This state is reached by a certain form of mental prayer in which the soul consciously refuses not only all discursive meditation but any distinct act such as desire for virtue, love of Christ, or adoration of the Divine Persons, but simply rests in the presence of God in pure faith. As this passive prayer expresses the height of perfection, it makes any outward acts of mortification, almsgiving, going to confession, etc. superfluous. Once a man has attained to it, sin is impossible, for then all he does or thinks is the work of God. The devil may, indeed, tempt him and even compel him to commit actions that would be sinful in others, but when his will has become completely annihilated they cease to be sins in him; on the contrary, the man who has reached this state must carefully guard against being disquieted by such distractions, lest he should be disturbed in his state of mystic death. The moral consequences of such teaching are almost indistinguishable from those of Pantheism.[89]

This teaching is supposed to be similar to the spirituality of British Quakers during their Quietist period, but, as Punshon argues, there are important differences between the two:

Continental Quietism was a mystical attitude, but it came very close to a doctrine of justification by pure faith, a view which Quakers have always strongly rejected. Moreover it was antinomian, and the Quakers were ever forthright moralists. This was because their experience of God was primarily one of leading and vocation, not of stillness and contemplation. Friends shared the Quietist distrust of human nature, but this was common across the whole of Christendom. Rather than encourage each Friend to cultivate his or her human garden in isolation, the Society of Friends understood itself to have a collective responsibility.[90]

Quietist Quaker spirituality is in fact best seen as an internal development within Quakerism, in which tendencies inherent in Quakerism from the beginning became stressed in an exaggerated fashion. The early Quaker message was that

---

[89]'Quietism'  *Oxford Dictionary of the Christian Church* 2nd ed. F.L. Cross and E.A. Livingstone (eds.) Oxford: OUP 1974. For further details on Quietism see R.A. Knox *Enthusiasm* Oxford: OUP 1950 chs XI and XII.

[90] Punshon op.cit. p.120

human beings need to go through a process of internal spiritual warfare in which God's light in their hearts, their internal monitor, shows them the evil in their life. They then become willing to forsake it, and they receive God's power to overcome it and to lead a life of moral perfection through obedience to the light's direction. The Quietist re-interpretation of this message stressed the need to go through a period of struggle, to overcome evil, and to obey the light, but it identified the overcoming of evil with the suppression of all human thought, effort, and desire since these were tainted by sin. The aim was the spiritual annihilation of the activity of the self so that all one's thoughts, efforts, and desires were those given by God through one's internal monitor. Thus while the early Quakers thought that the self had to become obedient to the light, the Quietists thought that the activity of the self had to be suppressed that the light might have free reign. In the words of Jones in *The later periods of Quakerism* vol.I:

> The true and essential preparation....for spiritual ministry, or for any action in the truth and life, seemed to the Quietist to be the repose of all one's own powers, the absence of all efforts of self-direction, of all strain and striving, the annihilation of all confidence in one's own capacities, the complete quiet of the 'creature'.[91]

A clear expression of such Quietist spirituality is to be found in the Epistle issued by London Yearly Meeting (the British Quaker General Assembly) in 1770. In this Epistle it is declared that:

> 'The manifestation of the Spirit is given to every man to profit withal' (1 Cor. XII. 7). The way to profit by it is to often diligently retire unto it. As it appears inwardly, it calls for inward retirement, and an abstraction from earthly objects, imaginations, and attachments. For, in the silence of all that is of the flesh, the still small voice of truth, the divine word nigh in the heart is heard, and by hearing with due _ observance, true faith is produced.[92]

---

[91] Jones op.cit. p.36

[92] London Yearly Meeting Epistle, 1770 in *Epistles from Yearly Meeting of Friends* vol 2 London: Edward Marsh 1858. For other examples of Quietist spirituality see *An account of the life and travels and Christian Experiences of Samuel Bownas* London: Luke Hinde 1756, *Some account of the Life and Religious Labours of Sarah Grubb* Dublin: R. Jackson 1792, *The Life of Mary Dudley* London: Elizabeth Dudley 1825, and the *Journal of the Life and Labours of Thomas Shillitoe* London: Harvey and Darton 1839

As can be seen from Benjamin Holmes *A serious call in Christian love to all people to turn to the Spirit of Christ in themselves*[93] Hugh Turford's *The Grounds of a Holy Life*[94] and the anonymous *The True Quakers' Principles defended from Scripture*[95] British Quakers of the quietist period held to the same theology as that put forward by the early Quakers and therefore stood in the same relation to the core of conviction. The influence of Quietist spirituality was the basic reason for British Quakerism's separation of itself from the world. To quote Jones, the ideals of Quietism:

> ...dwelt ... upon withdrawal from contact with the world and from responsibility for shaping the affairs of men and of nations - withdrawal even from an interest in politics. The conquests which best fitted these ideals of Quietism were conquests of the inner spirit. The world confronted them stubborn and unmalleable. It seemed a realm of darkness and hostility to spiritual aims. Their business, as it appeared to them, was to bring every power of heart and mind and will into obedience to the Light of Christ which shined in their souls, to build an inner kingdom where Christ might absolutely reign, and to this conquest they devoted all their energies.[96]

To British Quakers of the Quietist period interest in the world around them seemed inimical to spiritual activity, and so they withdrew from the world as much as possible to concentrate on perfecting their own spiritual lives. As the London Yearly Meeting Epistle of 1770 put it:

> Much hurt may accrue to the religious mind by long and frequent conversation upon temporal matters, and especially by interesting ourselves too much in them; for there is a leaven therein which _

---

[93] Benjamin Holmes *A serious call in Christian love to all people to turn to the Spirit of Christ in themselves* London: J.Sowle 1725

[94] Hugh Turford *The Grounds of a Holy Life* 16th ed London: James Phillips and Sons 1797

[95] Anon *The True Quakers' Principles defended from Scripture* Lewes: 1786

[96] Jones op.cit p.101

indisposes and benumbs the soul, and prevents its frequent ascending in living aspirations towards the fountain of eternal life.[97]

During this period, British Quakers maintained the distinctive Quaker form of worship based upon silent waiting upon God. They also maintained the distinctive Quaker 'Testimonies' but the significance of these changed. They ceased to be seen as a dynamic form of witness intended to convict the world of its unrighteousness, and came to be seen instead as marks of committed Christian discipleship and as rules designed to prevent the Christian being contaminated with the spirit of the world.

From 1738 onwards British Quakers began to issue Books of Discipline in which their beliefs and practices were authoritatively recorded. The task of ensuring that these beliefs and practices were adhered to was that of the Quaker Elders, aided from 1789 by the Overseers. The job of these Elders and Overseers was to provide pastoral supervision, given the absence of an ordained ministry within the Society of Friends. The Elders helped and encouraged those Quakers recorded as having a particular vocation to speak in Meetings for Worship and made sure that what was said in Meeting for Worship was in accordance with Quaker tradition. The Overseers were concerned with seeing that Quakers were observing Quaker standards in their daily lives.[98] The ultimate penalty for someone whose beliefs or conduct were deemed to be un-Quakerly was expulsion from the Society of Friends, technically known as 'disownment'. For example, during the Quietist period Quakers were regularly disowned for marrying outside the Quaker fold. A combination of such disownments, together with the effects of emigration, people deciding to leave the Society of Friends, and the decline in evangelistic zeal resulting in a lack of fresh converts, led to a serious decline in the number of British Quakers during the Quietist period. In chapter IV of *Quakerism Past and Present* John Stephenson Rowntree calculates that between 1680 and 1856 the number of Quakers in England and Wales fell from 60,000 to 14,350.

---

[97] Epistle for 1770 *Epistles from Yearly Meeting of Friends* Vol.2

[98] For details of these aspects of Quietist Quakerism see *Extracts from the Minutes and advices of Yearly Meeting* London: James Phillips 1783, and ditto London: William Phillips 1803, Brayshaw op.cit. chs XII + XIII, Jones op.cit. chs IV-VI, and Punshon op.cit. ch 6

**The Evangelical Period**

From the 1730's onwards the movement of religious renewal known as the Evangelical Revival began to affect the religious life of Britain. As John Walsh has argued, the Evangelical revival was the product of a number of different sources[99] and it was also theologically diverse, being marked by both Arminian and Calvinist tendencies. However, the Evangelicals had three emphases which transcended this diversity.

Firstly, they possessed a general commitment to the beliefs of the core of conviction. For instance, those involved in the Evangelical Revival held firmly to the Trinity of God, the Deity of Christ and the Fallenness of Man.

Secondly, they contended that the means of salvation was faith in the atoning death of Christ.

Thirdly, they stressed the importance of the Bible as the appointed means by which human beings might know about God and His will for humankind.

These emphases were not new. They had already been anticipated in the teaching of the Protestant Reformers. What the Evangelical Revival achieved was to promote a fresh acceptance of them.

Initially British Quakers mostly chose to remain aloof from the Evangelical Revival, believing its stress on active Evangelism rather than inward retirement to be incompatible with the tenets of Quietism. As Punshon notes, referring to the Revival by its alternative title of the 'Methodist Revival':

> The mighty rushing wind of the Methodist revival swept through the Eighteenth century as the Quaker revival had shaken its predecessor. After an intial welcome, Friends came to perceive correctly that the evangelical zeal of the Methodists was inimical to their own principles and security. So they closed ranks behind their birthright membership and began to reassess their position as no longer an apostolic missionary church, but a peculiar people, kept apart from the world as a sort of spiritual aristocracy.[100]

---

[99] J.D.Walsh 'Origins of the Evangelical Revival in G.V.Bennett and J.D.Walsh (eds.) *Essays in Modern English Church History* London: A & C Black 1966 pp.132-62

[100] Punshon op.cit. p.135

The Quakers at the time of the Evangelical Revival saw that opening themselves to what the Methodists were doing would entail having to change radically. They did not wish to do so, and chose instead to remain content with accepting the children of existing Quakers into membership rather than by going out to convert non-Christians.[101]

Although British Quakerism was thus initially unreceptive to the Evangelical Revival, nonetheless, as Jones argues in chapter IX of Volume I of *The Later Periods of Quakerism*, from 1775 onwards there appears:
"a clearly marked tendency to mould and formulate Quaker thought in the direction of Evangelical doctrine".[102] This tendency can be seen in the journals of the Quaker preachers Thomas Shillitoe and Mary Dudley, both of whom, interestingly combined both Quietist and Evangelical tendencies in their thought, and in Quaker writings such as Henry Tuke's *Principles of Religion,*[103] Joseph Gurney Bevan's *Thoughts on Reason and Revelation,*[104] and John Bevan's *A Defence of the Christian Doctrines of the Society of Friends against the charge of Socinianism*[105] all first published in 1805.

As the 19th century progressed, so the influence of Evangelical thought within British Quakerism grew until, from the end of the 1820's onwards, Evangelicalism became the dominant theological tendency within Quakerism in this country.[106]

This triumph of Evangelical thought is marked by the Epistle issued by London Yearly Meeting in 1836, which stated:

..the Holy Scriptures of the Old and New Testament were given by inspiration of God; that therefore the declaration contained in them

---

[101] For further details of Quaker-Methodist relations see Frank Baker *The relations between the Society of Friends and Early Methodism* London: Epworth Press 1948.

[102] Jones op. cit. p.275

[103] Henry Tuke *Principles of Religion* London: Phillips and Fardon 1805

[104] Joseph Gurney Bevan *Thoughts on Reason and Revelation* London: Phillips and Fardon 1805

[105] John Bevan *A Defence of the Christian Doctrines of the Society of Friends against the charge of Socinianism* London: William Phillips 1810

[106] John Bevan *A Defence of the Christian Doctrines of the Society of Friends against the charge of Socinianism* London: William Phillips 1810

> rest on the authority of God himself, - and there can be no appeal
> from them to any authority whatsoever : that they are able to make
> us wise unto salvation through faith which is in Christ Jesus; being
> the appointed means of making known to us the blessed truths of
> Christianity : that they are the only divinely authorized record of the
> doctrines which we are bound as Christians to believe, and of the
> moral principles which are to regulate our actions: that no doctrine
> which is not contained in them can be required of any one to be
> believed as an article of faith : that whatsoever any man says or
> does which is contrary to the Scriptures, though under profession
> of the immediate guide of the Spirit, must be reckoned and
> accounted a mere delusion.[107]

The emphasis found here on the authority of Scripture is typically Evangelical. It departs from previous Quaker tradition in two ways. It sees Scripture rather than the internal monitor as the means by which the truths of Christianity are made known, and it fails to stress the subordination of Scripture to the internal monitor.

Various suggestions have been made as to the reasons for the growth of Evangelicalism within British Quakerism. In her thesis on *Victorian Quakers* Elizabeth Isichei suggests "the most important factor (in the growth of Evangelicalism) was the eloquence and prestige of contemporary Anglican Evangelicalism".[108] This Anglican influence on Quaker Evangelicalism was noted by its contemporary critics. For instance, Shillitoe, in spite of the evangelical tendencies in his own thought, declared shortly before his death in 1836 that he apprehended that Joseph John Gurney, the leading Quaker Evangelical:

> ... is no Quaker in principle. Episcopalian views were imbibed from
> his education, and still remain with him. I love the man, for the
> work's sake, so far as it goes; but he has never been emptied from
> vessel to vessel, and from sieve to sieve, nor known the baptism of
> the Holy Ghost and of fire, to cleanse the floor of his heart from his
> Episcopalian notions.[109]

---

[107] Cited in *Christian Doctrine Practice and Discipline* London: Friends Book Depository 1864 pp.15-16

[108] Elizabeth Isichei *Victorian Quakers* Oxford: OUP 1970 p.4

[109] Quoted in William Hodgson *The Society of Friends in the Nineteenth Century* Philadelphia: Smith Elder and Co 1875 p.313

Punshon, in *Portrait in Grey*, accepts that there was an Anglican influence, but also suggests other reasons for the growth of Evangelical Quakerism in Britain. He argues that Quietism was deficient because it had become old fashioned and hidebound and had led to the isolation of British Quakerism; that the trend towards Evangelicalism was "strengthened and confirmed" by the work of "a quartet of powerful American Evangelical ministers", Rebecca Jones, David Sands, William Savery and Stephen Grellet, who had all paid pastoral visits to this country by 1820."[110]

Brayshaw, in *The Quakers their story and message*, states that:

> Early in the nineteenth century the contact of Friends with others, particularly in their work for slaves and prisoners, bringing them within the influence of the Evangelical and Methodist movements, began to open the eyes of many to a sense of Christian fellowship, to the value of the Scriptures and to a new conception of Jesus Christ. This uprising from spiritual inertia into life naturally took the form in which the life had been shown forth, the Evangelicalism which at the time was the most living religious influence in England.[111]

He also agrees that the influence of Grellet "gave a marked impetus to the Evangelical movement among those (Quakers) in England".[112]

I have already noted that Joseph John Gurney was the leading Evangelical Quaker. As Isichei puts it:

> Any account of the beliefs of Quaker evangelicals must be drawn largely from the writings of Joseph John Gurney... He was so pre-eminent in the movement that its opponents called Quaker Evangelicalism 'Gurneyism'.[113]

Gurney's most comprehensive statement of the beliefs which he held as an Evangelical Quaker was his *Observations on the Religious Peculiarities of the*

---

[110] Punshon op.cit. p.166

[111] Brayshaw op.cit. pp.197-8

[112] ibid p.1999

[113] *Victorian Quakers* pp.3-4

*Society of Friends*, first published in 1824.[114] It is a systematic statement of the Evangelical interpretation of Quakerism, and clearly indicates what 19th century British Evangelical Quakerism stood for.

In the seventh edition of this work, which contains an important new 'Introductory Chapter', Gurney endeavours to do three things.

Firstly, because previous editions of the work had stressed the distinctive aspects of Quaker theology, Gurney seeks to show in this introductory chapter that Quakers also hold to the theological emphasis common to all Evangelicals. He stresses the Quakers' commitment to the beliefs contained in the core of conviction, what he calls the "fundamental doctrines" accepted by all "true Christian believers"[115], explaining that although they have never subscribed to a creed, nevertheless in every period of Quaker history the faith of the Society of Friends has been:

> ... sound and unquestionable. Repeatedly have they confessed their belief in one ever-living God, all-wise, almighty, omnipresent, the Creator and Ruler of the universe; holy, just, true and merciful; in the immortality of the soul; in the resurrection of the dead; in the eternity of the future rewards and punishments; in the mysterious union and distinction of the Father, the Word and the Holy Spirit; in the deity of our Lord Jesus Christ; in his incarnation and birth of the Virgin Mary; in his sinless human nature; in his meritorious obedience, in sufferings and death; in his resurrection and ascension; in his supreme and universal reign; in his spiritual presence with his people; and in his glorious future coming to judge the quick and the dead.
> They are well aware of the fatal effects of the transgression of our first parents - that man is a fallen creature, by nature the child of wrath, prone to iniquity, and absolutely incapable of true holiness and happiness, unless born again of the Spirit.[116]

---

[114] The 7th ed has been republished as Joseph John Gurney *A Peculiar People* Richmond Indiana: Friends United Press 1979. and I shall quote from this re-publication.

[115] ibid pp.2-3.

[116] ibid pp.3-4.

Secondly, he contends that although the Quakers' emphasis on the principle
that "without holiness none can see the Lord or enter into his kingdom"[117]had led
some people to think that they underrated the importance of faith, in fact:

> ... there is probably no truth on which Friends have been more
> accustomed to dwell, that the Scripture doctrine that the 'just shall
> live by faith'. They freely acknowledge that FAITH is essential to
> man's ... salvation; and that as is the light bestowed upon us, so is
> the BELIEF required of us. They rejoice in the assurance of
> Scripture, that 'God was in Christ, RECONCILING the world unto
> himself, not imputing their trespasses unto them'; that 'we are
> justified freely by his grace, through the redemption which is in
> Christ Jesus', and that whosoever BELIEVETH in the Son of God,
> shall 'not perish' but shall 'have everlasting life'.[118]

Lastly, he maintains that the Quakers' belief that it is the Spirit who brings people
to God does not mean that they are equivocal about the importance of the Bible:

> There is probably no body of Christians who have taken more pains
> than Friends have done to enjoin upon their members a frequent
> perusal of the Scriptures of Truth. It is one of those duties which is
> annually brought home to us by a public inquiry addressed to all our
> inferior meetings; and it has been the subject of many a warm
> exhortation, and many a strong advice, issued by our Yearly
> Meeting itself. Nothing can have been more clear than the
> testimony of the Society to the divine origin of the book. Friends
> have always asserted that it was given by inspiration of God; and
> when our forefathers were defamed by their adversaries, and falsely
> accused of unsound principles, they always appealed to Scripture as
> the ONLY authoritative written testimony by which their
> sentiments could be tried. They boldly invited their hearers and
> readers to imitate the example of the noble Bereans - to search the
> Scriptures daily that they might know 'whether these things were
> so'.[119]

Having emphasised the beliefs which the Quakers share with other
Christians, Gurney goes on to outline the distinctive features of Quakerism, what

---

[117] ibid p.5.

[118] ibid p.5

[119] ibid pp.10-11.

the title of the seventh edition calls the Quakers' "Distinguishing Views and Practices". Three examples will serve to illustrate this point.

Firstly, Gurney explains that Quakers believe in direct inward guidance from God:

> The work of the Holy Spirit is not only immediate and direct, but perceptible. We believe that we are all furnished with an inward Guide or Monitor, who makes his voice known to us, and who, if faithfully obeyed and closely followed, will infallibly conduct us into true virtue and happiness, because he leads us into conformity with the will of God.[120]

Secondly, he defends the traditional Quaker belief that:

> ... the outward knowledge of Christ is not absolutely indispensable to salvation, and that other persons, who are COMPLETELY DESTITUTE of that knowledge, may ALSO be saved from sin, and from the penalties which are attached to it, through the secret operations of divine grace.[121]

Thirdly, he contends that it is the:"_ great Christian law that they who worship God, who is a spirit, 'must WORSHIP HIM IN SPIRIT AND IN TRUTH'" which has led Quakers to abandon the ordained Ministry and the use of liturgy in favour of the Quaker practice of 'waiting together upon the Lord in SILENCE'.[122]

Like other forms of Evangelicalism the Evangelical Quaker faith presented by Gurney is thus a hybrid. Just as the Anglican, Methodist and Congregationalist forms of Evangelicalism were a a mixture of common Evangelical beliefs with specific denominational features, so also the faith put forward by Gurney is a mixture of those beliefs held in common with other Evangelical Christians and distinctive Quaker ideas and practices. This faith differs from early and Quietist Quakerism in two ways.

---

[120] ibid p.76

[121] ibid p.27

[122] ibid p.430

Firstly, Gurney's view of the Bible comes closer to the core of conviction than did theirs. Like the Yearly Meeting Epistle of 1836 he emphasises the importance of the Bible as the authorised standard of religious truth without stressing its subordination to the internal monitor.

Secondly, Gurney's emphasis on the importance of faith for salvation comes closer to the mainstream Protestant concept of justification by faith than to the traditional Quaker belief in justification by sanctification. Gurney does indeed insist on the importance of sanctification, but it is not at the centre of his theological vision as it was for the early and Quietist Quakers. It is separate from, and subsequent to, justification.

Gurney's theology is therefore closer to the core of conviction and to mainstream Protestantism than was previous Quaker theology, and this is also true of Evangelical Quakerism as a whole. While retaining distinctive Quaker ideas and practices, Evangelical Quakerism put forward a theology which stressed the agreement, and minimised the difference, between Quaker beliefs and those held by other Protestant Christians.[123]

Evangelical Quakerism was, as I have indicated, the dominant force in British Quakerism from the end of the 1820s onwards. Its influence led Victorian Quakers to break out of the isolation of the Quietist period and to engage in widespread philanthropic activity and renewed missionary work at home and overseas.[124]

Although Evangelical Quakerism was thus dominant, its dominance was challenged in three directions.

Firstly, it was challenged throughout the nineteenth century by those who continued to hold to the Quietist understanding of Quakerism. These maintained the Quietist ideas and traditions of the previous century and criticised Evangelical Quakers for substituting a purely intellectual study of scripture for an experiential knowledge of Christ through the internal monitor. For instance, the Quietist Anne Jones visited the Men's Meeting at London Yearly Meeting in 1836 and declared:

---

[123] For other examples of Evangelical Quaker theology see E.Ash *The Christian Profession of the Society of Friends* London: John and Arthur Ash 1837, Richard Cadbury's *What is my Faith?* Carlisle: 1888 and the volumes of the Evangelical newspaper *The Friend* from 1843 onwards.

[124] For details on Victorian Quakerism see Isichei's *Victorian Quakers* throughout.

> There are those among us who are encouraging a carnal wisdom, a
> head knowledge, an outward learning which exalteth itself, and is
> ever endeavouring in its own strength to find out the way of
> salvation by the study of Scripture. This spirit has spread even
> among those who are making a very high profession - men who are
> robbing Christ. They talk much of a belief in the atoning sacrifice,
> but are setting at naught and despising Christ in his inward and
> spiritual appearance... [125]

In 1870 a small number of Quietist Quakers seceded from London Yearly
meeting and set up their own General Meeting at Fritchley in Derbyshire, but the
vast majority of Quietist Quakers remained as a small minority within the larger
body.[126]

Secondly, in 1835 the Manchester Quaker Isaac Crewdson reacted to the
extreme mysticism of the American Quaker Elias Hicks, which seemed to him to
denigrate the importance of Jesus Christ and of the Bible, by publishing a tract
entitled *A beacon to the Society of Friends*. In this tract Crewdson argues that the
root of Hicks' mysticism lies in the traditional Quaker idea that:

> ... we are authorised to expect to be taught the true knowledge of
> God and of his salvation - our duty to him, and to our fellow men,
> IMMEDIATELY by the SPIRIT independently of HIS
> REVELATION through the Scriptures. [127]

As Crewdson sees it, this idea "is unsupported by Scripture, contradicted by fact,
and one which renders its votaries a prey to many fatal delusions".[128]    He
therefore proposes that it should be replaced by the idea that the Bible has been
given "as the gracious message of God to us, to teach us the mind of the Spirit, as

---

[125] Quoted by Hodgson op.cit.p.298

[126] For details of Quietism in the 19th century and of the Fritchley Schism see Isichei op.cit.
pp.16-25 and 53-61, and for examples of Quietist thought see the journals of Sarah Lynes Grubb
and Thomas Shillitoe previously cited, Daniel Pickard *An Expostulation on behalf of the Truth*
London: A W Bennett 1864 and the volumes of *The British Friend* (the Quietists' newspaper)
from 1843-1891

[127] Isaac Crewdson *A beacon to the Society of Friends* Manchester: Henry Smith 1835 p.51

[128] ibid p.51

our sole and ultimate rule of faith and duty and as a guide to the Christian Church to the end of time".[129]

Crewdson's 'beacon' challenged the attempt by Evangelical Quakers to combine the traditional Quaker idea of the immediate guidance of the Spirit with an Evangelical insistence on the central importance of the Bible. Crewdson's challenge was, however, not accepted, and he and some three hundred of his supporters resigned from the Society of Friends in 1836. Most of these supporters joined other Churches, but some of them joined Crewdson in setting up a short lived Evangelical Friends Chapel in Manchester.[130]

The third challenge to Evangelical Quakerism came from those British Quakers who held Liberal views on theology and were sympathetic to the widespread questioning of Christian belief which was a feature of the Victorian era. This questioning seems to have had three main causes.

The first of these was the development in the natural sciences. As Owen Chadwick points out in his history of the Victorian Church, the precise effect of science on faith is difficult to determine and it would be a mistake to think of a clear conflict between science and religion, with all the scientists on one side and all the believers on the other [131] Nevertheless developments in the study of geology and Darwin's formulation of the theory of evolution in *The Origin of Species* do seem to have unsettled the faith of many people. They seemed to undermine the authority of the book of Genesis as an account of human origins by suggesting that its account of this subject was scientifically inaccurate. Also, as Horton Davies notes, Darwin's work in particular called into question the providence of God by "drawing attention to the disteleological aspects of nature" through exposing the apparent wastefulness and cruelty involved in the development of life on earth.[132]

The second cause was the development of the literary and historical criticism of the Bible in response to intellectual developments in Germany. This

---

[129] ibid p.10

[130] For details of this 'Beaconite' schism see Isichei op.cit. pp.45-53

[131] Owen Chadwick *The Victorian Church* vol 2 2ed. London: A & C Black 1972 Ch.I.

[132] Horton Davies *Worship and theology in England from Newman to Martineau,* 1850-1900 London: OUP 1962 pp.174-5.

again seemed to undermine the authority of the Bible by appearing to demonstrate that large parts of the Bible were not the work of their traditional authors and were historically inaccurate and internally contradictory.[133]

The third cause was moral doubt about some parts of the Bible and of traditional Christian doctrine. For example, objection was taken to the slaughter of the Canaanites by Joshua and to the fate of the Gadarene Swine, and as H.G.Wood notes in his study *Belief and Unbelief since 1850*, the development of a more humane penal policy in Victorian England and, more importantly, increasing emphasis on God as a loving Father caused people to question the notion that on the Cross Christ was punished by God for the sins of the world and the belief that after death the wicked would be punished eternally in Hell.[134]

In response to this questioning of Christian belief some people abandoned Christian faith altogether. Others rejected the questioning altogether, seeing it as inspired purely by impiety. Still others saw it as a challenge to re-shape Christian theology into a new and more acceptable form.

The Quaker Liberals belonged to this last group. Their views first came to prominence in connection with the Manchester Unitarian Schism of 1871. This was caused by the setting up of an independent Friends Meeting in Manchester by a group of Quakers with Unitarian views who had left the Society of Friends in protest against the disownment of a Quaker with Liberal ideas called David Duncan. In 1861 he had published an enthusiastic review of a volume of essays entitled *Essays and Reviews*[135] which had been produced the previous year by seven Anglican writers in an attempt to stimulate fresh thinking about theology, and which had caused a great furore for, among other things, urging the acceptance of Biblical criticism, questioning the apologetic value of miracles, and criticising any attempt to reconcile Genesis and geolog[136] Then in 1863 he had

---

[133] For the development and influence of Biblical criticism see J.Rogerson *Old Testament Criticism in the Nineteenth Century: England and Germany* London: SPCK 1984, S.C.Neill *The interpretation of the New Testament 1801-1961* Oxford: OUP 1966 and Chadwick op.cit. Ch.II.

[134] H.G.Wood *Belief and Unbelief since 1850* Cambridge: CUP 1955 p.28. See also Geoffrey Rowell *Hell and the Victorians* Oxford: OUP 1974

[135] David Duncan *Essays and Reviews* Manchester: Edward Slater 1861

[136] F.W.Temple et al *Essays and Reviews* London: John W.Parker 1860. For the furore it caused see Chadwick op.cit. Ch.II pt.4.

published an essay entitled *Can an outward revelation be perfect?* in which he rejected the idea of the infallibility of the Bible and argued for the abolition in theology "of any authority short of God, as He reveals Himself to the Spirit of the individual".[137]

The events in Manchester showed that British Quakerism as a whole was not yet ready to accept Liberal ideas, and after them Evangelicalism continued to dominate British Quakerism to the extent that Edward Grubb later recalled that after losing his Evangelical faith as a result of his university studies in Philosophy he sat:

> ... in a back seat during a meeting for worship at the Yearly Meeting of 1880, in tears because I felt myself utterly alone. I seemed to be living in a different world from all that company, and of what was said in ministry I could hardly believe one word.[138]

However, the Evangelical domination of British Quakerism was not to endure. Just as British Quakers had found it impossible to remain aloof for ever from the Evangelical Revival so also they were to find it impossible to ignore for ever the Victorian questioning of faith.

The first crack in the dam came a few years after Grubb's experience at Yearly Meeting with the publication of two books, *A reasonable faith* by Francis Frith, William Pollard and William Turner, published anonymously in 1884[139] and *The Gospel of Divine Help* by Edward Worsdell published in 1886.[140]

Both these books reflected the questioning of established belief which I noted above and challenged central tenets of Evangelical Quaker theology.

In *A reasonable faith* Frith, Pollard and Turner rejected the idea that the whole Bible was a perfect revelation from God in favour of the idea, influenced by evolutionary theory, that it is a "Progressive revelation" which is "necessarily

---

[137] David Duncan *Can an outward revelation be perfect?* 2ed. London: F.Bowyer Kitto p.23.

[138] Edward Grubb,'Some Personal Experiences' *Friends' Quarterly Examiner* vol. 72 October 1938 p.301.

[139] Francis Frith, William Pollard and William Turner *A reasonable Faith - by three Friends* London: Macmillan & Co 1884

[140] Edward Worsdell *The Gospel of Divine Help* London: Samuel Harris and co. 1886.

imperfect in its earlier stages" and contains "many distinctly human words" alongside "the words of God".[141]   In addition they also rejected the penal theory of the atonement in favour of the idea that the Cross is a demonstration of our sinfulness and God's love designed to lead us to penitence and faith and reduced belief in the Trinity to belief that God has manifested Himself in nature, history and the human heart.[142]

Worsdell too advocated the idea that the Bible is a progressive revelation containing material which was merely an accommodation to earlier and less advanced thought.  He also denied that "the presence of an assertion in Scripture" is "a guarantee of its truth".[143]  Furthermore, he rejected the penal theory of the atonement in favour of the belief that the purpose of the Cross was to show us "the awfulness of sin in the Divine sight" so that we can be saved by the example of the Cross leading us to "like self-sacrifice"[144] and held out the hope that those who died impenitent might still be saved in the next life.[145]

A reasonable Faith caused a great controversy[146] and Worsdell's essay was attacked in London Yearly Meeting and cost him the headship of Lancaster Friends' School[147], but the tide of opinion started to flow against Evangelicalism. In 1888 London Yearly Meeting declined to adopt a statement of Evangelical Quaker belief drawn up by a General Conference of Friends held at Richmond Indiana the previous year[148] Then in 1893 and 1894 the right to dissent from

---

[141] Frith, Pollard and Turner op.cit. p.101.

[142] ibid pp.26 and 75.

[143] Worsdell op.cit. p.63.

[144] ibid p.70.

[145] ibid p.70.

[146] See the correspondence about it in *The Friend* Second Series, vol. XXV 1885 and in *The British Friend* vol. XLIII 1885. See also the reports of the discussion it provoked at London Yearly Meeting in *The Friend* Second Series, vol. XXV 1885 sixth month 6, pp. 142-144, and in *The British Friend* vol. XLIII 1885 6 month 1st No. VI pp.127-130.

[147] Punshon op.cit. p.192.

[148] For the text of this declaration see the *Proceedings, including Declaration of Christian Doctrine, of the General Conference of Friends held in Richmond Indiana* Richmond Indiana: Nichols and Bro. 1887 and for the discussion of it in London Yearly Meeting see *The Friend* New Series, Sixth Month 9th 1888 pp.158-160 and *The British Friend* vol. 46 No. 6 6th Month 5th 1888 pp. 152-157

Evangelicalism was forcefully defended in London Yearly Meeting by speakers who were to become the leaders of Liberal Quakerism.

For example, Braithwaite declared in London Yearly Meeting in 1893 that:

> The Society (of Friends) was no longer secluded from the influences of the world around it; it was subject to the scientific spirit of the age. The fresh aspiration and thought of the world was brought to the interest of their members, and they could not be expected to look upon truth in the same way as their forefathers did.[149]

For another example, John Wilhelm Rowntree declared in London Yearly Meeting the following year:

> Our real basis of unity must be that of aim, not a mere uniformity of thought. We could meet together in practical work even while we thought differently. Even though one person might differ in thought from another, yet let his efforts be recognised if he were endeavouring to lead a pure and noble life. If there could be a freer atmosphere in our meeting - houses we should go forward with greater power than in the past ... in the belief of the acknowledged guidance of God in the heart there was enough unity for any church to base itself upon.[150]

Finally, in 1895 the Manchester Conference was held, "The first occasion on which 'Modern Thought' on religious matters was officially recognised by the Society." [151] In my next chapter I shall consider this conference and its consequences.

---

[149] *The Friend* New Series vol. XXXIII 2nd June 1893 p.350

[150] *The Friend* New Series vol. XXXIV No. 22 1st June 1894 p.34.

[151] Grubb 'Some Personal Experiences' p.307.

# Chapter Two
## Late Victorian Liberalism

In the last chapter I noted that the first sign that the Quakers were going to find it impossible to ignore permanently the Victorian questioning of faith was the publication of *A reasonable faith* and *The Gospel of Divine Help*. What the authors of these works were attempting to do was to re-interpret traditional Christian theology in order to make it more acceptable in the face of the contemporary challenges to Christian belief. As I have indicated, Liberal Quakers such as these authors were not the only people at the time attempting to re-interpret traditional beliefs. They were part of a group of Liberal theologians from across the various Christian denominations who in the last two decades of the nineteenth century sought to re-think their particular Christian traditions so as to try to integrate them with contemporary thought.

Two examples from different ends of the denominational spectrum will illustrate this point.

In 1889 a number of younger theologians from the Anglo-Catholic wing of the Church of England led by Charles Gore published a collection of essays called *Lux Mundi*[1]. In the preface to this work Gore declares that the contributors had written:

> ...with the conviction that the epoch in which we live is one of profound transformation, intellectual and social, abounding in new

---

[1] Charles Gore (ed) *Lux Mundi* London: John Murray 1889

needs, new points of view, new questions; and certain therefore to involve great changes in the outlying departments of theology, where it is linked to other sciences, and to necessitate some general restatement of its claim and meaning.[2]

In their view what this statement required was a new development in theology and this was what they had attempted in the studies contained in *Lux Mundi*

> ...theology must take a new development.  We grudge the name development on the one hand, to anything which fails to preserve the type of the Christian church; for development is not innovation, it is not heresy:  on the other hand, we cannot recognise as the 'true development of Christian doctrine' a movement which means merely an intensification of a current tendency from within, a narrowing and hardening of theology by simply giving it greater definiteness or multiplying its dogmas.
>
> The real development of theology is rather the process in which the Church, standing firm in her old truths, enters into the apprehension of the new social and intellectual movements of each age;  and because 'the truth makes her free' is able to assimilate all new material, to welcome and give its place to all new knowledge, to throw herself into the sanctification of each new social order, bringing forth out of her treasures things new and old, and showing again and again her power of witnessing under changed circumstances to the Catholic capacity of her faith and life.
>
> To study such a development these studies attempt to be a contribution.[3]

In 1891 the Congregational leader R.W.Dale, who stood in the tradition of Evangelical Non-Conformity, published a series of lectures entitled *The Living Christ and the Four Gospels*.[4]  In these lectures Dale addresses:

> ...large numbers of people who suppose that modern science and modern criticism have destroyed the foundation of faith, and who cannot understand how it is possible in these days for intelligent, open minded, educated men to belief in the Lord Jesus Christ.[5]

---

[2]  ibid p. VIII

[3] ibid pp. VIII-IX.

[4] R.W.Dale *The Living Christ and the Four Gospels* London: Hodder and Stoughton 1891

[5] ibid p.1

Dale's response to this sort of attitude is to appeal to experience as the basis for faith. Traditional Evangelical theology had based faith in Christ on the authority of the Bible understood as the infallible Word of God, but Dale argues that Christian experience can provide a basis for belief independent of any particular view of the Bible:

> ...the faith in the living Christ of those who have had the great experiences of His power and grace which I have described is not shaken by any assaults on the historical trustworthiness of the story of His earthly Ministry. Much less can it be shaken by discussions concerning the nature and origin of the ancient scriptures of the Jewish people. Their confidence in the books, both of the Old Testament and the New, may perhaps have to be suspended until the controversies of scholars are closed, or until they can see their own way to firm and definite conclusions about the main questions at issue, but not their confidence in Christ. They may be uncertain about the books; they are sure about Him. Both Christian scholars and the commonalty of Christian people approach the controversies with a settled faith in His power, His grace, His glory. Their faith in Him rests on foundations which lie far beyond the reach of scientific and historical criticism. They know for themselves that Christ is the saviour of men; for they have received through Him the remission of their own sins; He has translated them into the Divine Kingdom; He has given them strength for righteousness and through Him they have found God.[6]

I have noted that the publication of *A reasonable faith* and *The Gospel of Divine Help* provoked opposition within the Society of Friends. Liberal theology of the kind I have described also provoked similar opposition from conservatives in other denominations.

For example, in the edition of the Metropolitan Tabernacle magazine *The Sword and the Trowel* for August 1887 the eminent Baptist preacher C.H.Spurgeon declared that reading the Non-Conformist newspapers sympathetic to Liberal thought led one to ask:

> How much farther could they go? What doctrine remains to be abandoned? What other truth to be the object of contempt? A new religion has been initiated which is no more Christianity than chalk is cheese; and this religion, being destitute of moral honesty, passes

---

[6] ibid p.23

itself off as the old faith with slight improvements, and on this plea
usurps pulpits which were erected for Gospel preaching.   The
Atonement is scouted, the inspiration of Scripture is derided, the
Holy Spirit is degraded into an influence, the punishment of sin into
a myth, and yet these enemies of our faith expect us to call them
brethren and maintain a confederacy with them![7]

So seriously did Spurgeon feel about this issue that he resigned from the
Baptist Union in what became known as the 'Down-Grade' controversy in protest
against its refusal to exclude those who had abandoned strict Calvinist orthodoxy
and had accepted Biblical criticism.[8]

Again, after the publication of *Lux Mundi* Gore and the other contributors
attracted strong criticism from those who felt that their proposed development of
doctrine amounted to a betrayal of Anglo-Catholic principles.

Thus the Anglo-Catholic controversialist Archdeacon George Denison
asked in a pamphlet entitled *A letter to Rev C.Gore*:

What is to be the issue of the proposed never-ending, always-
increasing flux of the religious mind of a people in successive
generations?  It looks very like the adoption of evolution in respect
of the 'One Faith': or like a tribute needful to be paid by the Church
on the part of the faith, to the successive accumulations of the
'natural knowledge' of man.  I had believed, and do believe, that the
faith has been given once for all to the Church, to be by the Church
delivered as received - delivered to man for man to accept humbly
and thankfully for his use, unto life eternal, in correcting and
purifying and sanctifying all natural knowledge;  and in no manner
or degree whatsoever for subordination, adaptation,adjustment to
the 'inventions' of men.[9]

In 1892 Denison resigned from the Anglo-Catholic body the English
Church Union, which he had helped to found, because he could not persuade it to
censure the teaching of *Lux Mundi*[10]

---

[7] *The Sword and the Trowel* vol.XXIII No.272 August 1887 p.29.

[8] See I.H.Murray *The Forgotten Spurgeon* London: Banner of Truth 1966 ch.6.

[9] G.A.Denison *A letter to the Rev C. Gore* London: Longman Green and Co. 1890 P.5

[10] G.L.Prestige *The Life of Charles Gore* London: Heinemann 1935 pp.116-7

The resignations of Spurgeon and Denison indicated which way thought was moving. From the late 1880's onwards Liberal theology began to achieve widespread acceptance in most of the mainstream churches in this country. This process of acceptance began with the Church of England and the Congregationalists and other churches such as the Baptists and the Wesleyan Methodists then followed suit.[11] The notable exception to this acceptance of Liberal theology was the Roman Catholic Church in which the Liberal ideas held by the so-called 'Modernists' were eventually condemned in the Decree *Lamentabili* and the Encyclical *Pascendi* issued by Pope Pius X in 1907.[12]

In his book *Evangelical Nonconformists and Higher Criticism in the 19th Century* Willis Glover notes that the acceptance of Biblical criticism was facilitated by the fact that its acceptance did not involve: "_ any important theological issue"[13] and what was true for Biblical criticism seems to have been true for theology as a whole. That is to say, the reason why the ideas of Liberal theologians won acceptance in the churches is that to many people they seemed to offer the best of both worlds. On the one hand they provided a positive response to the developments of thought in the Victorian era. On the other hand they also appeared to leave the heart of the Christian faith substantially unchanged.

Thus in the preface to *Lux Mundi* Gore insists that theology needs to develop so as to respond positively to intellectual and social change, while at the same time he also stresses that such development must not mean heretical innovation and needs to be undertaken by a church: "standing firm in her old truths". Thus also in *The Living Christ and the Four Gospels* Dale allows for a suspension of judgement about the nature of the Bible in the face of scholarly controversy while maintaining that this need not undermine faith in Jesus Christ.

The attraction of this middle way between intellectual obscurantism and the wholesale abandonment of Christian beliefs is clearly illustrated in G.L.Prestige's

---

[11] See W.B.Glover *Evangelical Nonconformists and Higher Criticism in the 19th century* London: Independent Press 1954 and A.M.G.Stephenson *The rise and decline of English Modernism* London: SPCK 1984 ch.1

[12] A.R.Vidler *The Modernist Movement in the Catholic Church* Cambridge: C.U.P. 1934 ch.XXVI.

[13] Glover op.cit. p.285.

biography of Gore. In it Prestige explains how Gore's essay in *Lux Mundi* together with the strength of his personal faith provided Oxford undergraduates of the 1890's with an alternative to both the radicalism of Benjamin Jowett and the ultra-conservative Anglo-Catholicism of H.P.Liddon:

> To many undergraduates Gore appeared as an intellectual deliverer. It was plain to them that the old outlook on the Bible could no longer be maintained. Broad churchmen, like Jowett, afforded no refuge; the faith they had to offer did not seem worth having. If Dr.Liddon could only offer them a Christianity impossible to believe, and Dr.Jowett a Christianity not worth believing, what were young men to do? Gore provided the answer. To men like these his essay in *Lux Mundi* was a message of orthodoxy and hope. They learned from it for the first time that it was unnecessary to identify Catholic Christianity with the verbal inspiration of the Bible. They came to believe in the living reality of the Church, as they had never believed in it before. And if haunting doubts sprang up about the New Testament and they began to fear that Christian apologists might be prejudiced in their defence of the Gospel, it was enough for them to put Gore to the question. Did he, apart from all orthodox desire and traditional bias, genuinely believe that the evidence was sufficient to justify staking one's life on it? He assured them with a smile, that he did so think and believe, and he would end the interview with the comforting affirmation, 'Yes, I assure you that I have no skeleton in my cupboard'. He was a rock, says one of them, with a rock-like faith, built on most intimate communion with the Rock of Ages.[14]

## The Manchester Conference

The point after which British Quakerism began to follow the example of other churches by coming to accept Liberal theology was the Manchester Conference of 1895. In this chapter I shall explain what happened at this conference and how, in its wake, Liberal theology came to dominate British Quakerism. In the course of this explanation I shall demonstrate that Liberal Quakerism formed part of a wider movement of Liberal theology by showing the close links that existed between Liberal Quakers and Liberal theologians in other denominations. I shall argue that these links can be seen in the ideas put forward by Liberal Quakers, in the speakers at their conferences, in the books they read and

---

[14] Prestige op.cit. pp.118-9.

recommended and in the lecturers at the college they established. I shall also argue that the reasons for the acceptance of Liberal theology by the British Quakers were the same as the reasons for its acceptance in other churches.

The Manchester Conference was held at the suggestion of the Friends Home Mission Committee. This had been set up by London Yearly Meeting in 1882 to support and encourage the work that was being done, mostly by younger Quakers, to revive declining Quaker Meetings and to bring the unconverted to Christ.[15] As the reports of 1882 Yearly Meeting in *The Friend*,[16] and *The British Friend*[17] make clear, it was the influence of Evangelical Quakers that led to its formation in the face of the hesitations felt by traditionalist Quakers who thought that organised mission activity ran the risk of compromising Quaker principles. It is therefore ironic that it should have been an initiative by this particular committee that led to the convening of the Manchester Conference, and so indirectly to the eclipse of Evangelicalism within British Quakerism which resulted from it.

The Home Mission Committee suggested the holding of a conference such as the one which eventually met at Manchester because, at its meeting on the 7th-8th February 1895, it came to the conclusion that efforts needed to be made:

> ...to dispel the ignorance that, more or less, exists in the public mind with regard to the principles and practices of the Society, and to strengthen the attachment of its younger members to its work.[18]

The committee then sent a minute to London Yearly meeting setting out this conclusion and suggesting that they should be asked to organise a conference to discuss the matter.

At its meeting later in the year London Yearly Meeting agreed that such a conference should be held and that the Home Mission Committee should be asked to organise it. It produced a minute authorising the committee:

---

[15] See 'Extracts from the Minutes and Proceedings of the Yearly Meeting' in *The Friend* London: Edward Marsh 1882 pp 21-25

[16] *The Friend* vol. XXII No. 26 Sixth Month 8th 1882 pp 136-47

[17] *The British Friend* vol. XL No. VI Sixth Month 1st 1882

pp 139-46.

[18] *Proceedings of the Manchester Conference* London: Headley Brothers 1896 'Introductory'

....to arrange for a conference on the subjects of their Minute
during the coming Autumn, at such a time and place as they may
consider best, the conference to be composed of members of the
Home Mission Committee together with the representatives
appointed by the Quarterly Meetings of Men and Women Friends,
in equal numbers to those usually appointed to the Yearly Meeting.
The conference is, however, to be open to the attendance of all
Friends, Men and Women. It is required to report to this Meeting
next year.[19]

The importance of this Minute is that it indicates the nature of the
Manchester Conference. The Conference was not a private one organised by a
particular party or group within British Quakerism. It was an official and
representative gathering of British Quakers authorised by, and reporting to,
London Yearly Meeting. As the Clerk to the Conference, Charles Brady, said at
its opening session: "This is a Conference appointed by the Yearly Meeting and
ordered to report to Yearly Meeting".[20]

The Conference was held at Manchester because Lancashire and Cheshire
Quarterly Meeting, having heard that such a conference might be organised, issued
an invitation for it to be held there,[21] and according to the published account of the
proceedings the attendance was 'very large, varying, at a rough estimate, from
1,000 to 1,300 persons."[22]

During the course of its sessions the Manchester Conference considered
the following eight subjects:

"Early Quakerism - its spirit and power."

"Has Quakerism a message for the world today?"

"The relations between Adult Schools and Mission Meetings and the
organisation of the Society of Friends."

"The attitude of the Society of Friends towards Social Questions."

"The attitude of the Society of Friends towards Modern Thought."

"The more effective presentation of spiritual truth."

---

[19] *Extracts from the Minutes and Proceedings of the Yearly Meeting of Friends 1895*  London:
Office of the Society of Friends  pp 54-55.

[20] *Proceedings of the Manchester Conference* p.17

[21] ibid p.12

[22] ibid *'Introductory'*

"The vitalising of our Meetings for Worship."

"The message of Christianity to the world."[23]

From the official record of the Conference it appears that, if we exclude contributions which were concerned with the working of the conference itself, there were 139 contributions to the Conference on those subjects by a total of 108 speakers. These contributions ranged from lengthy papers prepared in advance to short spontaneous comments made from the floor of the Conference, and they may be usefully divided into three categories. These categories are: theologically uncontroversial contributions, contributions expressing

The vast majority of contributions, 92 out of 139, came under the first category. Either they expressed no theological opinions at all, or they expressed theological opinions which would have been acceptable to all British Quakers of that period whatever their particular theological standpoint.

Examples of contributions expressing no theological opinions are the presentation by Ellwood Brockbank of information concerning the existence and status of unofficial "Christian Societies" on the fringe of the Society of Friends; the presentation by George Newman of the results of an inquiry into the lives of the London poor, and the suggestion by Hannah Cadbury that "great benefit" would result from the presence of male Quakers on the "Boards of Guardians" who administered the Poor Law.[24]

Examples of contributions expressing generally acceptable theological opinions are the contributions to the Conference by Elizabeth Cadbury, Joshua Rowntree and Anne Richardson.

Speaking on the subject "Has Quakerism a Message to the World Today?", Elizabeth Cadbury declared:

> I feel very thankful for the discussion of this subject this morning, for I feel that we do need more of the individual reception of the Holy Spirit filling our hearts, so that our meetings may be

---

[23] ibid pp. VI-VII

[24] ibid pp 101-9, 194-6 and 197

collectively what God would have them to be, and that we may rightly deliver our message to the world.[25]

In his address on the topic "The Society of Friends in relation to Social Questions", Joshua Rowntree told the Conference that:

> Granting, as we modestly may do, that Friends have a fair amount of common sense, it seems to be true that what is especially requisite for the adoption of a right attitude of mind towards social questions, is a mind resolutely free from the trammels of conventionalism and worldlyism, and a spirit lighted with the love of Christ towards our fellow men.[26]

As part of her address on "The Message of Christianity to the World" Anne Richardson stated that:

> The work of George Fox, a work committed to him by God, as many others besides our own Society now see, was to recall men's souls and spirits, weary of shells and husks, to the truth that the redemption wrought in Christ must be made a spiritual reality in the inmost heart of each. The early Quakers discovered once again that the one great endowment for a spiritual ministry, as for a spiritual life, was the direct influence of the Holy Spirit of God, and that every human soul who had life in Christ by faith became thereby, in the apostle's words, a "priest unto God".[27]

As I have indicated, such statements were theologically uncontroversial and would have been acceptable to Quakers holding a range of differing theological viewpoints. All Quakers at the end of the nineteenth century would, for example, have agreed that individual Quakers needed to be filled with the Holy Spirit, and that a right attitude to "Social Questions" demanded "a spirit lighted with the love of Christ towards our fellow men". All Quakers at that time would, I think, also have agreed that the work of George Fox was to recall man to the "truth that the redemption wrought by Christ must be made a spiritual reality in the heart of each", and that "the one great endowment for a spiritual ministry" was

---

[25] ibid p.65

[26] ibid p.147

[27] 27. ibid p.371

"the direct influence of the Holy Spirit of God". Sentiments such as these would have been common ground among Quakers of all theological persuasions because they express basic Quaker beliefs.

If the vast majority of the contributions to the Manchester Conference were thus theologically uncontroversial, twenty five of them put forward a specifically Evangelical point of view. We can see this point of view expressed, for example, in papers given by Frederick Sessions, J. Bevan Braithwaite and John T. Dorland which contain features characteristic of Evangelical Quakerism.

As I indicated in the last chapter, Evangelical Quakerism was a mixture of traditional Quaker ideas and practices with beliefs common to Evangelical Christians across the Protestant denominations. It is this combination we see in these three papers.

In the papers by Braithwaite and Dorland we see a commitment to Quaker traditions in theology and worship.

Braithwaite was the leading Evangelical Quaker of his day and is described by Rufus Jones as "... in type of thought and spirit .. a genuine successor of Joseph John Gurney".[28] In his paper on 'The attitude of Friends towards Modern Thought' Braithwaite declared that he assumed that the intention behind the Conference's discussion of this topic was not:

> ...to suggest any change in the position which our religious society has ever maintained in relation to all that our Heavenly Father has been pleased to reveal concerning Himself in the Gospel of His Beloved Son. Rather would we desire afresh to re-affirm our deepening sense of the importance and necessity of this position, and of the high and glorious privileges involved in its faithful maintenance.[29]

In other words, traditional Quaker doctrine must be upheld.

Dorland was a Canadian engaged in Home Mission work in this country[30] In his paper on 'The vitalizing of our Meetings for Worship' he reflected the traditional Quaker emphasis on simplicity and immediacy in worship when he

---

[28] Jones *The Later Periods of Quakerism* vol.II London: Macmillan 1921 p.930.

[29] *Proceedings of the Manchester Conference* p.209.

[30] See W.K.Baker *John T.Dorland* London: Headley Bros. 1898.

stressed that Quakers could gladly leave to others "magnificent architecture" and
"all the gorgeous accompaniments of a sensuous worship" because:

> ...our plain meeting places will be made the birthplaces of souls,
> they will be 'lit with their loving and aflame with God' and we shall
> say again in no pride or arrogancy, 'it seemed good unto the Holy
> Ghost and to us - a worship and service that have in them the
> immanency and immediateness of God Himself'.[31]

In the papers by all three speakers we also see an emphasis on beliefs held
in common by all Evangelical Christians.

Firstly in the paper by Frederick Sessions on the theme "Has Quakerism a
message to the world today?" we find an emphasis on the essential orthodoxy of
the Society of Friends similar to that which we noted in Gurney's *Observations on
the religious peculiarities of the Society of Friends*:

> Friends have never, from their beginning until now, professed to
> have any new revelation or new teaching respecting the great
> central Christian beliefs.   On all these points they have taken
> especial pains to prove their unity with orthodox Protestant
> Churches in an apostolic series of apologies, confessions,
> declarations, Yearly Meetings' Epistles.[32]

Secondly, in all three papers we see a Christ centred and Biblically based
theology expressed through the use of Biblical quotations and Biblical
phraseology.  For example, Braithwaite told the conference:

> The great facts are irreversible which belong to our position as men
> and as Christians.  We cannot uncreate ourselves.   We cannot
> uncrucify Christ, or set aside His own declaration, 'I am He that
> liveth and was dead, and, behold, I am alive for evermore'. (Rev.
> 1:18).  As creatures we cannot be independent.  As those who have
> been 'bought with a price' we cannot deny that we 'are not our own'
> (1 Cor.vi,19,20).  Our growth and prosperity as a Christian Church
> are inseparably bound up with a whole-hearted allegiance to our

---

[31] *Proceedings of the Manchester Conference* p.321.

[32] ibid pp.36

living head, and a subjection to His truth as our Saviour and King at
one fearless, truthful and unwavering.[33]

Thirdly, in line with the 1836 Yearly Meeting Epistle, Sessions emphasised
the authority of the Bible, maintaining that any alleged revelation from God to an
individual had to be subject to: "the authority of the Scriptures of Truth as ultimate
tests of doctrine".[34]    In addition Braithwaite contended that the critical
investigation of the Old Testament need not lead to any re-assessment of the
Quaker attitude towards it:

> The researches which are still being diligently prosecuted into the
> character and authentication of the books of the Old Testament,
> and the verification of their contents from the monuments of the
> other ancient civilizations cannot yet be said to be fully completed,
> but they have already produced results which tend both to enlarge
> and confirm the views, which as a Religious Society we have ever
> entertained of the Old Testament.  On the one hand, although in
> Professor Driver's recent important, and in many respects VERY
> VALUABLE 'Introduction to the literature of the Old Testament'
> we may find suggestions which we are at liberty to treat with the
> same freedom which he has thought it right to apply to some
> portions of the Old Testament, and from some of which I may be
> allowed respectfully to dissent – we may listen with no small
> satisfaction to his testimony in reference to what is popularly styled
> 'the Higher Criticism'.  'These conclusions', says he, 'affect not the
> fact of Revelation, but only its form.  They help to determine the
> stages through which it passed, the different phases which it
> assumed, and the processes by which the record of it was built up.
> They do not touch either the authority or the inspiration of the
> Scriptures of the Old Testament.  They imply no change in respect
> to the Divine attributes recorded in the Old Testament;  no change
> in the lessons of human duty to be derived from it;  no change as to
> the general position (apart from the interpretation of particular
> passages) that the Old Testament points forward prophetically to
> Christ'.      On the other hand men like Professors Sayce and
> Flinders Petrie have by their researches triumphantly demonstrated
> the substantial accordance of Old Testament history with the facts
> disclosed by the tablets and monuments of Ancient Egypt and
> Assyria.[35]

---

[33] ibid p.210

[34] ibid p.39

[35] ibid pp 215-16

This quotation reflects two points of particular interest.  Firstly, the fact that Braithwaite defends a conservative view of the Old Testament reflects the fact that it was the Old Testament that was the focus of controversy at the time.

Mainly as a result of the work of the Cambridge trio of New Testament scholars J.B.Lightfoot, B.F.Westcott and F.J.A.Hort, a fairly traditional view of the dating and historicity of the New Testament was still widely accepted at the end of the nineteenth century.  It was the traditional view of the Old Testament that was coming under pressure.[36]

Secondly, it is noteworthy that although Braitwaite's overall approach to the Old Testament was conservative he was nevertheless prepared to accept the principle of critical investigation of it and was even prepared to say complimentary things about the work of Driver, which popularised in Britain the radical approach to Old Testament criticism developed in Germany by Karl Graf and Julius Wellhausen.[37] Braithwaite's willingness to accept the principle of Old Testament criticism parallels the attitude of other Free Church leaders such as R.W.Dale, the Baptist John Clifford and the Presbyterian W.G.Elmslie.[38]  It also helps to explain why other Evangelical Quakers were able to come to terms with the whole hearted acceptance of the results of Old Testament criticism advocated by the Quaker Liberals.  Once the principle of Old Testament criticism had been conceded by an Evangelical leader such as Braithwaite it was then easier for other Evangelicals to accept the results of Old Testament criticism even when these challenged traditional views of the Bible.

---

[36] See Chadwick op.cit.pp.71-2 and for the work of Lightfoot, Westcott and Hart see Neill op.cit.ch.II.

[37] The work by Driver referred to here is S.R.Driver *Introduction to the Literature of the Old Testament* Edinburgh: T & T Clark 1891.  For its context and importance see R.K.Harrison *Introduction to the Old Testament* Leicester: I.V.P. 1969 ch.II.

[38] See C.T.Bateman *John Clifford - Free Church Leader and Preacher* London: National Council of Evangelical Free Churches 1904 pp.163-4, A.W.W.Dale *The Life of R.W.Dale* London: Hodder & Stoughton 1898 pp.349-50 and W.R.Nicoll and A.N.Macnicoll (eds.) *W.G.Elmslie -Memoir and Sermons* London: Hodder & Stoughton 1890 pp.45-6.

**The Liberal Contribution**

Alongside the uncontroversial and Evangelical contributions to the conference there were also twenty two Liberal contributions. Although this was the smallest category of contributions it was also the most significant because the Liberal understanding of Quakerism was to shape the way that British Quaker theology was to develop until the beginning of the 1960's.

Although the Evangelical and Liberal forms of Quakerism differed markedly in their theology they can both be understood as attempts to combine Quaker traditions with wider currents of thought. As I have noted, for Liberal Quakerism this meant combining them with beliefs common to Liberal theologians in the latter part of the nineteenth century. It is this second combination we see in the Liberal contributions to the Manchester Conference.

The Liberal speakers at the conference did not make specific reference to the works of any particular theologians. However, seven beliefs common to Liberal theologians in general can be found in their contributions.

The first and most characteristic of these was the belief that religion had to adapt to fit the changing patterns of contemporary thought.

This was the idea that underlay Gore's Preface to *Lux Mundi* It was also, for example, the idea put forward by the Congregationalist theologian Andrew Fairbairn in his 1878 lecture on 'Faith and Modern Thought' in which he declared that:

> Our religious beliefs can never be dissociated from our conceptions of the Universe; and as the latter grow larger and truer, the former must be transfigured so that they may live and shine in the new light. Hence it is not by affirming the faith in the forms fixed by the past that living thought is to be penetrated and possessed by religion, but by carrying the religious idea into the regions that thought explores, proving its right to live there, it claim to be the only rational interpreter of the universe.[39]

In a similar vein John Wilhelm Rowntree, whom we have already encountered putting the Liberal point of view at Yearly Meeting in 1893, and who

---

[39] A.M.Fairbairn *The City of God* London: Hodder & Stoughton 1883 p.25.

was to be the leading figure in the development of British Quakerism until his early
death in 1905[40] told the Manchester Conference:

> If the age of the faith which comes by tradition and authority is
> gone, and men can no longer believe without knowing why they
> believe, if they are expanding those partial views of the truth that
> were inevitable in earlier times, then such a change will bring, as its
> ultimate result, not weakness but new strength.
>     At the root of this great movement is the longing for reality,
> for a more real and human touch with God.  We must not - we dare
> not - continue in a spirit of timid conservatism.   We must
> understand sympathetically if we would convince and lead.
>     Those who, having the ability, refuse to acquaint themselves
> with the modern development of thought, sadly limit the scope of
> their service.  That faith alone will satisfy which, triumphant and
> aggressive, fights no longer with 'bows and arrow' but arms itself
> with the weapons of the time.[41]

The second of these beliefs, and one which followed on from the first, was
the belief that the theory of evolution put forward by Darwin should be accepted.
Although there were conservative Christians who refused to accept the theory
because they believed it to be incompatible with the Biblical record, by the end of
the last century many educated Christians had come to terms with it and sought to
integrate it with their religious beliefs.[42]

Thus in his 1884 Bampton lectures the Bishop of Exeter, Frederick
Temple, declared that the notion of evolution:

> ... leaves the argument for an intelligent Creator and Governor of
> the world stronger than it was before.  There is still as much as ever
> the proof of an intelligent purpose pervading all creation.   The
> difference is that the execution of the purpose belongs more to the
> original act of creation, less to acts of government since.[43]

---

[40] See Richenda C. Scott 'Authority or experience, John Wilhelm Rowntree and the dilemma of
19th century British Quakerism' *Journal of the Friends Historical Society* XLIX Spring 1960
pp.75-95

[41] *Proceedings of the Manchester Conference* pp.82-3.

[42] For details see J.R.Moore *The Post Darwinian Controversies* Cambridge: CUP 1979.

[43] F.W.Temple *The relations between religion and science* London: Macmillan 1884 pp.122-3.

At the Manchester Conference the Biblical scholar and orientalist J.Rendel Harris urged British Quakers officially to accept the theory of evolution because:

> A generous statement of our belief in the correctness of the evolutionary interpretation of the world, without pretending that it is 'all the keys of all the creeds' (it certainly is one big key), would do much to redeem us from the reproach of conservative timidity, which is usually characteristic of religious organisations, and to set us in our right place amongst the intellectual forces of the world.[44]

The third Liberal belief was that it was impossible to reconcile a literal reading of the early chapters of the book of Genesis with the advances that had taken place in scientific knowledge.  As I indicated in the last chapter, the development of Geology and the emergence of the theory of evolution called into question the scientific accuracy of these chapters as an account of the early history of the world and in the latter half of the nineteenth century many people came to believe that their literal accuracy could no longer be maintained.

This was the view taken by C.W.Godwin in his essay 'On the Mosaic Cosmogony' in *Essays and Reviews* and it was also the view taken, for instance by the report on 'Definite teaching of the Faith' which was submitted to the Lambeth Conference of 1888 and which declared that:

> ...when we call upon men to accept the Lord Jesus as the one Saviour, we do not require them, as part of their belief in Him, to say that the account of the Creation is not only a lesson in the great ideas of the omnipotence of God in making all things out of nothing, the order and harmony of all His working, the subordination of the material to the spiritual, but is also an enunciation of scientific truth in the modern sense of these words [45]

In similar fashion Thomas Hodgkin, a Quaker elder statesman and a noted historian[46], told the Manchester Conference that all intelligent Christians had come

---

[44] *Proceedings of the Manchester Conference* pp.224-5.

[45] Quotation in Stephenson op.cit. p.38.

[46] See Louise Creighton *Life and Letters of Thomas Hodgkin* London: Longmans Green and Co. 1917

to see that although the Hebrew Scriptures are of great value spiritually they are nevertheless:

> ...the work of men in a state of childish ignorance (ignorance which they shared with Plato and Cicero) as to the real constitution and past history of the universe; that their words, all aglow with filial piety and love towards the Creator, and full of deepest insight into His relation to the Soul of Man, do nevertheless reflect this ignorance, and that it is time and labour lost to try to fit in the words of those old Hebrew scribes into the discoveries of modern science.[47]

The fourth belief was that there should be an acceptance of the results achieved by Biblical criticism. This was the position taken by the contributors to *Lux Mundi* who, to quote Alec Vidler, accepted "not only the methods of biblical criticism but its assured results as they seemed to stand".[48] It was also the position taken at the Manchester Conference by John W.Graham and Rendel Harris.

Graham, a tutor at Dalton Hall, the Quaker Hall at the Owens College, Victoria University (now the University of Manchester), described the effect of Biblical criticism as being like the removal of a "uniform coat of speckless and infallible whitewash" to reveal the truth about the nature and development of some ancient building.[49]

Rendel Harris conceded that the Biblical critics "have not done criticising their own criticisms yet, and in many points they will probably turn out to be wrong all round" but he also dismissed those who opposed the findings of Biblical criticism as ecclesiastical obscurantists, declaring that their voices:

> ...may be sonorous enough in Church Congress, but amongst the thoughtful they are 'thin, like voices from the grave'; they may have authoritative episcopal resonance and yet be the 'bat-like shrillings of the dead'[50]

---

[47] *Proceedings of the Manchester Conference* p.208.

[48] A.R.Vidler *The Church in an Age of Revolution* Harmondsworth: Penguin 1961 p.192.

[49] *Proceedings of the Manchester Conference* p.245.

[50] ibid p.224.

Harris is probably making reference to the Episcopal opposition to Lux Mundi and to the attacks made on Gore and Driver at the Church Congresses in 1893 and 1894.[51]In addition he rejected the Evangelical belief in the infallibility of Scripture, stating that "_ the internal discords of all scriptures, and of all explanations of Scriptures, ought to be enough to convince us that we have no infallibility in the house, not a drop!"[52]

The fifth belief was that the historical investigation of the Gospels that had taken place in the nineteenth century had resulted in a greater knowledge and understanding of Jesus as a historical figure than had ever been achieved before.[53] In his book *Christ in Modern Theology* Fairbairn claimed that the late Victorian era knew Jesus:

> ...as no other age has done, as He lived and as He lives in history, a Being who looked before and after within the limits and under the conditions of time and space, influenced by what preceded Him, determining what followed.[54]

At the Manchester Conference this belief was reflected in Rendel Harris's claim that the nineteenth century understood the "outward", or historical, Christ "better than any century since the first"[55]

The sixth belief was a belief in the immanence of God. This had always been part of the Christian tradition, but, to quote Horton Davies, in the later nineteenth century "as the older theology had emphasised God's transcendence so the newer theology emphasised His immanence, His in-dwelling".[56]

---

[51] See Chadwick op.cit. pp.102 and 105.

[52] *Proceedings of the Manchester Conference* p.225

[53] The classic account of this investigation remains A.Schweitzer *The Quest of the Historical Jesus* London: S.C.M. 1954.

[54] A.M.Fairbairn *Christ in Modern Theology* London: Hodder & Stoughton 1893, pp.20-21.

[53] The classic account of this investigation remains A.Schweitzer *The Quest of the Historical Jesus* London: S.C.M. 1954.

[54] A.M.Fairbairn *Christ in Modern Theology* London: Hodder & Stoughton 1893, pp.20-21.

[55] *Proceedings of the Manchester Conference* p.222

[56] Davies op.cit. p.192.

In large part this emphasis on the Divine immanence seems to have resulted from the acceptance of the theory of evolution.  To those who accepted it it seemed necessary to see God at work in and through the evolutionary process rather than as making occasional interventions into His creation.  For example, Aubrey Moore argued in his contribution to *Lux Mundi* that evolutionary science:

> ...has conferred upon philosophy an inestimable benefit, by showing us that we must choose between two alternatives.  Either God is everywhere present, or He is nowhere.  He cannot be here and not here.[57]

In his contribution to the Manchester Conference Graham echoed this new emphasis on God's immanence when he declared that modern thought had come to see God as immanent in the world, and as constantly rather than occasionally at work in it.[58]

The last of the beliefs reflected by the Liberals at the Manchester Conference was that theology had ultimately to be based on an appeal to immediate experience of God.  In a world where science and Biblical criticism had made it increasingly difficult to appeal either to miracles or the Bible to prove the validity of the Christian religion, some other way of justifying Christian faith had to be found and theologians increasingly turned to religious experience to provide it.

Thus, as we have seen, Dale argues in *The Living Christ and the Four Gospels* that Christian faith can be based on the Christian's experience of Christ.  Thus also Temple argues in his Bampton Lectures that the principle reason for belief in God is because:

> There is within us a voice which tells of a supreme law unchanged throughout all space and all time, which speaks with an authority entirely its own;  which finds corroboration in the revelation of science, but which never relies on these revelations as its primary or its ultimate sanction;  which is no inference from observations from the senses external or internal, but a direct communication from the spiritual kingdom, the kingdom, as philosophers call it, of things in themselves;  which commands belief as a duty, and by necessary

---

[57] *Lux Mundi* p.99.

[58] *Proceedings of the Manchester Conference* pp.240-2.

consequence leaves it possible to disobedience; and in listening to which we are rightly said to walk not by sight but by faith.[59]

Graham drew attention to this sort of apologetic at the Manchester Conference when he stated that "Men have got down to the bedrock of faith, so that the religious world has come round to the indwelling voice as its central conception."[60]

As I indicated, the Liberal speakers at the conference sought to combine these common beliefs with specifically Quaker traditions. Three examples will illustrate this.

Firstly, Hodgkin argued that abandonment of belief in the scientific accuracy of the Old Testament need not cause Quakers concern because the fact that George Fox and the other early Quakers were providentially guided to refuse to call the Bible the Word of God meant that it could be said:

> ....it is a conclusion to which our forefathers were led by the Spirit of Christ Himself, that we need not ask you to accept the Hebrew chronology or Hebrew cosmogony as a necessary part of an all-rounded and infallible Word of God.[61]

Secondly, in his contribution to the conference on the subject 'Can a scientific man be a sincere Friend?' the Quaker scientist and Fellow of the Royal Society Silvanus P. Thompson followed John Wilhelm Rowntree in urging Quakers to be open to "modern thought". He argued that they ought to see it as sent by God Himself to sweep away a multitude of theological errors. Furthermore, he also maintained that Quakers did not need to be perturbed by this sweeping away of error because most of the things which would be swept away had: "already been renounced by Friends". As examples of errors already abandoned by Friends he cited belief in the resurrection of the body, the

---

[59] Temple op.cit. pp.37-8.

[60] *Proceedings of the Manchester Conference* p.241.

[61] ibid p.209. Hodgkin was being slightly misleading here. Although, following the Preface to John's Gospel, the early Quakers reserved the title 'Word of God' for Christ Himself they were nevertheless insistent that the words of the Bible were the words of God. See Fox *Journal* pp.159 & 604.

Athanasian Creed, and a priesthood set apart through Apostolic succession, and pointless disputation about the Eucharist, the Trinity and the Incarnation.[62]

Thirdly, Graham identified the Liberal appeal to direct experience of God with the traditional Quaker belief in the witness of the internal monitor. This identification enabled him to claim that the contemporary emphasis on religious experience meant that: "... essential Quakerism holds the future in the hollow of its hand".[63]

## The Influence of the Liberal Contribution

The atttempt by the Liberal speakers at the Manchester Conference to combine Quaker tradition with Liberal theology was not received with universal approbation. At the end of the conference session on "The Society of Friends and Modern Thought", during which the case for Liberal Quakerism was put forward by Hodgkin, Rendel Harris, Thompson and Graham, an anonymous Friend declared:

> I feel concerned to utter my earnest protest against the views
> uttered here tonight. It seems to me that this conference,
> representing London Yearly Meeting, cannot do justice to itself
> without placing on record a protest.[64]

In the end the conference neither endorsed nor rejected the ideas put forward by the Quaker Liberals but merely re-emphasised that "it assumes no responsibility for the opinions expressed in any of the papers read before it".[65]

However, although there were those who thus objected to the views expressed by the Liberals, and although Liberal views were not endorsed by the Conference, or by London Yearly Meeting when it came to consider the report of the conference the following year, these views seem to have had the support of a

---

[62] *Proceedings of the Manchester Conference* pp.237-8. Thompson's assertion that Quakers had abandoned belief in the resurrection of the body seems to refer to the fact that the early Quakers followed Paul in 1.Cor 15:36-44 in emphasising the spiritual nature of the resurrection body. See Barclay *Catechism* ch.XIV Question 113.

[63] *Proceedings of the Manchester Conference* p.241.

[64] ibid p.247

[65] ibid p.249

sizeable number of Quakers. At the end of the session on"The Society of Friends and Modern Thought" Samuel J.Capper declared: "Many of us feel that never in our lives have we so appreciated the privilege of being Quakers as tonight".[66] and an anonymous Friend stated: "Many of us feel that there is widespread sympathy with these papers read tonight especially among our younger Friends".[67]

Although a fair number of Quakers were thus sympathetic to the ideas put forward by the Liberal speakers at the Manchester Conference, they would still have been a minority within British Quakerism, but as Howard Hodgkin wrote in a letter to *The Friend* in December 1895 what the Manchester Conference showed was that " it has now become possible for earnest-minded Friends to differ from the opinions of the majority and yet be regarded as loyal members of the Society."[68] The fact that Quaker Liberals were able to express their views to an official and representative Quaker gathering without attracting censure or condemnation showed that Liberalism was not seen as incompatible with loyalty to Quakerism.

The reference to "our younger Friends" by the anonymous speaker quoted above is significant because it supports other evidence that it was the younger generation of Quakers who were especially receptive to Liberal theology.

For instance, many of the leaders of the Liberal movement within British Quakerism were themselves still comparatively young. At the time of the Manchester Conference John Wilhelm Rowntree was twenty seven, William Bevan Braithwaite was thirty three and John W. Graham was thirty six.

Furthermore, Rufus Jones, whose evidence is valuable because he took a leading part in the development of Quakerism in this country[69] tells us that the openness to Liberal ideas shown at the Manchester Conference was felt to be liberating by "the Young Friends who were being prepared in the excellent schools of the Society, and who were being educated at the Universities"
because it meant they could:

---

[66] ibid p.247

[67] ibid p.247.

[68] *The Friend* vol.XXXV No.50 13th December 1895 p.825.

[69] See E.G.Vining *Friend of Life- The biography of Rufus M. Jones* London: Michael Joseph 1959 and Punshon *Portrait in Grey* pp.225-9.

...pursue their search for truth fearlessly without feeling themselves
forced either to adopt a hypocritical position to revolt from a
theological scheme incompatible with their accepted scientific
conclusions, having no refuge left for the soul but barren
agnoticism.[70]

The point that Jones is making in this quotation is clearly illustrated by
Laurence Richardson in his autobiographical article 'Newcastle upon Tyne Friends
and Scientific Thought' published in the *The Journal of the Friends Historical
Society* in 1953.

In this article Richardson recalls that shortly after he left boarding school,
in about 1887, the editor of the Evangelical Quaker newspaper The Friend came to
Newcastle to conduct a mission at the Quaker Meeting House:

....and I heard him explain Christianity in these words - 'God was so
just that he HAD to punish someone for the sin of Adam; but he
loved mankind so much that he put all the punishment on to his
own son Jesus, so that those who believed on Him might be saved
from future punishment.' I am quite sure now that many other
members would have disliked that as much as I did, but no one told
me so. I was much puzzled and worried greatly over many points
ofdoctrine
        The final upshot was that I revolted rather violently. If
Christianity meant that sort of creed, then I must give up
Christianity. No doubt I was crude; and pugnacious - but I was
having to fight for my spiritual and intellectual life against
influences that would have stifled it. There are some rather sore
memories and I cannot but feel that Newcastle Meeting and the
Society in general failed rather badly in its dealings with those of us
who revolted. There was pity for misled youth; there was not
understanding. It was not persecution and was well meant, but
there was painful social pressure; we were not irreverent or
irreligious, but such views must not be allowed to feel themselves at
home; so it meant feeling like a fish out of water in any religious
gathering; it meant going out into the wilderness for 10 or 12
years.Thomas Hodgkin asked half a dozen of us to his house once
or twice and that was definitely understanding and helpful; he knew
the difference between Jahwist and Elohist in Genesis (which is the
ABC of Biblical origins); what he said in meeting was always
interesting, though he was not so outspoken as I wished; I think he
was very anxious to avoid controversy.
        My attendance at meeting became very irregular. But for
my friendship with John Wilhelm Rowntree ('that dangerous young

---

[70] Jones *The Later Periods of Quakerism* Vol.II p.977.

man' as some called him) I should probably have resigned my membership and might have drifted into indifference. I have heard Neave Brayshaw say that the Society lost a whole generation of young people.[71]

In 1901, Richardson attended the Liberal Summer School held at Scarborough.

I got to the second Summer School at Scarborough in 1901 and what a revelation it was! - a company in which one could speak freely, ask any questions; devotional meetings where one did NOT feel like a fish out of water; lectures by experts as to the origins of the Bible, which made it far more interesting and therefore - a group of human documents with contradictions and errors in plenty, savage atrocities even - but from which one could wash out the gold and let the rest go. Rendel Harris on the quarrels of St. Peter and St. Paul made the latter far more human and understandable if still often not profitable.[72]

The Scarborough Summer School of 1901 was the third in a series of six summer schools in theology organised by the Quaker Liberals from 1897 onwards. The idea of holding a summer school in theology was not new. For example, Fairbairn, following an American precedent, had held summer schools in Oxford for Free Church Ministers in 1892 and 1894.[73] The Quaker summer schools, however, seem to have been a result of the Manchester Conference. At the conference itself Joseph Rowntree suggested that:

... some intelligent study of the scriptures and of great moral questions under competent direction would be an immense help to the majority of those who long that their ministry should be effective.[74]

---

[71] Lawrence Richardson 'Newcastle Upon Tyne Friends and Scientific Thought' *Journal of the Friends Historical Society* vol. XLV 1953 p.41-2.

[72] ibid p.42

[73] W.B.Selbie *The Life of Andrew Martin Fairbairn* London: Hodder & Stoughton 1914 pp.222-228.

[74] *Proceedings of the Manchester Conference* p.269

After it was over Rendel Harris wrote in a letter about the conference published in *The Friend* of the 29th November 1895:

> ....a summer school of Theology or criticism should be assembled in some healthful locality to be held for a given length of time under the management of experts.[75]

In line with these suggestions a 'Summer School for Religious Study' was held at Scarborough from the 4th to 18th August 1897. It was advertised as being intended to:

> ...stimulate thought, promote healthful reading and study, and....to awaken in the Society a fuller conception of the place in the service of Christ of the trained and consecrated intellect.[76]

However, the aim of the Summer School was in fact less straight-forward than these words might lead one to think. Unlike the Manchester Conference the School was not an official and representative gathering. Although it was open to anyone who wished to attend, it was organized privately by a committee of Quaker Liberals including Joshua and John Wilhelm Rowntree, Rendel Harris, and William Charles Braithwaite, and the programme of the School reflected their beliefs and concerns. As a result the School was intended not only to stimulate thought, but also to guide it in a specifically Liberal direction.

Rufus Jones states in *The Later Periods of Quakerism* vol. II that at the Scarborough Summer School of 1897: "The teaching was distinctly on the modern lines, facing frankly and boldly the central questions of the day".[77] Decoded, this means that the teaching followed the path laid down by the Liberals at the Manchester Conference by looking to Liberal theology to meet the challenges posed by contemporary life and thought.

The teaching at Scarborough came under three main headings, "General subjects with special reference to the Old Testament", "New Testament Subjects",

---

[75] *The Friend* vol. XXXV No.48 29th November 1895 p.784

[76] Supplement to *The Friend* 30th April 1897

[77] Jones *The Later Periods of Quakerism* vol. II p.977.

and "Exegesis, Church History, and Social Questions". In addition to the lectures given under these headings there were also a number of "Special lectures and discussions" on subjects ranging from "Armenia" to "How to follow up the work of the Summer School", two public meetings on "Inspiration" and "Christianity in Daily Life", and a meeting for scholars from the Quaker Adult Sunday Schools.

Alongside the teaching given by Quaker speakers such as J.Rendel Harris, Thomas Hodgkin and Edward Grubb, teaching was also provided by eminent scholars from outside the Society of Friends, such as the Congregationalist George Buchanan Grey who was Old Testament Professor at Mansfield College, Oxford, the Baptist T.R.Glover who was an Ancient Historian and a Fellow of St.John's College, Cambridge, and George Adam Smith who was a member of the Free Church of Scotland and Professor of Hebrew at their College in Edinburgh, a fact which once again emphasises that Liberal Quakerism did not exist in isolation but was part of a wider Liberal movement within the British Churches of the day.[78]

The general tenor of the School is illustrated by the following three extracts from papers which were given to it by William Littleboy, Thomas Hodgkin and William Charles Braithwaite.

In a paper on "Teaching from the Old Testament" William Littleboy argued that:

> We must, moreover, cultivate an openness of mind to receive the best results of modern criticism. It is not always needful or expedient to introduce into our lessons in detail even the most assured critical conclusions, but it is often useful to do so; and I know of nothing that has so smoothed the path of the student of the Old Testament in the solving of problems which used to appear almost hopeless, as many of the results worked out by our leading critics, who are indeed the Adult School teacher's best friends. Such books as Robertson Smith's 'Old Testament in the Jewish Church', and 'Prophets of Israel', Driver's 'Introduction to the literature of the Old Testament', and G.A.Smith's 'Historical Geography of the Holy Land' (not to mention many others), should find a place on the shelves of every teacher who can purchase or borrow them. And when we feel it right to use such modern material, let us never commit the fatal blunder of adopting an apologetic tone as if we were half ashamed or half suspicious of the

---

[78] For details concerning the teaching and teachers at Scarborough in 1897 see *Echoes from Scarborough* London: Headley Bros. 1898 pp.V-VIII.

novelties we are propounding, but one rather of joyful satisfaction
that so much additional light has been shed on the sacred page.[79]

Speaking on the "The Inspiration of the Bible" Thomas Hodgkin developed
further the point he had made at the Manchester Conference about the childish
nature of the Old Testament:

> The Revelation, then, of the will of the Most High was made not
> only TO MEN but THROUGH MEN, and necessarily partook of
> the limitations of the human understanding.  Like all things human,
> it was subject to the law of growth and development, and in the
> childhood of the human race it could not be couched in the same
> words which might have been used to it in its maturity.  Let anyone
> try to explain to a little child the bearings of a complicated social
> question, or the details of a political revolution, and he will find at
> every turn that he has to use language which does not fit closely to
> the actual relations of things, but only by somewhat distant
> analogies helps the child to follow his own line of thought.  Such
> was probably the character of the Revelation made to the early
> Hebrew writers, and it is in this way that we must understand the
> 'Anthropomorphisms' which have probably puzzled most of us in
> their pages:   the passages which seem to attribute to God,
> passionate anger, jealousy, changes of purpose, delight in the odour
> of sacrifice and so forth.  And we must always remember that the
> story was not only told to children but has been repeated to us by
> children, - by men, that is to say, in the early stage of spiritual
> development:  and their words come to us sometimes not only with
> that touching simplicity which we call 'childlike', but with that
> ignorance and feebleness of thought which we call by the less
> commendatory word 'childish'.[80]

Lastly, talking on the subject of "Inspiration" William Charles Braithwaite
told his audience that:

> Our modified views of revelation and inspiration make the Bible
> again a modern book.  Its writers are no longer men standing apart
> from our life, cut off from our experiences;  the Bible is no longer
> separated by an impassable gulf from all other books.[81]

---

[79] ibid p.8

[80] ibid pp 5-6

[81] ibid p 13

and declared:

> We recognise that its inspiration varies in quality and degree; and it
> is not different in kind from the wisdom that has come to holy souls
> in all ages, 'making them friends of God and prophets': we
> understand that that which makes the Bible pre-eminent over other
> inspired literature is not any fundamental difference in the kind or
> manner of inspiration of its writers - but partly in the relative purity
> and fulness of the inspiration, and partly in the unique importance
> of the subject matter which the writers treat.[82]

These extracts are typical of the overall teaching at Scarborough. Like the
Liberal contributions to the Manchester Conference they show that Liberal
Quakers were enthusiastic about the results of Biblical criticism and they also
demonstrate that they, like other Liberal theologians of the time, sought to develop
new understandings of the nature and inspiration of the Bible to replace the
traditional Christian emphasis on its perfection and unique inspiration.[83]

The extracts by Littleboy and Hodgkin contain two points worthy of
particular note.

Firstly, the books by Robertson Smith and G.A.Smith mentioned by
Littleboy are, like the book by Driver, works of Biblical criticism by non-Quaker
scholars. This again indicates the dependence of Liberal Quakerism upon outside
scholarship.

Secondly, Hodgkin's emphasis on the childish nature of the Old Testament
enables him to find a solution to some of the moral doubts about the Bible
mentioned in Chapter One. He is able to explain away Old Testament passages
which contain unacceptably "anthropomorphic" pictures of God as being due to
the inevitably immature character of the Old Testament revelation.

The Scarborough Summer School was a great success with seven hundred
people attending its sessions.[84] Its deliberations even attracted favourable editorial
comment from *The Friend* which was traditionally the mouthpiece for Evangelical

---

[82] ibid p.13.

[83] For attempts by non-Quaker Liberal theologians to develop new views of the Bible see
R.F.Horton *Inspiration and the Bible* London: T.Fisher Unwin 1888, Gore's essay on 'The Holy
Spirit and Inspiration' in *Lux Mundi* and W.R.Sanday *Inspiration* Oxford: O.U.P. 1893.

[84] *The Friend* vol. XXXVII No.36 3rd September 1897 p.586

opinion within British Quakerism.[85]   In view of this success a 'Summer School
Continuation Committee' was set up to continue the work begun at Scarborough.
It did this in two ways.

Firstly, it organised more Summer Schools and Settlements on the
Scarborough pattern.  These were held at Birmingham in 1899, Scarborough again
in 1901, Windermere in 1902, Woodbrooke Birmingham in 1903, and lastly at
Sidcot in 1905.  National Summer Schools were discontinued after 1905, but by
then the Summer School idea had become well established in British Quakerism
and smaller local Summer Schools had begun to be organised.  For example there
were local Summer Schools held at Kirkby Moorside in 1904 and at Reigate,
Scalby and Ilkley in 1905.

Secondly, the Summer School Continuation Committee encouraged the
creation of reading circles and lecture courses to propagate more widely the ideas
put forward at the Summer Schools.  Thus the first annual report of the Committee
in June 1898 noted that:  "Reading circles under the auspices of the Committee"
had been formed at Croydon, Dublin, Falmouth, Great Ayton, Jarrow-on-Tyne,
Saffron Walden, Scarborough, and Southport, and in Witney Monthly Meeting.[86]
It also noted that official courses of lectures:  "have been given or are in progress"
at sixteen places, including Birkenhead, Cardiff and Southport, and that unofficial
lecture courses were also in progress as well.[87]

To support these reading circles and lecture courses the committee drew
up lists of suitable and available lecturers and of recommended reading.  For
instance, the third annual report of the committee in 1900 contains "Biblical" and
"Christian Ethics" lecture lists and a "Book List" of recommended literature.  The
lecture lists contain the same mixture of outside experts and Liberal Quaker
speakers as was the case at Scarborough.  The "Biblical" lecture list, for example,
notes that J.V.Bartlett, the Congregationalist Professor of Church History at
Mansfield College Oxford, is willing to give lectures on "The historical study of
the New Testament", "The Book of Acts", "From Primitive Christianity to

---

[85] *The Friend* vol. XXVII No.35 27th August 1897 pp.559-60

[86] Summer School Continuation Committee *First Annual Report 1898* p.1

[87] ibid pp.1-2

Catholicism", and "The Return to the Bible in the 16th Century", and that William Charles Braithwaite is willing to give lectures on "The New Testament, its form, text, and composition", "How we got our New Testament", "The Synoptic Problem", and "Studies in the life and writings of Paul".[88]   The "Book List"[89] mostly consists of works by eminent Liberal scholars from outside the Society of Friends such as Dale's *The Atonement*,[90] and Driver's *An Introduction to the literature of the Old Testament*. However, it also contains works by conservative non-Quaker scholars such as the High Anglican H.P.Liddon's *The Divinity of Our Lord and Saviour Jesus Christ*. The paucity  and derivative nature of Quaker theological scholarship at that time is indicated by the presence on the list of only one work by a Quaker author, Edward Grubb's *First lessons on the Hebrew Prophets*[91] which was a popularisation of the work of Driver.

According to the tenth annual report of the committee in 1907 it also produced a series of "Notes or lesson sheets on Biblical History" and a correspondence class for the study of New Testament Greek.[92]

In 1899 John Wilhelm Rountree  wrote an essay entitled 'The Problem of a Free Ministry' in which he considered the problems involved in upholding the Quaker tradition of a non-professional ministry.  In the course of this essay he suggested that:

> There must be means placed within the reach of any Friend, who feels the call to the Ministry, for still further equipment and for closer study.

As a means to this end he further proposed that "There should be established a PERMANENT Summer School ... This must not be a Theological College, but a permanent Bible School, open to either sex and to persons of any age."[93]

---

[88] Summer School Continuation Committee *Third Annual Report 1900* pp.13 & 14

[89] ibid pp.26-29

[90] R.W. Dale *The Atonement* London: Congregational Union  1894

[91] Edward Grubb *First Lessons on the Hebrew Prophets* London: Headley Bros. 1897.

[92] Summer School Continuation Committee *10th Annual Report* 1907 p.4

[93] J W Rowntree 'The Problems of a Free Ministry' *Present Day Papers* vol II  J.W. Rowntree

This idea of a permanent Summer School had also been advocated by John W.Graham and was of interest to William Charles Braithwaite. It became a reality in 1903. The Quaker chocolate manufacturer George Cadbury had read about Bible Schools in America and became interested in the idea of starting something similar in this country. To this end he placed his former home, called Woodbrooke (near Selly Oak, Birmingham) at the disposal of the Summer School Continuation Committee to be used initially as a venue for the 1903 Summer School, and thereafter as a home for a "settlement for students, who might reside there for a time for purposes of religious study under competent direction".[94]

In this way the 'Woodbrooke Permanent Settlement', later to be known as Woodbrooke College, came into existence in 1903.[95] Rendel Harris became the first director of studies, and the settlement was run by a committee consisting of the executive of the Summer School Continuation Committee and several Birmingham Quakers. The subjects offered for study at Woodbrooke were similar to those being offered at the Summer Schools. There was a core of Biblical Studies supplemented by courses concerned with other aspects of the study of Religion and Society. For instance, in the Spring Term of 1905 Rendel Harris gave lectures on 'Introduction to the New Testament' and 'Greek Testament (advanced)', but there were also lectures by George Shann on 'The remuneration of the Agents of Production', and by Annie H.Small on 'Aspects of the life of a Modern Missionary'.[96] The lecturers at Woodbrooke were also similar to those at the Summer Schools in that they were a mixture of Quakers and sympathetic non-Quaker scholars. Thus in the early days at Woodbrooke lectures were given by Quakers such as Rendel Harris and A. Neave Brayshaw, but they were also given by such non-Quaker scholars as R.S.Franks, who was a Congregationalist, and T.H.Robinson, who was a Baptist. As Punshon notes in *Portrait in Grey,*

---

[94] Summer School Continuation Committee *6th Annual Report 1903* p.2

[95] For more details on the origin of Woodbrooke see Chapter I of Robert Davis (ed.) *Woodbrooke 1903-1953* London: Bannisdale Press 1953

[96] *Woodbrooke Settlement for Religious and Social Study - Programme of Lectures* Spring Term 1905.

Woodbrooke was "not a Quaker ghetto but part of the Liberal Christian think tank."[97]

Because the creation of Woodbrooke was what H.G.Wood calls a "private venture"[98] by the Summer School Continuation Committee the teaching at Woodbrooke unsurprisingly reflected the Liberal ideals of this committee. For example, one of the major concerns of the committee had been to introduce British Quakers to the findings of modern critical scholarship concerning the Bible and early Christian history, and one of the earliest students at Woodbrooke, Ethel M.Heath, later recalled being introduced to these findings during her time there. In her recollections she wrote of learning about modern criticism of the Pentateuch by engaging in "the mild and mechanical occupation of underlining the 'J.E.+ P' portion of the Pentateuch in different coloured inks" and of the lectures by Neave Brayshaw in which he "enlightened us on the work of modern scholars and explorers in confirming or re-shaping our knowledge of Old Testament History". She also wrote of the talks given by Rendel Harris:

> ....on the somewhat recently discovered 'Teaching of the Twelve Apostles' and others on the 'Sayings of Jesus', unearthed by Grenfell and Hunt among their other papyrus finds at Oxyrhynchus

which were memorable:

> ....not only for the startling nature of their content, but because of the background they evoked of the life and  great personalities of the early church.  One also became aware for the first time of the sphere of textual criticism, of manuscript groupings, of versions, of variations, and above all of 'conjectural emendations'![99]

In 1907 the 'Summer School Continuation Committee' became the 'Woodbrooke Extension Committee'. To quote from the chapter on 'Woodbrooke extension work' by J.Roland Whiting and Robert Davis in the history of

---

[97] Punshon op.cit. p.212

[98] Davis op.cit. p.18

[99] ibid pp.118-119

Woodbrooke *Woodbrooke 1903-1953*, this new committee continued the work of the old one by making available:

> ...a small panel of travelling lecturers....to visit meetings, to conduct lecture courses and to give help at locally arranged lecture schools and week-end conferences. The subjects were varied but were usually biblical or concerned with the Quaker interpretation of the Christian faith. The following are typical programmes: Three lectures on 'Psychology of Religious Experience' by A.Barratt Brown at Heys Farm Guest House. Eight lectures on 'Friends' Principles' given by Edward Grubb at several centres. Lectures on 'The Fourth Gospel' and 'The Appeal of Quakerism to the non-mystic' by Wm.Littleboy.[100]

In addition to arranging this pool of travelling lecturers the Woodbrooke Extension Committee also set up the Swarthmore Lectures. I have referred to the purpose of the Lectures, but the point to note here is that all the early lectures were given by those who were part of the Liberal movement within British Quakerism. For example, the first four Swarthmore Lectures, from 1908 - 1911, were given by Rufus Jones, William Charles Braithwaite, Joan M.Fry and Thomas Hodgkin, all of whom were prominent members of this movement.

As one would expect, the content of these early Swarthmore Lectures reflects the Liberal theology of the lecturers. Two examples will serve to illustrate this fact. Firstly, in his 1909 lecture *Spiritual Guidance in Quaker Experience* William Charles Braithwaite argues that the early Quaker idea of the internal divine monitor:

> ... had been verified along the lines of science as well as in the experience of the soul. We are coming to recognise that the gradual development of Man out of lower forms of life made him, at the appropriate stage of that development, responsive to a higher form of consciousness than other animals possess: he became the vehicle through which the universal consciousness could express itself as mind and spirit.[101]

---

[100] ibid p.106

[101] William Charles Braithwaite *Spiritual Guidance in Quaker Experience* London: Headley Bros. 1909 p.87

This linking of evolution with seventeenth century Quaker theology is typical of Liberal Quakerism since, as we saw with reference to the Manchester Conference, it sought to combine Quaker tradition with Liberal theology and acceptance of evolution was a central element in Liberal theology.

Secondly, in her 1910 lecture *The Communion of Life* Joan M. Fry declared that:

> ... some who love the Lord Jesus in sincerity and truth will do well to exercise a larger charity to those who cannot take upon their lips the usual expressions about Him .... the church must learn to make wide her channels, to welcome all sincere seekers, before she can know the flood-tide of fellowship which is waiting to pour over her barred harbour gates.[102]

This welcoming attitude to those unable to assent to traditional doctrine is again typical of Quaker Liberalism because Quaker Liberalism was itself in revolt against the Evangelical insistence on correct belief.

As well as supporting lectures and lecture courses, the Woodbrooke extension committee also produced literature, starting off with a series of Bible notes on the books of the Old Testament, the teaching of Jesus, and the teaching of the Apostle Paul which were published in 1910.[103] Moreover, the literature produced by Woodbrooke was not the only literature produced within British Quakerism in support of the new ideas. The 'Yorkshire 1905 Committee' of Yorkshire Quarterly Meeting produced pamphlets such as William Charles Braithwaite's *What does the Society of Friends stand for?*[104] in support of these new ideas, and books such as Edward Grubb's *Authority and the Light Within*, which contrasts the authority of the Inner Light with that of the Catholic Church and of a supposedly infallible Bible, were also written to justify the new thinking. In addition the liberal understanding of Quakerism was supported by the periodical *Present day Papers* which was produced by John Wilhelm Rowntree between

---

[102] Joan M. Fry *The Communion of Life* London: The Swarthmore Press 2ed. 1925 p.33

[103] Davis op.cit. pp.106-7

[104] William Charles Braithwaite *What does the Society of Friends stand for?* Bannisdale Malton: Yorkshire 1905 Committee N.D

1898 and 1902,[105] and by *The British Friend* during the editorship of Edward Grubb,from 1901-13.[106]

By a tragic irony the early death from pneumonia of John Wilhelm Rowntree in 1905 seems to have strengthened the Liberal party within British Quakerism. As Richenda C. Scott puts it in her article 'Authority or experience - John Wilhelm Rowntree and the Dilemma of 19th century British Quakerism':

> The death of John Wilhelm Rowntree in 1905 shook the Society of Friends as nothing had done since the death of Edward Burrough in Newgate gaol in 1662 - but the effect of that death upon his contemporaries is one of the most amazing witnesses to the creative power of John Wilhelm Rowntree's dedicated life. To all who have left a record of that time it came as a challenge and a spur to increased effort that the things for which he had cared and worked should be carried forward and not die with him.
>
> 'His death, so unexpected and so moving, carried me further perhaps than his continued life could have done' wrote Rufus Jones. 'I felt at once that I had to live and work for both of us and no longer as one person. I felt his concerns laid upon me as though they were mine by birth'.
>
> 'It rests with us to do what is in our power to further the work which he had at heart, and to keep alive the ideals and enthusiasms of 'one who never turned his back but moved breast forward'': said Lawrence Richardson.
>
> 'Seebohm (John Wilhelm Rowntree's brother) is perfectly wonderful, he thinks all the time of how John's work is to be carried on, and is full of plans for holding meetings to put the necessity before the younger Friends who are in sympathy with it', wrote Edward Grubb.
>
> 'His sudden death has drawn us all together who knew him, and to many of us it has brought deep heart-searchings and aspirations after the higher ways', wrote Henry Bryan Binns. 'His memory and life seemed not....to cast a bewildering gloom on everyone, but just the reverse, it seemed to stimulate and encourage everyone', wrote Herbert Standing.[107]

A major consequence of the determination to continue the work of John Wilhelm Rowntree noted by Richenda C. Scott in this article was the production of

---

[105] J.W.Rowntree and H.B.Binns (eds.) *Present day Papers* vols. I-V
1898-1902

[106] *The British Friend* vols.10-22 1901-1913.

[107] Richenda C. Scott 'Authority or Experience' pp.92-3

the seven volume 'Rowntree' history of Quakerism between 1909 and 1921. This consisted of the work of four writers. William Charles Braithwaite wrote *The Beginnings of Quakerism* and *The Second Period of Quakerism* Rufus Jones produced *Studies in Mystical Religion*,[108] *Spiritual Reformers in the 16th and 17th centuries*,[109] and *The later periods of Quakerism* vols. I and II. Lastly, Rufus Jones, Isaac Sharpless and Amelia Gummere were responsible for *The Quakers in the American Colonies*.[110]

As Punshon points out in *Portrait in Grey*, the beginning of this century saw a renaissance of interest in Quaker history, marked by the appearance of *The Journal of the Friends Historical Society* and its supplements from 1903 onwards, the work of Norman Penney in producing editions of early Quaker documents, and the purchase for London Yearly Meeting of George Fox's home, Swarthmore Hall, in 1912.[111] John Wilhelm Rowntree had shared this renewed interest in Quaker history and planned with Rufus Jones the production of a new history of Quakerism. After his death this project was continued under the editorial direction of Rufus Jones and the 'Rowntree' history was the result.

The 'Rowntree' history operates on two levels. On one level it is an extremely thorough piece of historical research which became, and remains, the standard history of Quakerism. On another level, though, it is an extended apology for Liberal Quakerism. Evangelical Quakerism understood itself as being part of Protestant orthodoxy and justified its existence on this basis by arguing that for the most part its beliefs were the same as those of Protestant orthodoxy and where they differed the Quaker position was supported by Holy Scripture. Liberal Quakerism, however, did not wish to see itself as part of Protestant orthodoxy because it believed that this had been discredited by the findings of contemporary thought. It therefore needed a new way of understanding Quakerism and a new justification for its existence. The 'Rowntree' history sought to provide it with both.

---

[108] Rufus Jones *Studies in Mystical Religion* London: Macmillan 1909

[109] Rufus Jones *Spiritual Reformers in the 16th and 17th centuries* London: Macmillan 1914

[110] Rufus Jones, Isaac Sharpless and Amelia Gummere *The Quakers in the American Colonies* London: Macmillan 1911

[111] Punshon op.cit. pp.223-5

Two extracts from Rufus Jones's concluding 'Review and Forecast' at the end of volume II of *The Later Periods of Quakerism* show how it sought to do this.

In the first of these extracts Rufus Jones declares that:

> Quakerism, as has often been said, is one of the numerous attempts in history to revive primitive, apostolic Christianity. The distinct forerunners of it were the Christian mystics and the spiritual reformers of the sixteenth and seventeenth centuries. They, too, endeavoured to revive the experience and power of new-born Christianity - the Christianity of the 'upper room'. They loosened their hold on systems and external authorities, and restored to a place of first importance the seeing eye, the hearing ear, the acutely sensitive soul of the individual Christian. More important for them than any event of the past was the present experience of the Day-dawn within, and the consciousness that the Day-star had risen in their own souls. Their individualism, their lack of organising leaders, and their reliance on the uncharted and unpredictable wind of the spirit, blowing as it listed, kept the earlier movement fluid and prevented it from becoming unified and integrated into a 'church'. George Fox, on the other hand, was a constructive leader, and he succeeded in bringing together into one loosely-knit society men and women who had been 'Seekers', 'Anabaptists', 'Familists', 'Behemites', or members of some others of the hundred and ninety nine varieties of 'sects' and 'schisms' described in Edward's 'Gangraena'.[112]

The argument that Rufus Jones advances here is that Quakerism is the organised form of a religious tradition going back to the Christian Mystics of the Patristic and Mediaeval periods and the Spiritual Reformers of the sixteenth and seventeenth centuries, which laid stress on the present apprehension of God by the individual soul rather than on the importance of historical events, theological systems, and external authorities. Reference to *Studies in Mystical Religion* and *Spiritual Reformers of the Sixteenth and Seventeenth Centuries* makes it clear that the Mystics and Spiritual Reformers mentioned here are figures like Meister Eckhart, The Brethren of the Common Life, Sebastian Franck, and Jacob Boehme.[113]

---

[112] Jones *Later Periods of Quakerism* vol.II p.980

[113] See Jones *Studies in Mystical Religion* chs XII and XIV and *Spiritual Reformers in the Sixteenth and Seventeenth Centuries* chs. IV and IX

This argument formed the first part of the apology for Liberal Quakerism contained in the 'Rowntree' histories.   As I noted in my examination of the Manchester Conference, the Quaker Liberals sought to link Quakerism with the general Liberal emphasis on the importance of religious experience.   Jones' argument supports this linkage by presenting Quakerism not as part of a discredited Protestant orthodoxy, but as part of an alternative 'mystical' and 'spiritual' religion based on direct experience of God.

In the second of these extracts Rufus Jones stated that in so far as the early Quakers:

> ....tried to expound their faith philosophically, they involved it in an inadequate and passing system of thought, and they tied it up to a bad psychology.  Vast changes have been made, especially during the nineteenth century, in the way of interpreting the deepest nature of the universe and the fundamental life of man.  We can use neither the metaphysics nor the psychology of the seventeenth and eighteenth centuries any more than we can use their science, or their systems of transportation.  But the simple direct testimony of these Friends to a God revealed to them experimentally still rings true and carries conviction now.  The Light within is no abstract phrase.  It is an experience of God revealed in the soul of man. What is needed at the present time is a renewal of this first-hand, living experience of God and a vital interpretation of it in the terms of thought which are live and current in the world of our day.[114]

Rufus Jones is saying here that while the religious experience of the early Quakers still carries conviction their metaphysics do not.   Therefore, what is wanted is a renewal of the religious experience they had had, coupled with an interpretation of that experience in terms relevant to contemporary thought.  This argument constituted the second part of the Liberal Quaker apologetic.  As I have indicated, the Quaker Liberals sought both to affirm Quaker tradition and to adapt their theology to fit in with current ways of thinking.   Separating the early Quakers' experience of God from their interpretation of it enabled Quaker Liberals to achieve both of these aims because it allowed them to uphold the basic validity of the Quaker form of religion while re-interpreting it in terms more congenial to contemporary thought.

---

[114]Jones *Later Periods of Quakerism* vol. II p.994

Therefore, to sum up the apology for Liberal Quakerism contained in the 'Rowntree' history of Quakerism we can say that this apology came in two parts. In the first part it was argued that Quakerism was not part of Protestant orthodoxy, but part of an alternative 'mystical' and 'spiritual' form of religion. In the second part it was argued that the early Quaker experience of God still carried conviction, but it needed to be reinterpreted in contemporary terms. This apologetic enabled Quaker Liberals to be both Quakers and Liberals. It enabled them to be Quakers because the experience of God upon which early Quakerism was based was a valid one. It enabled them to be Liberals because the Evangelical understanding of Quakerism as being part of Protestant orthodoxy was mistaken, and because the Liberal desire to re-state Quakerism in up-to-date terms was justified.

Eventually all the efforts made by the Quaker Liberals to publicise and commend their interpretations of Quakerism bore fruit as the Liberal interpretation of Quakerism gradually became prevalent among British Quakers. In the words of Isichei, Liberal Theology "silently and invisibly became an orthodoxy among Friends".[115]

The explanation for this triumph of Liberalism within British Quakerism is the same as the explanation for its acceptance in other denominations. As I have argued, Liberalism was accepted by the Churches in general because it seemed to provide a viable middle path between obscurantism and the wholesale abandonment of traditional beliefs. This was also the reason for its success within British Quakerism.

On the one hand, the willingness of the Quaker Liberals to call into question aspects of traditional belief was welcomed by radical young Quakers such as Lawrence Richardson because it sanctioned their theological questioning and exploration and their desire to jettison those tenets of Evangelical Quakerism they found intellectually incredible.

On the other hand, Liberal Quakerism was also acceptable to many Evangelical Quakers. In the words of Whiting and Davis in the history of

---

[115] Isichei op.cit. 42

Woodbrooke already quoted "many leading evangelical Friends of the time welcomed the new teaching".[116]

This was because the ideas put forward by the Quaker Liberals seemed to be compatible with Evangelical beliefs. This comes out in the editorial comments on the Scarborough Summer School by *The Friend* to which I referred earlier in this chapter.

In the first place it declares that:

> ...the firm conclusion at the Summer School was that 'we are losing little and gaining much' by the new light which has been brought to bear upon the reverent study of the inspired records.[117]

As I have noted, the example of J. Bevan Braithwaite shows that Biblical criticism was already acceptable in principle to Evangelicals at the time of the Manchester Conference; many of them were able to go on to accept the critical approach to the Bible advocated by the Quaker Liberals because the desire to understand the Bible was fundamental to Evangelicalism and this approach seemed to shed fresh light on the Bible's meaning.

In the second place it argues that the change in thinking reflected by Liberal Quakerism had led "in the direction of the exaltation of Christ Jesus our Lord as the consummation of all devout thought".[118] Devotion to Christ lay at the heart of Evangelicalism and Liberal Quakerism was acceptable to many Evangelicals because, as we shall see, it placed Christ firmly at the centre of its theology.

It was because Quaker Liberalism had an appeal both for radical young Quakers and also for many Evangelicals that it won over British Quakerism as a whole and the schisms that had marked British Quakerism in the nineteenth century were not repeated.

---

[116] Davis op.cit. p.105

[117] *The Friend* vol. XXVIII No.35 London 27th August 1897 p.559

[118] ibid p.559

**The Revision of the Disciplines**

The triumph of Quaker Liberalism was clearly revealed when the *Book of Christian Discipline* was revised between 1906 and 1921.

I noted earlier that from 1738 onwards British Quakers began to issue a series of Books of Discipline which authoritatively recorded Quaker beliefs and practices, and which were periodically revised as these changed. The last Victorian Book of Discipline was issued in 1883.[119] Like Roman Gaul it was divided into three parts, 'Christian Doctrine' which recorded what Quakers believed, 'Christian Practice' which advised Quakers how they should behave, and 'Church Government' which, as its title suggests, outlined Quaker Church Government.

Revisions of the part concerned with 'Church Government' were issued by London Yearly Meeting in 1906 and 1917,[120] and a revision of 'Christian Practice' was issued in 1911,[121] in spite of protests from Evangelicals who were concerned that alterations to sections on Bible reading and the upbringing of children indicated a lack of commitment to orthodox views of Christ's life and work and Man's fallenness.[122] However, the section of the 1883 Discipline to do with 'Christian Doctrine', which was highly valued by Evangelicals as a summary of their understanding of Quakerism, remained unrevised until after World War One.

The Friends' Commission charged with preparing the Quaker approach to the planned "World Conference on Faith and Order" (a precursor of the present World Council of Churches) reported to London Yearly Meeting in 1917 that 'Christian Doctrine' needed to be revised: "especially in view of the large amount of interest in the Society of Friends which is now being taken by those who have but little knowledge of our position on matters other than that of war".[123] During the

---

[119] *Book of Christian Discipline of the Religious Society of Friends in Great Britain* London: Samuel Harris and Co.1883

[120] *Christian Discipline of the Religious Society of Friends in Great Britain and Australia - Part III Church Government* London: Headley Bros.1906 and *Christian Discipline of London Yearly Meeting of the Religious Society of Friends - Part III Church Government* London: Friends' Bookshop 1917

[121] *Christian Discipline of London Yearly Meeting of the Religious Society of Friends - Part II Christian Practice* London: Headley Bros. 1911

[122] *The Friend* vol. LI No. 46 17th November 1911 pp.742 & 4

[123] *Extracts from the Minutes and Proceedings of London Yearly Meeting of Friends* London: Office of the Society of Friends 1917

First World War many people had become interested in Quakerism because of its pacifism and the Commission felt that this section of the Book of Discipline particularly needed updating in order to give these people a greater knowledge of what Quakerism stood for. Because of the attachment of Evangelical Quakers to the old section its proposed revision was a highly controversial matter, but a representative conference set up by London Yearly Meeting in 1919 to resolve the controversy eventually succeeded in producing a document acceptable to both Liberals and Evangelicals and, after further revision, this was adopted by London Yearly Meeting in 1921.[124] However, although this new section of the Discipline, now called *Christian Life Faith and Thought*,[125] was acceptable to both the Liberal and Evangelical wings of British Quakerism it nevertheless showed that Liberal thought had become predominant among Quakers in this country.

*Christian Life Faith and Thought* retained two-thirds of the content of 'Christian Doctrine' but, as its preface declared, it also contained "so much additional material from the writings of deceased Friends and from Society documents that it is substantially a new book".[126]

This substantially new book was made up of two parts. Just under half of it consisted of the "Illustrative Spiritual Experiences" of a selection of Quakers ranging from George Fox and William Penn to Joseph Bevan Braithwaite, John Wilhelm Rowntree, and Thomas Hodgkin.[127] In the words of the Preface, these were intended as "a limited selection of a few vital experiences sufficient to illustrate the varied ways in which the heavenly vision has come with living power to the souls of men."[128]

Having a record of Quaker religious experience as a part of the *Book of Discipline* was an innovation which was suggested by William Charles

---

[124] For details see E.H.Milligan 'How we got our Book of Discipline: the revision of 1921 - from doctrine to experience' *The Friends' Quarterly* vol. 23 No. 3 July 1988 pp.110-117

[125] *Christian Life Faith and Thought in the Society of Friends - Being the First Part of the Book of Christian Discipline of the Religious Society of Friends in Great Britain* London: The Friends Bookshop 1922

[126] ibid Preface p.7

[127] ibid pp.15-69

[128] ibid Preface p.8.

Braithwaite,[129] and which reflected the Liberal Quaker emphasis on the importance of religious experience.[130] Evangelical Quakers, like other Evangelical Christians, placed emphasis upon the authoritative teaching contained in the Bible. This emphasis was reflected in the statements of belief contained in the 1883 *Christian Doctrine*, which were based on Biblical texts and echoed the language of the Authorised Version. Liberal Quakers such as William Charles Braithwaite, on the other hand, held that both the demands of the contemporary religious situation and the witness of the early Quakers meant that Quakers should lay stress not on the Bible, important though the Bible was, but on direct, personal, Christian experience. It was this belief which was expressed in the presence of the "Illustrative Spiritual Experiences" in *Christian Life Faith and Thought* in 1921. The inclusion of this part of *Christian Life Faith and Thought* was an innovation which marked a shift from an Evangelical emphasis on Biblical teaching to a Liberal stress on Quaker experience.

The remainder of *Christian Life Faith and Thought* consisted of an anthology of short extracts which were drawn from a variety of Quaker sources, and which were concerned with various aspects of Christian faith and thought. The largest proportion of these extracts were Liberal in outlook. Thirty seven extracts put forward the convictions of Liberal Quakerism compared with twenty four which reflected the beliefs of the early Quakers, and twenty one which expressed the Evangelical Quaker point of view. The following extract, taken from the writings of John Wilhelm Rowntree, is typical of those which advocated Liberal Quaker ideas.

In his posthumously published *Essays and Addresses* John Wilhelm Rowntree writes:

> (Jesus says): 'I and the Father are one'. That means to me that I think of God in terms of Jesus Christ, that I pray to Jesus as representing the Father to my consciousness, or to the Father as I see Him in Jesus. Carry that thought through to Calvary itself. See

---

[129] Milligan 'How we got our Discipline' p.116

[130] See for instance Braithwaite *The Second Period of Quakerism* ch.XIV, Brayshaw op.cit. ch.1V, E.Grubb 'The Society of Friends' in

W.B.Selbie (ed.)*Evangelical Christianity its history and witness* London: Hodder and Stoughton 1911 and Rufus M.Jones *Quakerism a religion of life* London: Headley Bros. 1908

in the crucifixion not merely a martyr's death, nor merely a passing gleam of God's love, certainly not a sacrifice to God carrying a legal significance, but in truth the flashing into light of an eternal fact, the nature of God's relation to Sin, of the pain we inflict on His heart by our own wrongdoing. Here is the wonderful dynamic of the Cross. God calls you to Him. He shows you His suffering, He shows you the hatefulness of the sin that caused it, and in showing you His love, shows you the punishment of alienation from Him, the hell of the unrepentant, in which we must remain until repentance opens the gate for the prodigal and gives entrance to the free forgiveness and love of the Father's house. In Jesus, in His life and His death upon the Cross, we are shown the nature of God and the possibilities that are within our reach. We are shown the world as the Father sees it, are called to live in harmony with His will and purpose, to hate the sins which made Him mourn, to scale the barrier of sin and discover that the way of penitence lies open and direct to the Fatherly heart. No legal bargain, but a spiritual conflict, and inward change, the rejection of the living death of sin, the choice of the new birth, of the purified self, the conversion from a low and earthly life to a high and spiritual standard of life and conduct - here you have the practical conditions of salvation, and in the active, free and holy love of God, ever seeking entrance, ever powerful if we but yield the gateway of our heart, is the substance of the Gospel. The revelation of God's Fatherhood and the possibility of unity with Him through Christ, meet the deep need of the soul for a centre of repose apart from the transitory interests and things of time. Hear then the gentle appeal 'Come unto me and rest'.[131]

In *Portrait in Grey* Punshon notes that:

It was no part of the liberals' intention to cast doubt on the Christian revelation. They were in search of an expression of it more adequate to the idiom of their times.[132]

Just as the 'Rowntree History' sought to maintain the basic validity of the Quaker form of religion while reinterpreting it in terms acceptable to modern thought, so Liberal Quakerism in general took the same approach to Christian belief as a

---

[131] ibid pp.95-6

[132] ibid pp.95-6

whole. For example, this is what we have seen in William Charles Braithwaite's paper at the Scarborough Summer School. He did not reject the traditional Christian belief that the Bible is inspired but re-interpreted it in such a way as to minimise the difference between the Bible and other writings.

This is also what we see in the quotation from Rowntree. He retains the traditional belief that the Cross reveals the nature of God, Man's alienation from Him and the way this alienation can be overcome. However, he reflects the Victorian moral critique of the penal understanding of the Cross by rejecting the Evangelical conviction that the Cross brought salvation because it was "a sacrifice to God carrying legal significance". Instead, influenced by the thought of the eighteenth century, writer William Law[133] he puts forward the idea that it brings salvation because it causes people to repent of their sins and adopt a new and holy way of life.

The largest proportion of the anthology of extracts concerned with various aspects of Christian faith and thought was dated after 1899 and represented recent developments in Quaker thought. These extracts all advocate the sort of Liberal theology expressed by Rowntree and demonstrate that, after the beginning of this century, the mainstream of British Quaker thought had developed in a Liberal direction. Whereas at the Manchester Conference Liberal views were advocated by a radical minority and the viewpoint of the Quaker establishment was Evangelical, by the early years of this century Liberalism had become the establishment point of view.

Evangelical Quakerism did not, of course, die out overnight. As I shall show in the next chapter, Evangelical Quakers maintained a vigorous defence of their understanding of Quakerism well into this century, but their beliefs ceased to influence the overall development of British Quaker theology.

I have said that Liberal Quakerism, as in the case of Rowntree, attempted to combine a commitment to, and a reinterpretation of, traditional Christian belief. In the next chapter I shall examine the extent to which the attempt to reinterpret Christian belief led Liberal Quakers to move away from both the core of conviction and its previous Christian tradition.

---

[133] See Joshua Rowntree ( ed.) *J.W.Rowntree Essays and Addresses* London Headley Bros. 1905 pp.399-400

# Chapter Three
## The Theology of Liberal Quakerism

I shall demonstrate the extent to which Liberal Quakers moved away from the core of conviction and previous Quaker thought by examining six works by five influential Quaker writers. These are *Quaker Strongholds* by Caroline E.Stephen, published in 1891;[1] *A dynamic faith* by Rufus Jones, published in 1901;[2] *A not impossible Religion* by Silvanus P.Thompson, published in 1918;[3] *The Faith of a Quaker* by John W.Graham, published in 1920;[4] and *Christianity as Life* and *Christianity as Truth* by Edward Grubb, published in 1927 and 1928 respectively.[5] These six works provide a reliable witness to the theology of Liberal Quakerism because they are representative of the thought of their authors, and their authors's thinking was representative of Liberal Quakerism as a whole. In this chapter I will first of all examine the teaching given in these works. I shall then summarise this teaching and show how it represents a move away from the core of conviction and previous Quaker thought.

---

[1] C.E.Stephen *Quaker Strongholds* 3ed London: Edward Hicks 1891

[2] R.M.Jones *A dynamic faith* London: Headley Brothers 1901

[3] S.P.Thompson *A not impossible Religion* London: The Bodley Head 1918

[4] J.W.Graham *The Faith of a Quaker* Cambridge: CUP 1920

[5] E.Grubb *Christianity as Life* and *Christianity as Truth* London: The Swarthmore Press 1927 and 1928

**'Quaker Strongholds'**

Caroline Stephen was an Anglican who converted to Quakerism because she found the Quaker form of worship more spiritually congenial than the services of the Church of England.[6]  She exercised a great influence over Quaker students at Cambridge while a member of the Quaker Meeting there, and, in the words of Rufus Jones, she "turned the attention of many serious seekers to the Friends as a religious body and to their way of life and worship".[7]

In Chapter VI, entitled 'Our calling' Stephen seeks to show the contemporary importance of Quaker principles and practices. In this chapter she puts forward four main points.

Firstly, she takes a positive view of the Victorian questioning of Christian belief, declaring that:

> ...though full of danger, this is on the whole a natural, a necessary, and, in the main, a beneficial process.  Throw a load of fuel on a clear fire and for a time it may seem doubtful whether it is not extinguished;  but if the flame be strong enough it will rise again through the smoke and dust, and burn the stronger for what it has mastered.  And so assuredly will faith in whatever is truly eternal rise above all present confusions and darkenings of counsel, and burn with fresh power in those hearts which have steadfastly cleaved to truth, be its requirements what they may.[8]

Secondly, she contends that in the face of this contemporary challenge to faith what people want is a form of worship based on direct religious experience:

> a manner of worship which shall be simpler, more living and actual - truly higher and purer because less intellectually ambitious, and more freshly inspired by human needs and Divine help;  and a manner of speaking about Divine things less conventional, less technical and artificial, arising more visibly from actual experience, and based more solidly upon common ground.  They want not authorised teachers but competent witnesses;  not to listen to sermons and religious 'services', however admirable, which are

---

[6] Stephen op.cit.'Introduction' pp.10-13

[7] Jones *The Later Periods of Quakerism* vol II p.970.  For details of Caroline Stephen's life and influence see the essays by Katherine Stephen and Thomas Hodgkin in C.E.Stephen *The Vision of Faith* Cambridge:  Heffers 1911

[8] Stephen *Quaker Strongholds* p.163

delivered in fulfilment of a professional engagement, within
prescribed bounds of orthodoxy, at stated times and in regular
amount; but to come into personal contact with those who have
seen, felt, encountered, the things of which they speak; and who
speak not because they are officially appointed to speak, but out of
the fulness of the heart because they must - people who dare be
silent when they have nothing to say, and who are not afraid to
acknowledge their ignorance, their doubts or their perplexities.[9]

Thirdly, she maintains that modern questioning of the Christian faith means
that Quakers are fortunate in not possessing creeds and in knowing about the
importance of silence:

We Christians have been roughly awakened by the storm and are
beginning to recognise that we needed such a correcting and sifting
of our thought and language as modern attacks are abundantly
supplying. At such a moment it is surely an unspeakable privilege
for any religious body to be entirely unshackled by creeds and
formularies; to have nothing in its traditions or practices to hinder
it from profiting by this process of correction, or from uttering its
perennial and unalterable testimony in the freshest and most flexible
and modern language it can command. And perhaps it is a still
greater privilege to have learnt the thrice-blessed power of silence;
to have secured both in private and in public the opportunity and
the practice of dwelling silently upon that which is unspeakable and
unchangeable; of witnessing to the light in that stillness which most
clearly reflects the Divine glory, in which the accusations of the
enemy are most effectually quenched.[10]

Finally, she holds that what is needed to help people in their religious
difficulties is that practical evidence of the power of faith in people's lives, to which
Quakers have always been taught to attach importance:

It is not by supplying people with the wisest and truest replies to
their difficulties that they can be effectually armed against them.
Second-hand belief is poor comfort in days when authority of all
kinds is freely discredited. And at all times and under all
circumstances something more than theory is required for victory.
For what, after all, is this 'faith', which above all things we who
have even a grain of it must desire to hold forth to others? 'This is
the victory which overcometh the world, even our faith'. It is a

---

[9] ibid p.165

[10] ibid pp.166-7

power, not a mere belief: and power can be shown only in action, only in overcoming resistance. Power that shall lift us one by one over temptations, above cares, above selfishness; power that shall make all things new, and subdue all things unto itself; power, by which loss is transmuted into gain, tribulation into rejoicing, death itself into the gate of everlasting life; is not this the true meaning of faith?[11]

The positive view which Stephen takes of the contemporary questioning of faith and her emphasis on the importance of religious experience both anticipate points made by Liberal speakers at the Manchester Conference four years later, as does her stress on the contemporary importance of aspects of the Quaker tradition.

However, in spite of her anticipation of later Quaker Liberalism, Stephen was in many ways quite conservative theologically. As I shall show, later Quaker Liberals were to challenge radically the beliefs held by the core of conviction and by previous Quaker tradition. Stephen, on the other hand, does not do this. Indeed, she sounds almost Evangelical when she argues in the Preface to the third edition of *Quaker Strongholds* that Quakers are basically orthodox in their beliefs in spite of their refusal to subscribe to any of the creeds, and affirms in the Biblical terminology typical of both the Quaker tradition and the core of conviction that:

If we do not always utter freely, or confidently define, our belief as to the nature and work of our Lord Jesus Christ, it is not for want of absolute and adoring trust in Him as the Lamb of God that taketh away the sins of the world: but because the mystery is the greater and the trust deeper - fuller, broader, more powerful - than words can utter: because we dare not limit or define in terms of the intellect that which can be understood only by the child-like heart, because as we 'look upon Him whom we have pierced', but who gave Himself for us, that the love of the Father to us sinners might be lovingly revealed to us - as we look upon Him, the only language possible to us is the language of penitence, of praise, of love and of adoration.[12]

Despite her overall theological conservatism there is, nevertheless, one topic on which she departs from the core of conviction and the Quaker tradition. This topic is the Bible. She accepts the traditional Quaker view that the Bible is

---

[11] ibid p.168

[12] ibid Preface

"the one common standard by which their practice and teaching may be judged".[13]
However, she rejects the idea of the verbal inspiration of the Bible accepted by
both the core of conviction and the Quaker tradition, [14] dismissing it as an
"exceedingly crude and mechanical conception".[15]

### 'A Dynamic Faith'

As might be inferred from their style, the five papers which make up *A
Dynamic Faith* are American in origin, and were first delivered at Haverford
College and the Earlham Biblical Institute in the United States.[16]   However,
because Jones was such an important figure in the development of Quakerism in
this country as well in America (L.Hugh Doncaster declared that he "made the
greatest contribution to the life and thought of Friends this century"),[17] I judge it
legitimate to consider his work as part of this study of British Quaker theology, its
American origin notwithstanding.

Jones was theologically   less conservative   than Stephen, and his re-
interpretation of Christianity in *A Dynamic Faith* differs markedly from the core of
conviction and previous Quaker thought on the three issues of the basis of religion,
Christ, and the nature of Biblical inspiration.  I shall look at each of these issues in
turn.

### The Basis of Religion

Jones begins *A Dynamic Faith* by asking:

What is the explanation, the ground, the basis of religion?[18]

---

[13] ibid p.151

[14] See G.B.Bentley *The Resurrection of the Bible* London: Dacre Press 1940 and Fox *Journal*
p.604

[15] Stephen  *Quaker Strongholds* p.32

[16] Jones *A Dynamic Faith* p.1X

[17] L.Hugh Doncaster 'Rufus Jones 1863-1948' *The Friend* January 25th 1963 vol. 121 No. 4
p.92

[18] Jones  *A Dynamic Faith*  p.2

Rejecting the traditional Protestant and Catholic answers that the basis of religion lies either in the authority of the Bible or in the authority of the Church, Jones argues instead that its basis lies in the fact that it is in the nature of God to reveal and give Himself to Man, and in the nature of Man to be able to receive, and respond to, this revelation and self-giving:

> The basis of religion...is to be sought in the primary fact that God Himself is love - a self-revealing and self-giving Being, and that man, by the very constitution of his being, is capable of receiving Him, of responding to Him, of uniting with Him and of being taken into the divine life. The soul no more needs a proof of His love and His presence than the eye does of the existence of the sunlight which it sees. Deep calls into deep; the deep in God calls to the deep in Man, and they know each other.[19]

Having made this point, he then defines it more precisely in his chapter on 'Mysticism and the Mystics'.[20] This chapter reflects an interest in mysticism which Jones had developed through reading the works of the American poet and essayist Ralph Waldo Emerson as an undergraduate and which was to be central to his subsequent theology.[21] In it he declares that mysticism:

> ...is grounded on the fact that a direct intercourse between the human soul and God is possible; and its ultimate goal is the attainment of a state in which God shall cease to be an external object and shall be known by an experience of the heart.[22]

He then attempts to explain how this 'direct intercourse' between Man and God is possible, by arguing that everyone possesses a 'subconscious' or 'subliminal' self and that:

> ...every man's subliminal self OPENS Godward, as the inlet opens to the sea, but the mystics are they who have found it out as a fact because the surges of the eternal self broke upon the shores of their

---

[19] ibid p.21

[20] ibid chapter III

[21] For the importance of Emerson see R.M.Jones *The trail of life in college* London: Macmillan & Co. 1929 pp.89-92.

[22] Jones *A Dynamic Faith* p.45

personal being, and they have realised that only sin could separate
Man and God.[23]

Finally, at the end of *A Dynamic Faith*, Jones summarises his argument
about the basis of religion by reiterating that:

> We have come at last to see, if we are Christians, that God is self-
> revealing, that it belongs to His very mature and essence to show    nature ?
> Himself i.e. He could not be God and stay self-contained and self-
> regarding. This is the first fact of the Christian religion, and it is a
> fact which is grounded in the divine nature. There is a second fact
> which is grounded in HUMAN nature, and that is that Man has a
> capacity for knowing God when he reveals Himself, i.e. that truth is
> self-demonstrative when it comes to us. There is no other proof
> that the sun is shining except that we feel it. There is no foreign
> evidence that love is of supreme worth except the heart's own
> testimony. There is no other proof that there is beauty in the world
> than this, that we perceive it and that our hearts beat for joy at it. It
> is just this same 'demonstration of the Spirit' which is the
> unassailable stronghold of the faith - the citadel of religion.[24]

For Jones it is this perception of God that enables Christians to meet "all the
questions, the doubts, the scepticism of our time".[25] because neither the historical
criticism of the Bible nor the discoveries of psychology or natural sciences can
invalidate the witness of an individual's personal experience of God.[26] In putting
forward an account of the basis of religion which he thinks can meet contemporary
questions, doubts, and scepticism, Jones is in agreement with Quaker Liberalism,
but the account which he puts forward disagrees both with the core of conviction
and the Quaker tradition. It disagrees with the core of conviction because, in
accordance with early and Quietist Quakerism, it emphasises that the basis of
religion is to be found in direct personal experience of God rather than in the
authority of the Bible.

It disagrees with the Quaker tradition in its explanation of how human
beings can have direct personal experience of God. According to Jones this is
possible because human beings have direct access to God through their

---

[23] ibid p.53

[24] ibid p.89

[25] ibid p.98

[26] ibid pp.100-2

subconscious selves, and are capable of receiving and responding to the Divine self-revelation given through their subconscious.    According to the Quaker tradition, on the other hand, it is possible because Christ speaks to all Men through the Divine internal monitor which God has placed in their hearts.   Jones sees the possibility of direct personal experience of God as based on the nature and psychology of Man, whereas the Quaker tradition sees it as based on the supernatural activity of God.

**Christ**

Jones concurs with both the core of conviction and the Quaker tradition in giving Christ a central place in his theology.  He declares that:

> The Christian religion centres around a Personality, who claims to reveal or manifest God as no book ever could

and he describes Christ's Incarnation as the "supreme revelation" of God.[27] However, he departs from the core of conviction and Quaker tradition in his explanations of the nature and purpose of the Incarnation.

His explanation of the incarnation is that:

> There have been men through whom He could speak because He could move them spiritually.   We find at length one single Personality who was sinless, who lived entirely open to God, who had a sole purpose - to do His will, and from it this truth emerges that this Personality is a complete expression of Divinity and Humanity.  It is no metaphysical puzzle, it is a concrete fact - the fact of facts - that one life has expressed both God and Man.  The moment humanity is perfected and lifted, as here, to its supreme height, and no mark of the beast is on it, it can equally well call itself divinity, and the moment God shows Himself adequately to the world He does it in terms of humanity.  The two natures belong together, and in Christ they were together - not as two natures, but as one nature expressing both.[28]

This interpretation of the Incarnation agrees with the core of conviction and Quaker tradition that Christ was sinless and was simultaneously God and Man.

---

[27] ibid p.12

[28] ibid p.13

It dissents from them in holding that what took place in Christ was a union between God and Man that resulted in the existence of one nature that was both Divine and human. This idea differs from the belief of the core of conviction, expressed in the Chalcedonian definition, that Christ had two distinct natures, one human and one Divine. It also differs from the Quaker tradition, because, although the Quakers did not subscribe to a Chalcedonian Christology, they nevertheless distinguished between Christ's humanity and the Divine Spirit which was present in Him and constituted His Divinity.

Jones' interpretation of the purpose of the Incarnation is contained in his discussion of the message of early Quakerism. In the course of this discussion he declares:

> In regard to the historic basis of Christianity, it may be said that the early Friends took practically the same position which the Apostle Paul took. The earthly life of Christ was to them a fact of supreme importance. It was the culmination of the manifestation of the self-revealing God. It showed once for all what God was like and what He would do to bring men to Him. The real purpose of His coming was to make men like Himself, not to enact a divine drama as a spectacle. In order to make men like Himself, He had completely to reveal Himself, and then to give such a mighty motive and spiritual impulse as should move men forever to Himself. Both Paul and Fox find THAT in the Cross of Christ. 'He loved me and gave Himself for me', therefore, 'the life I now live in the flesh I live by the faith of the Son of God'.[29]

In short, the purpose of the Incarnation was to completely reveal God, and through the Cross to motivate people to come to God that they might become like Him. Whatever merits this may have as an interpretation of the theology of St. Paul, it is inadequate as a representation of the thought of the early Friends. While they would have agreed with Jones that the Incarnation reveals what God is like, and that the Cross motivates men to return to Him, they also maintained that Christ's death on the Cross brought the enmity between God and Man to an end by paying the penalty for human sin. As I have indicated, this was a view of the Cross which the early Quakers shared with the core of conviction and so Jones'

---

[29] ibid pp.71-2

interpretation of the purpose of Incarnation also disagrees with the core of
conviction.

**Biblical Inspiration**

Although Jones does not see the Bible as the basis of religion it is
nevertheless important in his theology. This can be seen from the fact that he
devotes the whole of Chapter II of *A Dynamic Faith*, 'Sources of Quakerism in the
Scriptures', to showing that the message of the early Quakers can be seen as
Biblically based. For example, he argues that the statement in Psalm 36:9 that "In
thy light we see light" means that "the light by which we see God and spiritual
things is a light which comes from God".[30] and that this was what Fox called the
Light Within. He also contends that the idea of the royal priesthood of all
believers found in I Peter 2:9 and Revelation 1:5-6 is:

> ...an essential feature of Quakerism. It underlies the conception of
> membership, the idea of Ministry and the method of conducting the
> business of the Church.[31]

The importance which he attaches to the Bible is in line with the core of
conviction and the Quaker tradition. However, he differs from these in what he
says about the nature of the Bible's inspiration. In his view:

> The only biblical definition of inspiration which we have is this, that
> 'God spoke through holy men who were moved.' This means that
> the 'holy men' were capable of apprehending divine truth and of
> expressing it in human terms. They came to such a spiritual
> condition that they SAW...When a mathematician has learned the
> fundamental nature of the figures of space and their relation he
> comes at last to see the whole curve involved in the small arc and
> he finds the new planet because he sees that it MUST BE there.
> So the man who has obeyed his heavenly visions, who has been
> crowding out his old self by the spiritual method of forming a new
> life within - who at length has taken degrees in the divine school -
> sees truth because now he has an organ to see it with. He is not
> less of a man, but rather more of one. God does not use him as a

---

[30] ibid p.27

[31] ibid p.38

telephone to talk through, or as a caligraph to write through, or as a
passive window to send light through, or as a stringed instrument to
send music through.  He uses him because he is a HOLY MAN
who can grasp spiritual truth and put it into human terms.  He
'moves upon' him and the holy man apprehends what the moving
means.[32]

Because the Biblical revelation comes to us through the spiritual perception of holy
men it:

> ...cannot all be on a single level.  It depends for its height wholly
> upon the person through whom it comes, as the sure breath through
> a flute gives a high note or a low note according to the stop that is
> fingered.  If this be so - and it is hard to see how any other view
> could be held - then the thing we are to look for in a revelation is
> not infallibility, not a dictated word, but a divine message spoken
> through a human personality, tested in a personal life and preserved
> for our use today because it has proved its supreme worth through
> all the siftings of the ages.[33]

The doctrine of verbal inspiration contained within both the core of
conviction and the Quaker tradition saw the very words of the Biblical writers as
directly inspired by God,and had, as its corollary, the further belief that what the
Biblical writings said was infallibly true.  Like Stephen, Jones rejects this idea of
verbal inspiration, which he caricatures in his references to "a telephone", "a
caligraph", "a passive window", a "stringed instrument", and a "dictated word",
because he feels that it underestimates the human element in the process of
inspiration.  Echoing the contribution of Hodgkin and Braithwaite at the
Scarborough Summer School, he instead re-interprets inspiration as meaning the
apprehension and expression of spiritual truth by holy men, and sees it as being on
a par with the discovery of a new planet by a mathematician.  As in his explanation
of the possibility of experience of God, Jones has shifted the emphasis away from
the supernatural activity of God towards the religious capacities of human beings,
and  this shift of emphasis has led him away from the core of conviction and the
Quaker tradition.

---

[32] ibid pp.8-9

[33] ibid p.9

In summary, in *A Dynamic Faith* Jones expounds a religion based on direct religious experience which he thinks is capable of withstanding contemporary challenges to faith.  On the subject of the basis of religion he agrees with the Quaker tradition in basing religion on first-hand experience, but he disagrees with the core of conviction in elevating experience above the Bible.  He also disagrees with the Quaker tradition in his explanation of how experience of God is possible.  On the subject of Christ he follows the core of conviction and the Quaker tradition in giving Christ a central place in his theology and in seeing Him as both human and divine.  However, he differs from them in his account of the nature and purpose of the Incarnation.  Finally, although the Bible is important in Jones' theology, he moves away from the core of conviction and the Quaker tradition in rejecting the doctrine of verbal inspiration.

## A Not Impossible Religion

As I noted in the last chapter, the physicist Silvanus P.Thompson was one of the Liberal speakers at the Manchester Conference, and he also gave the 1915 Swarthmore Lecture.[34]  *A Not Impossible Religion* is his summary of his theological thought, published by his friends after his death.

Like Stephen and Jones before him, Thompson seeks to put forward a theology that can stand up to contemporary questioning of the Christian faith.  In his 'Introductory Statement' he declares that the refusal of theologians to face up to the advances of modern science and the discoveries of Biblical Criticism has:

> ...made orthodox religion impossible to men of thought and sincerity.  But it has not destroyed religion, nor has it made the following of Christ impossible.  This indeed is the theme of the following chapters.  There is a large and increasing class of thoughtful men and women who, while profoundly dissatisfied with the teaching of the Churches are nevertheless deeply conscious of the need for their own souls of a religion that shall bring them nearer to the inmost truth of things. To these outcasts of orthodoxy, to the honest and reverential thinkers after spiritual enlightenment, does the author now address himself.[35]

---

[34] Silvanus P. Thompson *The Quest for Truth* London: Headley Bros. 1917

[35] Thompson *A Not Impossible Religion*  pp.X1V-XV

Thompson attempts to answer the spiritual needs of these people by returning to the teaching of the New Testament and writing off all subsequent theology as a corruption of this teaching.  The theology which results is similar to that put forward by Stephen and Jones.  It both agrees and disagrees with the core of conviction and the Quaker tradition in the following ways:

It agrees with the Quaker tradition as a whole in rejecting the sacraments, the priesthood, and the creeds.

It agrees with the tradition of the early and Quietist Quakers in stressing the importance of first-hand religious experience, but in so doing it disagrees with Evangelical Quakerism and the core of conviction.

It agrees with both the Quaker tradition and the core of conviction in emphasising the central importance of Christ.

It disagrees with both the Quaker tradition and the core of conviction in its attitude to the Fall, Miracles, Salvation, Christology, and the Trinity.

### Sacraments, Priesthood and Creeds

One of the distinctive features of the early Quakers was their ultra-Protestant rejection of the Sacraments, the Priesthood, and the Creeds. Subsequent Quaker tradition followed them in this rejection, and Thompson does likewise, declaring:

> The religion we seek must be one that binds the human soul to
> God, and human souls to one another in a Divine fellowship,
> without the intervention of any priest or priestly order of men.  The
> mummeries and magical efficacy of the sacraments, the repetition of
> formal creeds which have mostly become meaningless, the claims of
> a priesthood to pronounce absolution and remission of sin, all these
> must go.  They are sheer stumbling blocks in the way of the sincere
> seeker after truth.[36]

---

[36] ibid p.176

**Experience**

In accordance with the tradition of the early and Quietist Quakers, Thompson stresses the fundamental importance of first hand religious experience. He argues that the:

> ...great fact of the immediate and interior revelation of God to the soul, the vision of the Unseen and Eternal, is the essence of all real religion.[37]

and that:

> One such genuine spiritual experience outweighs ten thousandfold in the problems of life and conduct the acceptance of any formal creed.[38]

He also declares that the reward for sincerely following Christ is a new form of religious experience:

> ...the follower of Christ who has been willing to leave the nearest and dearest, to renounce himself and to become a partaker in His suffering, becomes a sharer, too, in His transfiguration. He will know in his own experience that new birth to righteousness, in which, under the transforming work of the Holy Spirit, he has become a new creature, from whom all the old things have passed away. He will have put to death the old sinful nature and have risen with Christ to newness of life. He will have learned in a new and joyful sense how fellowship in the Kingdom of Heaven binds him by ties of sacred love and duty to all his fellow creatures. He will have found in the community of those whose hearts are illuminated by the spirit of Jesus a true communion of faith, a church of the first born whose names are written in heaven.[39]

Although this stress on the importance of first-hand religious experience is in accord with the thought of the early and Quietist Quakers, it differs from Evangelical Quakerism and the core of conviction in not being qualified by any

---

[37] ibid p.171

[38] ibid p.171

[39] ibid pp.183-4

counter-balancing emphasis on the central importance of the Bible for Christian life
and thought.

### The Centrality of Christ

Following his rejection of the sacraments, the priesthood, and the creeds,
Thompson then asks what sort of religion is left if these are abandoned.  In his
answer to this question he follows the core of conviction and the Quaker tradition
by advocating a religion centred on the figure of Christ:

> In the life and work of Jesus Christ we have, if we may reverently
> so express it, a working model of a human life, a perfect example of
> what a human life may be.  The perfect obedience to the Divine
> will, the complete absorption into the Divine life, the entire
> devotion to the service of Man, revealed in the character of Jesus;
> that is a revelation that has never been surpassed: so that in spite of
> all the dogmas and all the rituals with which theologians and
> ecclesiastics have overlaid it, we can still see the light of the
> knowledge of the glory of God in the face of Jesus Christ.  He who
> has caught a glimpse of that face, who has heard but the echo of
> that voice cannot choose but to follow whither He leads.  He needs
> no 'proof' of Christ's divinity to whom Christ thus reveals Himself in
> His Divine radiance.[40]

### The Fall

While he is thus in agreement with the Quaker tradition and the core of
conviction in his advocacy of a Christ-centred form of religion, Thompson departs
from them in what he writes about the Fall of Man.

Both the core of conviction and the Quaker tradition accepted the account
of the Fall of Man given in Genesis 3 as historical.  However, as William Hordern
points out in his article on the Christian doctrine of Man in *A Dictionary of
Christian Theology* "nineteenth century biblical criticism discredited the historical
nature of the Adam and Eve story".[41]  Thompson accepts this discrediting of the
historical nature of the Fall.  He describes the Fall as legendary, and asks why it is

---

[40] ibid pp.176-7

[41] William Hordern 'Man, Doctrine of' in Alan Richardson (ed.) *A Dictionary of Christian
Theology* London:SCM 1967 p.204

necessary to argue about it, given the clear evidence of human sinfulness to be found in our lives: "Why dispute about a legendary fall when the sad scenes of human degradation and the bitter consequences of proneness to sin are patent facts in our own lives?"[42]

## Miracles

Not only does Thompson think it unnecessary to argue about the Fall, he also maintains that it is unnecessary to argue about the historicity of Miracles. He thinks we do not need miraculous proof of God's activity in the world when we can see evidence of this in the way that people's lives are changed through the love of Christ:

> Why quarrel about miracles when every day, if we have eyes to see, we may observe the spirit of God working miracles not on the winds and waves,[43] but on the lives of men and women redeemed from the degradation of sin and renewed in their minds through the love that Christ bore to them?[44]

This agnostic attitude to the miraculous differs from the core of conviction and the Quaker tradition because they accepted the historicity of at least the Biblical miracles as part of their belief in the infallibility of the Bible.[45]

## Salvation

The understanding of salvation which Thompson advances agrees with the core of conviction and the Quaker tradition in affirming that it is Christ who saves. It parts company with them in what it says about how He saves.

Thompson goes against the core of conviction and the Quaker tradition by denying that Christ saves us through His death on the Cross. He regards Christ's

---

[42] Thompson *A not impossible Religion* p.182

[43] See Mk 4:35-41, Mk 8:18, 23-7, Lk 8:22-25

[44] Thompson *A not impossible Religion* p.183

[45] Indeed, as Henry J. Cadbury (ed.) *George Fox's Book of Miracles* Cambridge: CUP 1948 makes clear, there is evidence that the early Quakers believed that miracles similar to the ones recorded in the Bible were taking place as part of their Ministry.

crucifixion as simply  a: "fearful murder",[46] and rejects what he calls "man-made doctrines of sacrificial atonements and plans of salvation by death".[47] by which he means the ideas that Christ's death was a sacrifice and part of God's plan for our salvation.

He also maintains that the correct understanding of salvation, put forward by the early Church and by Christ Himself, is that Christ was:

> the saviour who should save His people from their sins - not from the consequences of their sins, but from sinning - by putting into them a new life of righteousness that they might bring forth the fruit of the Kingdom.[48]

Both the core of conviction and the Quaker tradition would have agreed that Christ saves people from sinning. Indeed, as I have indicated, this was one of the major emphases of early Quakerism.  However, they would also have held that Christ *does* save people from the consequences of their sins by, for example, offering a sacrifice for them.

### Christ and the Trinity

Thompson's final disagreement with the core of conviction and the Quaker tradition is on the subjects of Christ and the Trinity.

On the subject of Christ he disagrees with them in three ways.

Firstly, while they accepted the Biblical testimony that Christ was born of a virgin, Thompson argues that it is wrong to insist on this belief because it unnecessarily undermines Christ's full humanity:

> Why try to force belief in a miraculous birth which, if believed in, robs the humanity of Jesus of half its force, when it is recognised that a revelation of the wholly Divine may be immanent in one who was also in this nature wholly human?[49]

---

[46] Thompson *A not impossible Religion* p.183

[47] ibid p.57

[48] ibid p.10

[49] ibid p.182

Secondly, both the core of conviction and the Quaker tradition accepted the Biblical testimony that Christ's bodily resurrection resulted in His tomb being empty. Thompson, on the other hand, cites 'an empty tomb' as being one of the things on which Christian faith does not need to be based.

Thirdly, while Thompson is prepared to talk about 'Christ's divinity' and His 'Divine radiance', he does not follow the core of conviction and the Quaker tradition in seeing Him as God. He contends that Christ did not think He was God[50] and that the idea of the Divinity of Christ means: "Divinity manifested through humanity".[51] Christ was not God, but rather a man through whom God manifested Himself. He illustrates this idea with a mathematical analogy:

> A plane figure in two dimensions, a mere shadow or projection, can suggest to us the form belonging to the three dimensional solid figure. It has even been possible for acute minds to form some dim conception of the figures of four dimensions, by considering how the solids of three dimensions can be regarded as their projections in three dimensional space. Is it not possible, then, to suggest an analogy with higher things? Can one conceive of the Divine fullness 'projected' upon the plan of the human; like a plane figure suggesting in the limitations of two dimensions a form belonging to three?[52]

Having dispensed with the belief that Christ was God, he also states that Christ did not: "attribute a separate personality to the Spirit of the Lord".[53] That is to say, Christ did not see the Spirit as constituting a second Person in the Godhead alongside God the Father, but saw Him merely as an aspect of the Father's being. Seeing things in this light, Thompson, unlike the core of conviction and the Quaker tradition, has no place for the doctrine of the Trinity and seems instead to opt for a unitarian view of God.

---

[50] ibid p.322

[51] ibid p.74

[52] ibid pp.77-8

[53] ibid.p.249

## The Faith of a Quaker

Like Thompson, John W. Graham was one of the Liberal speakers at the
Manchester Conference and was subsequently a Swarthmore lecturer.[54]  He was
also like Thompson in being concerned for those who were disatisfied with
mainstream Christianity.  In the conclusion to *The Faith of a Quaker* he makes
clear that his brand of Quakerism is aimed at those:

> ....men and women who are religious, who believe in God, and
> know something of His communion, which they rightly identify
> with the love of man, who love Christ and wish to obey His
> commandments,[55]

but who also:

> ...see through every ecclesiastical claim, who are too sincere and
> original to appreciate a religion of routine, to whom theology has
> become extremely simple, but correspondingly penetrating in its
> appeal, whose religion must needs survive, if it is to survive at all,
> in friendly contact with history and science.[56]

Like the theology of Stephen, Jones, and Thompson, the theology which
Graham offers these men and women falls partly within, and partly without, the
core of conviction and the Quaker tradition.  This can be seen in his treatment of
the topics of the basis of theology, God and Man's relationship with Him, Christ,
the Atonement, and the Bible.

## The Basis of Theology

Graham begins *The Faith of a Quaker* by declaring :

> The Quaker search for God begins from the beginning and bases
> whatever it builds on the sure foundation of experience.  Even if
> what we build thereon should be found to be no much better than
> wood, hay or stubble, we shall even then be safe after its
> destruction, though saved as from fire, for nothing, however

---

[54] John W. Graham *The Quaker Ministry* London: The Swarthmore Press 1925

[55] Graham *The Faith of a Quaker* p.417

[56] ibid p.417 .

foolish, which is based upon direct experience, can ever fall with so overwhelming a destruction, or produce a desolation so hopeless, as that which is based not on the facts of life but on fancy and tradition. Our walls may crash and our floors flame, but through them we shall fall down to the gentle common earth from which we began to build. We will do as the wise Pope in 'The Ring and the Book' did in his own heart, we will
'correct the portrait by the living face
Man's God by God's God in the mind of Man'[57]

This basing of the search for God on experience runs counter to the core of conviction and to Evangelical Quakerism in that it gives no place to the Bible as the authoritative basis for our knowledge of God. It also runs counter to the Quaker tradition as a whole in that the experience on which the search for God is to be based seems to be experience of the "facts of life" rather than experience of Christ speaking through the internal monitor. The supposition that Graham is not basing his search for God on hearing the voice of Christ is confirmed as his argument in *The Faith of a Quaker* develops. He does not base his theology on the revelation of Christ through the internal monitor, but on "_ the reality of the three experiences of consecration, of love, and of Prayer"[58] each of which he uses to build up his picture of God and Man's relationship with Him.

The picture of God which Graham develops is in some ways a quite traditional one. For instance, in accordance with the view of God pre-supposed by both the core of conviction and the Quaker tradition, he argues that we are justified in seeing God as personal:

...it is a Person that we want; or to speak more carefully that it is a humanlike relationship with our humanity that we seek, 'A heart behind creation beating'. Nor is this a blind cry of the emotional nature only, an unjustifiable 'will to believe'. The highest we can touch through the personal faculties must be personal; it can, at any rate, be nothing smaller or simpler; how much larger and more complex it may be is impossible to determine.[59]

---

[57] ibid p.3

[58] ibid p.27

[59] ibid p.11

However, Graham's understanding of God also goes against the core of conviction and the Quaker tradition in that he rejects a Trinitarian view of God. Noting that in his discussion of the person of Christ he has "left outside the Doctrine of the Trinity in its complete theological form_".He states:

> It is better so. The doctrine of Nicaea may have been a useful thought-form for the time when it arose; it may have crystallised experience and speculation in the best shape then possible - but it is not a living part of contemporary thought; and I doubt the usefulness of the washed out or attenuated forms of the doctrine in which triple manifestations of some kind can be noted or discovered in God. These are really only more polite and less dangerous ways of denying the old conception. This reduced doctrine really darkens counsel, as it is to most people unintelligible, though it is doubtless convenient to keep the traditional word even if you alter its meaning. It has, of course, no more authority than a Roman Emperor and a Church Council under his presidency and control can give it. It was no part of the thought of Jesus nor of Paul. The two passages where it occurs are interpolations of the usual doctrinal type - the one in I John,[60] now deleted, confessedly so; the other, the baptismal formula in the last words of Matthew's Gospel [Mt 28:19], held so by a large consensus of scholars. But the doctrine represents one of those hard and fast lines of division and classification which are never of more than temporary use as scaffolding, and are really in their permanence the bane of theology.[61]

In this quotation Graham not only disagrees with the core of conviction by denying the Nicene doctrine of the Trinity, but also disagrees with the Quaker tradition by dismissing all forms of Trinitarian doctrine as unbiblical and unhelpful.

In support of his rejection of the Nicene doctrine of the Trinity Graham refers his readers to Rendel Harris' work *The Origin of the Prologue to John's Gospel* in which Harris argues that the Christology of Athanasius, which was fundamental to the Nicene doctrine of the Trinity, was based on a faulty exegesis of the Septuagint text of Proverbs 8:22[62]

---

[60] 1 Jn 5:7

[61] Graham *The Faith of a Quaker* pp.64-5

[62] J.Rendel Harris *The Origin of the Prologue to John's Gospel* Cambridge: C.U.P. 1917 p.49.

Graham also departs from the core of conviction and the Quaker tradition in what he writes about God's relationship to Mankind. He contends that we should see God as "...an infinite Personality of which we are a part, as a leaf is of a tree. We are leaves of the tree which is God".[63]

In addition, influenced by the book *The Biology of War* by the German biologist G.F.Nicolai[64], he suggests that the locus of God's presence in humanity is the 'germ-plasm' - the nuclear part of the human cell by means of which hereditary characteristics are transmitted from one generation to the next. As he sees it, this germ-plasm is what links all human beings in a common humanity made in the image of God, and is also the "true vehiculum Dei, the nearest we can get to the secret place of the Most High".[65] This organic and biological explanation of the relationship between God and Man differs from the core of conviction and the Quaker tradition because they tend to see this relationship as analogous to that between two separate human beings.[66]

## Christ

Graham follows the core of conviction and the Quaker tradition in stressing the religious importance of Christ. He insists that in our attitude to Christ we may:

> safely, rationally, love, reverence, and obey - we may worship and bow down in discipleship - to the fullest extent of which we are capable. It is historically true that His is the Name which is above every name, at which every knee shall bow, and shall confess that Jesus Christ is Lord, to the glory of God the Father.[67]

However, he departs from the core of conviction and the Quaker tradition in other aspects of his treatment of Christ.

---

[63] Graham *The Faith of a Quaker* p.5

[64] G.F.Nicolai: *The biology of War* London: J.M.Dent 1919

[65] Graham *The Faith of a Quaker* p.26

[66] For examples see Augustine *City of God*. Luther *Lectures on Romans* Tr. Wilhelm Pauck Philadelphia: Westminster Press 1961 and Emil Brunner *The Divine Human Encounter* Tr. Amadus W. Loos London: SCM 1944 and on the Quaker side, Fox's *Journal* and Barclay's *Apology*

[67] Graham The Faith of a Quaker p.66.

Firstly, like Jones, he rejects any distinction between Christ's divine and human natures:

> His nature cannot have had in it elements of contradiction, the divine and the human checking and limiting one another, mixed together in debatable proportions, the Divine spoiling the completeness of the human nature, and the human limiting the infinity of the Divine; not purely human, yet 'laden with attributes that make not God'. It was one nature, single - probably indeed simple if we only knew - powerful without hesitation - self conquered in inward harmony - poised and pure - unhampered by haunting doubt - calm in its great claim - certainly wholly and perfectly human - yet able to say 'Come _. and I will give you rest' - leave houses and lands 'for my sake' - 'Everyone therefore who shall confess me before men, him will I also confess before my Father'.
>    There need be no compound of human and Divine, and there can be no antithesis; for they are of the same stuff - the human has a share of the Divine; and the larger and more perfect a man's humanity, the larger and more perfect his share in divinity too.[68]

As in the case of Jones' Christology, the Christology Graham puts forward in this quotation agrees with the core of conviction in asserting that Christ was both human and divine, but disagrees with them in not making any distinction between His human and divine natures.

The second example of his departure from the core of conviction and Quaker tradition is when he comes to explain in detail precisely how Christ could be both human and divine. Graham follows the theory put forward by the Oxford New Testament scholar W.R.Sanday in his book *Christologies Ancient and Modern*.[69] This theory had two parts: (1) that the point of contact between God and Man lies in the subliminal self possessed by all human beings; (2) that what was distinctive about Jesus Christ was that He was a man whose subliminal self was completely open and obedient to God. In Graham's words, what this theory means for our understanding of Christ is that:

> We thus have in Jesus Christ a personality falling into the same general scheme as our bodies; but whilst the divine subliminal endowment we possess is a glimmering and struggling light, we find

---

[68] ibid p.51

[69] W.R.Sanday *Christologies Ancient and Modern* Oxford: Clarendon Press 1910.

behind the human personality of Jesus a subliminal soul to whom the Spirit is given without measure, one whose meat and drink was to the will of His Father, one who was able to say at the hardest crisis of His life 'Not my will, but thine, be done', one in whom the divine had frictionless way. We have the Son of Man, and if our thought of God be broadly correct, we have a Son of God too in a soul so endowed.[70]

This Christology differs from the core of conviction in that it does not see Christ as someone who was uniquely and paradoxically both God and Man, but as someone who was a man like all other men apart from His limitless endowment with the Spirit and His complete submission to the will of God. It could be argued that this Christology resembles the early Quaker belief that Christ was a uniquely Spirit filled man, but the theory of the subliminal endowment of Man on which it is based cannot be found in early Quaker writings, and is contrary to the Quaker belief in a supernatural internal monitor as the basis of human knowledge of God.

Thirdly, like Thompson, he rejects the idea of Christ's bodily resurrection. He follows the Anglican theologians B.F.Westcott and Kirsopp Lake in their books *The Gospel of the Resurrection* and *The Resurrection of Jesus Christ*[71] in arguing that it was a spiritual rather than a physical event. It needs to be:

understood as Bishop Westcott and Professor Lake and others understand it, as the raising of a spiritual, not a fleshly, body. On this view the parallel drawn by the apostle gains its validity - 'If Christ rose, then we shall rise'. Otherwise it loses its validity.[72]

In other words, the apostle, by whom Graham means St. Paul, said that Christ's resurrection foreshadows our own, and also said that our resurrection will be spiritual rather than physical. Therefore Christ's resurrection must have been spiritual and not physical.

Whatever its validity as an interpretation of the thought of St. Paul, Graham's argument on this matter takes him away from the core of conviction and

---

[70] Graham *The Faith of a Quaker* p.76.

[71] B.F.Westcott *The Gospel of the Resurrection* 4th ed London: Macmillan 1879 and K.Lake *The Resurrection of Jesus Christ* London: Wiliams and Norgate 1912.

[72] Graham *The Faith of a Quaker* p.81.

the Quaker tradition.  As I indicated in my comments on Thompson, they both accepted the Biblical witness to the physical nature of the resurrection.

## The Atonement

On the subject of the Atonement Graham coincides with the core of conviction and the Quaker tradition in seeing Christ as the one who makes Atonement, but differs from them in his understanding of how He does so.

His account of the Atonement is as follows:

> The mission of our Lord was to reunite in family reconciliation, restoring love and order and peace in the Father's house, replacing the communion marred by sin.  Sin is separation from God; and He came to conquer sin.  Sin is the self-assertion of the flesh and of the mind of the flesh - the undivine self - which should only be the instrument, the necessary clothing and vehicle of the soul;  and needs to be voluntarily submitted in a heavenly obedience, and to conform to this central Divine Order with which our souls have organic union. Every theory of the Atonment breaks down which assumes the separateness of God and Man, as two parties to a bargain.  Therein Christ is made to be the victim of a colossal injustice - discreditable to the other two principals in the transaction.  But it is all needless - a lawyer's scrupulous quibble - the result of an ignorant people accepting primitive teaching.  If, however, the mission of Jesus was to restore, wherever His Gospel penetrated, a unity of purpose, a harmony of motive, a Divine obedience, in the heart of the believer - the At-one-ment, the reconciliation, is therein achieved.[73]

This account of the Atonement agrees with the core of conviction and the Quaker tradition in seeing the restoration of communion between Man and God as the purpose of Christ's mission.  This idea is central to all Christian accounts of the Atonement.  However, there are also two points on which this account differs from them.  It assumes that there is an organic relation between God and the human soul.  As I have noted, this understanding of the relationship between Man and God differs from that held by the core of conviction and the Quaker tradition.  It also rejects by implication the beliefs, which they accept, that Christ's death was a sacrifice for our sins, made satisfaction for them, or paid the penalty for them.

---

[73] ibid pp.30-31

This is because these beliefs assume: "the separateness of God and Man, as two parties to a bargain", in that they see Christ as performing an action on behalf of Mankind which is then accepted by God.

### The Bible

Graham's final disagreement with the core of conviction and the Quaker tradition is on the subject of the Bible. As I observed in Chapter 3, the early Quakers modified their subordination of the Bible to the inward Monitor in line with the core of conviction by insisting that any action which was contrary to Biblical teaching was inspired not by the inward Monitor but by the Devil. This idea is rejected by Graham.

As part of a review of Barclay's *Apology* he contends that Barclay was right when he declared that the scriptures are only a secondary authority subordinate to the enlightenment given by the Spirit, but that he was wrong when he further maintained that: "whatsoever any do, pretending to the Spirit, which is contrary to the scriptures, is to be accounted and reckoned a delusion of the devil". According to Graham there are two reasons why Barclay is wrong. Firstly, Graham accepts the Liberal belief that the Biblical material developed progressively over an extensive period of time and declares that this means:

> ...the Scriptures do not speak with a single voice on either faith or practice. Their morality is progressive, and so is their faith. They are not a book written systematically to cover a certain ground and meet the needs of a flock for guidance, as was the Koran. They are the literature of a mixed race, extending over eight or nine hundred years and recognisably Hebrew or Greek in their origin. They began with primitive and barbarous proceedings, and with equally primitive science and history. They were not written to form parts of any single volume, and they do not constitute a book, but are the anthology of great religious experience.[74]

Secondly, the diversity of the Biblical teaching means that:

> We cannot go to the Bible to find detailed guidance, easy of apprehension, on monogamy, on the bringing up of children, on total abstinence, on war, on reading frivolous literature, on

---

[74] ibid p.140

gambling and speculating, on national rights, on slavery, on the right use of Sunday, to say nothing of such issues as the cure of poverty, individualism, or socialism, or the rights of women to share in the franchise or the ministry.[75]

As a result:

On all these points we are thrown back on spiritual enlightenment, able to guide and inspire us apart from the Scriptures. When we turn to the Scriptures the same enlightenment guides us in the help we can select from them, guidance which an enlightened spirit will have no difficulty in finding there on all these subjects. But the unenlightened, as we know, have found there texts to support every form of obsolete tyranny and cruel evil. We may and do, therefore, accept Barclay's principle of secondary authority and proceed to use the Scriptures in the only way now possible to us.[76]

Furthermore, Graham also contends that, whatever they may have officially believed, in practice the early Quakers ignored the authority of the Bible when it was convenient for them to do so. As he puts it:

From the beginning, in fact, Friends allowed themselves as much liberty as they required in dealing with Scripture passages, in obedience to the dictates and the divine enlightenment within them.[77]

He cites as examples of this the Quakers' rejection of war, predestination, and oaths in spite of the fact that these find clear support in the Bible, and he argues that had the early Quakers:

lived in these days in which the Scriptures are better understood as literature, they would doubtless have exercised a correspondingly larger freedom.[78]

---

[75] ibid p.140

[76] ibid p.140

[77] ibid p.141

[78] ibid p.141

As I have just noted, the early Quakers' insistence on the binding authority of all Biblical teaching represented a convergence with the core of conviction. Therefore, in advocating a selective acceptance of Biblical teaching, Graham not only departs from the Quaker tradition, but from the core of conviction as well.

**Christianity as Life**

Edward Grubb was one of the leading contributors to the development of Liberal Quakerism.  He was not only the editor of *The British Friend* and the Swarthmore Lecturer in 1914,[79] but also wrote numerous books and articles defending and expounding the Liberal Quaker point of view.[80]

In the preface to his book *Christianity as Life* Grubb states its purpose as follows:

> Christianity entered the world of men in the form not of a philosophy or a dogma but of a Personal Life, and proved its worth not as an institution but as an inspiration.  The purpose of this book is to amplify this statement in the light of history:  to indicate the characteristics of our religion in its Golden Age, and some aspects of its human development;  and to estimate its effects on the lives of individuals and on human society.[81]

In accordance with the Liberal rejection of the dogmatic and institutional aspects of Christianity noted in the work of Thompson, Grubb holds that Christianity is at the root a non-dogmatic and non-institutional form of religion, and he attempts to show how the history of Christianity supports this contention. Just like the Rowntree history, *Christianity as Life* is an attempt to develop an apology for Liberal Quakerism based on history.

This apology agrees with the Quaker tradition in its account of the early Church.

It agrees with both the core of conviction and the Quaker tradition in affirming human immortality.  It disagrees with them in what it says about Christ, the Kingdom of God, the Cross and the resurrection.

---

[79] Grubb  *The Historic and Inward Christ*

[80] For details see Dudley  *The Life of Edward Grubb*

[81] Grubb  *Christianity as Life*  p.7

**The Early Church**

On the basis of the evidence provided by the book of Acts, Grubb draws a
picture of the first Christian community. This picture follows the Quaker tradition
in portraying the early Church as a community based on the experience of direct
inspiration by the Spirit, just like the Society of Friends:

> Early Christianity was, then, essentially an experience, individual
> and collective, of new life with God and new relations to men -
> relations based on 'the love of God shed abroad in our hearts
> through the Holy Spirit which was given unto us' (Rom.v.5). Its
> real content was this experience of the Spirit, bringing with it a
> glorious release from the old world-order of self-preservation, a
> new power of self-abandoning love and self-forgetful service. The
> Christian Fellowship was a community of inspired people, who
> trusted the Spirit of Christ to lead them both in their personal
> concerns and in their collective life, and who felt that God was ever
> calling and enabling them to bring others into the fellowship of
> love. It was only indirectly a matter of intellectual beliefs or of
> outward organisation.[82]

Grubb also combined Quaker tradition with the work of the nineteenth
century Anglican writer Edwin Hatch and argues that the early Church knew
neither a monarchical episcopate nor a separate order of priesthood:

> ...the Christian community in its early days was essentially the
> Fellowship which consisted of true followers of Jesus, united by
> living faith in a common Lord, and by the inspiration of his living
> spirit in their individual and corporate life _ But this unity was
> inward and vital not external and governmental. It depended on the
> one Divine life that flowed through the whole, as the sap circulates
> through the vine. There is no sign in the New Testament of the
> monarchical bishop, ruling with an authority derived by formal
> ceremony from the Apostles, or of a clerical and priestly order,
> through which alone spiritual blessings could be mediated to the
> laity. In the Church of the first century there was no laity, for all
> true disciples of Christ were priests. 'The Kingdom of God' says
> Hatch, 'was a kingdom of priests...and only in that sense was
> priesthood predicable of Christian men. For the shadows had

---

[82] ibid p.96

passed; the Reality had come: the one High Priest of Christianity was Christ'.[83]

In his view the emergence of Episcopacy and Creeds in the early Church was due to a failure to trust the guidance of the Spirit to safeguard the unity of the Church and the truth of its teaching.

Lastly, he is in line with the Quaker tradition in taking a negative view of the development of fixed forms of church service, and in contending that the sacraments of Baptism and the Eucharist are dispensable. He declares that:

> The gradual substitution of a fixed order of 'service' in the hands of Church officials, for the original freedom of the Spirit, was due in part to the decay of the genuine gift of prophecy, and in part to the consequent loss of faith in the power of the Spirit to preserve order and harmony.[84]

and further maintains that because the sacraments of Baptism and Eucharist were not instituted by Christ Himself,

> The continuance of these rites in the Church is a matter not of obedience but expediency. The Church has at various times exercised freedom in altering the ceremonies both of Baptism and the Eucharist, as new circumstances and new needs seem to have required. Should it not claim an equal freedom to dispense with their formal observance altogether, if it should appear that its life can be better maintained by seeking the Reality without the Symbol?[85]

---

[83] ibid pp.144-5 quoting E.Hatch *The Organisation of the Early Christian Churches* 3ed London: Rivingtons 1888

[84] ibid p.161

[85] ibid p.275. Grubb's argument that Baptism and the Eucharist were not rites instituted by Christ Himself is based on the belief that Mt 28:19 is a late interpolation and that the Lukan account of the last supper is dependent on Pauline theology and therefore not historically reliable.

## Human Immortality

Both the core of conviction and the Quaker tradition accept the idea that there is life after death.[86] Grubb also accepts this. He argues that God intends to make Mankind perfect, and that:

> ...we find the necessary place and function of Christian belief in Immortal Life. Whether, as the Platonists held, this is an endowment of 'the soul' as such, or whether, as the New Testament seems rather to teach, it is a gift to be striven for and attained, it contains the assurance that spiritual progress, the creative work of perfecting manhood, is not to be cut short by the mere accident of physical death. 'God is not the God of the dead but of the living', and even the cessation of physical life on this earth, by the slow cooling of the ages, or a sudden impact with another star, could not destroy His purpose to bring all men into communion with Himself.[87]

## Christ

Reflecting the confidence in the historical reliability of the Synoptic Gospels which was a feature off British New Testament scholarship between the wars[88]Grubb declares that when we study the Synoptic Gospels:

> The outlines of the portrait they leave us blend into a consistent and intelligible whole. Jesus is there before us as a real man, subject to the conditions and limitations of a particular time, yet so far transcending them as to speak the language of universal truth, and to lay the foundations of a universal religious morality. His life of perfect love brought to man a new and adequate revelation of the nature and character of God. He felt himself to be fulfilling, in a deeper and truer sense than anyone else understood, his people's expectation of a Divinely sent Deliverer. And this sense of Messiahship rested on his inward knowledge of God as His Father, and on the conscious-ness of an unbroken filial relation to Him. In the clear light of the Divine Communion he spoke and acted with the certitude and authority of one who saw the truth with unclouded vision. Because of the new experience he brought to

---

[86] See for example the *Apostles' Creed* text in Leith   op.cit. pp.24-25, the *Westminster Confession* ch. XXII text in Leith ibid pp.228-9 and Barclay *Catechism* ch. XIV

[87] Grubb *Christianity as Life* p.281

[88] See, for example, B.H.Streeter *The Four Gospels* London: Macmillan 1924.

> men - the outward experience of his radiant life and the inward
> knowledge of a blissful relation with God - they began to call him
> Lord and Saviour.  He had done for their souls what only God
> could do, and henceforth they could only speak of him in terms that
> had hitherto been applied to God.[89]

All that is positively affirmed in this quotation agrees with the core of conviction
and the Quaker tradition.  For example, both would accept that Christ's life:
"brought to man a new and adequate revelation of the nature and character of
God".  Where this quotation departs from the core of conviction and the Quaker
tradition is in describing Christ in purely human terms.  Although Grubb admits
that people began to describe Christ in terms previously reserved for God, it
appears from the quotation that they were using these terms of one who was in
fact merely a man.  This portrayal of a purely human Christ contrasts with the
consistent portrayal of Him as incarnate God by the core of conviction and the
Quaker tradition.

**The Kingdom of God**

Basing his argument on texts such as John 3:19-20, 8:15-16, and 12:47-49
Grubb argues that Christ probably did not associate the idea of the Kingdom of
God with that of the vengeance of God upon sinners, and states:

> If this is a possible interpretation, the teaching concerning the
> Kingdom becomes a consistent whole.  When the Father of all sets
> up His Kingdom on the earth it will not be with the purpose of
> condemning men to destruction but of delivering them from it, He
> will not force their wills, even by threats of impending doom, but
> will win them by love to the uttermost.  He will Himself, in the
> person of His Son, suffer for and with them in the final struggle
> with evil.  Love is the last appeal, the final reaction of the Father
> against the moral evil in men's hearts.  Those who reject it He will
> never overwhelm with irresistible might, but will suffer with them
> until they repent.  'Father forgive them for they know not what they
> do' - this prayer must surely be answered.  Jesus overcomes his
> adversaries not by destroying them but by converting them - as his
> living spirit converted Saul of Tarsus.  In the fourth Gospel Jesus
> looks forward to the time when even his enemies will acknowledge

---

[89] ibid pp.31-2

him (John viii:28) and when he will 'draw all men unto himself'(xii:32).[90]

This interpretation of Christ's teaching on the Kingdom of God, implying that in the end all men will repent and be saved, differs from the core of conviction and the Quaker tradition which accept the possibility that some people may continue to resist God and so be damned.

## The Cross

In an interpretation of the Cross similar to that by Rowntree noted in the previous chapter, Grubb portrays the Cross as a morally transforming example of judgement, love, and obedience:

> If men are to be effectually brought to repentance and reconciled to God, these things at least need to be stabbed into their consciousness: the moral loathsomeness of sin; the Divine holiness that inevitably condemns it; the outreaching love that forgives it and restores; and the perfect human obedience that has been and can be rendered. The Cross of Christ is unique as a moral dynamic because it fills all these needs.[91]

As with his writing about Christ, everything that Grubb affirms in this quotation is in accordance with the core of conviction and the Quaker tradition. They would agree with all that he writes here about the: "moral dynamic of the Cross". They would however differ from him in saying more about the meaning of the Cross than he does here. The various images they use to describe Christ's death portray it not only as a subjective moral dynamic, but also as the means by which the barriers separating Man from God were objectively overcome.

## The Resurrection

Grubb's understanding of the resurrection is similar to that of Thompson and of Graham in that, like them, he dispenses with the idea of a physical resurrection. Like Graham he believes that the resurrection occurred, but departs

---

[90] ibid p.51

[91] ibid p.64

from the core of conviction and the Quaker tradition by not accepting that it was a physical event.  Building on the work of the Society for Psychical Research he argues instead that it was a psychical one, and declares:

> The theory that the appearances were psychical rather than physical implies that Jesus, a living personality, was purposely impressing his real presence on the minds of the disciples in such a way that they seemed to see (and Thomas possibly to touch) his body.   It preserves what is after all the essential thing - that Jesus was living after death, and actively at work carrying forward the great task on which he had previously been engaged.  It fulfils the paramount need of the situation - that for the accomplishment of his work of setting up the Kingdom the faith of the disciples should be restored by indubitable evidence that death had not ended his career.[92]

## Christianity as Truth

In *Christianity as Truth* Grubb looks at the question of whether that: "new outlook on the universe" which Christianity gave to the world can: "bear examination in the light of history and of known facts".[93]  Some of what he says in answer to this question overlaps with what he writes in *Christianity as Life* and so I shall not comment on it.  I shall instead examine those areas of agreement or disagreement with the core of conviction and the Quaker tradition that were not covered in his previous volume.  These areas are: Revelation, the Trinity, the meaning of the Incarnation, and the Fall of Man.

## Revelation

In his treatment of Revelation Grubb agrees with the core of conviction and the Quaker tradition in maintaining that God has revealed Himself in a special way in Christ:

> While...we are not to confine the thought of Revelation to that which Jesus brought to men - while with the Apostle we recognise that God has not 'left himself without witness' (Acts 14:17) in all

---

[92] ibid p.67

[93] E.Grubb *Christianity as Truth* p.9

human history - it seems that in a very special way He revealed Himself in Christ.[94]

He differs from them in what he says about Revelation and the Bible. He contends that the revelation of God in Christ was preceded by a gradual process of revelation in the history of Israel intended to prepare the way for it, and declares:

> ...it is as the record of this gradual process of revelation that the Bible is unique in human literature, and indispensable for the understanding of Christianity.[95]

However, although the Bible is thus a record of Revelation:

> The Bible is not the Revelation itself; it is a profound misfortune that it was ever called the 'Word of God'. The 'Word of God' is CHRIST: it is in him, not in the Bible, that the substance of Revelation is to be found. Revelation is not in words, not even in such inspired and inspiring words as those which the prophets and psalmists were led to use in recounting their experience of God|; it comes to us through a personal life of perfect beauty, perfect fidelity to truth, perfect devotion to God and Man. It is in Christ and nowhere else that redeeming Divine love comes to find expression; it is through him alone that we are able to believe with full conviction that 'God is love'.[96]

While both the core of conviction and the Quaker tradition would endorse what Grubb says about Christ in this quotation, neither would agree with him that Revelation comes to us **only** through Christ, and not through the Bible as well. The core of conviction holds that the definitive Revelation of God is given to us through **both** Christ **and** the Bible. Likewise, although the Quaker tradition reserved the title 'Word of God' for Christ rather than for the Bible, and in its early and Quietist forms did subordinate the Bible to the Revelation of Christ through the inward monitor, it never denied that the Bible contains the self-revelation of God. As we have seen, although the early Quakers did not call the Bible the 'Word

---

[94] ibid pp.87-8

[95] ibid p.88

[96] ibid p.88

of God' they were insistent that its words were nevertheless the words of God Himself.

## The Trinity

In his thoughts on the Trinity, Grubb is dubious about the idea found in the core of conviction that the Father, the Son, and the Holy Spirit should be described as 'Persons'. Grubb is unhappy about this for two reasons. Firstly, to describe them as 'Persons' in the modern sense of the term would mean seeing them as: "conscious selves", which would lead to an unorthodox and philosophically unacceptable tritheism.[97]  Secondly, while it may be acceptable to describe the Father and the Son as conscious selves, to say that the Holy Spirit: "is conscious of a distinct Personality would be to affirm what we cannot know".[98]  In Grubb's view, when the New Testament ascribes personality to the Holy Spirit this is because He is seen as the channel of the personality of Jesus, and we cannot deduce anything from this about whether the Holy Spirit Himself has personality.

His conclusion about the Trinity is that we may be:

> ...content, in company with the New Testament writers, to acknowledge experience of God as Father, Son, and Holy Spirit, without attempting to 'rationalise' these concepts any further than experience warrants.  We may recognise a threefold manifestation of God - in Nature, in History, and in the Christian life - without committing ourselves to a Trinitarian formula.[99]

Grubb's unhappiness with the use of the term 'person' to describe the members of the Trinity, and his argument that our three-fold experience of God need not commit us to a "Trinitarian formula" conflict with both the core of conviction and the Quaker tradition.  The core of conviction uses the term 'Person' to describe the members of the Trinity, and is committed to the Trinitarian formula contained in the 'Nicene' creed.  The Quaker tradition, whilst sharing Grubb's doubts about the use of the term 'Person' and not accepting the 'Nicene' formula,

---

[97] ibid p.173

[98] ibid pp.173-4

[99] ibid p.174

nevertheless went beyond Grubb in insisting not only that we experience God in a three-fold way, but that God in Himself actually is Father, Son, and Holy Ghost, and yet still one God.

### The Meaning of the Incarnation

Grubb agrees with the core of conviction and the Quaker tradition that God was incarnate in Christ. He argues that this was possible because:

> ...in becoming Man through self-limitation, God did not cease to be God. In relation to us, at any rate, He became on the contrary more truly and fully God than ever before, because His nature was now capable of being more adequately understood and known. The more completely He became Man, the deeper the humiliation and self-sacrifice, the greater was the love displayed, the fuller the revelation of Himself. That is why it has mattered so much to the Church to safeguard the complete humanity of Jesus. She has never really glorified her Lord by denying it or explaining it away; for the more truly human God became the more adequately He expressed in Christ His nature, which is love.[100]

However, having affirmed the truth of the incarnation, Grubb then states:

> ...the real meaning and worth of the confession of the Divine Humanity of Christ is the conviction which it brings us that in Him we have a REVELATION of God in terms that we can understand - not by the intellect only but by the response of our whole personality to the revelation. May it not be said that anyone whose inward eyes are opened to perceive and accept this revelation - who is able to think of God in terms of Jesus Christ, and feels that without Christ his knowledge of God would be vague and uncertain - and whose will is captured for living out in his own life what he has seen in Jesus - is fundamentally an ORTHODOX Christian, whatever may be his intellectual attitude towards the Creeds of the Church?[101]

This statement goes against the core of conviction and the Quaker tradition because neither would accept that confessing Christ's Divine humanity really means being convinced that in Him we have an understandable revelation of God.

---

[100] ibid pp.57-8

[101] ibid p.58

They would say that it really means believing that Christ was God and Man, and that being orthodox means accepting this.

## The Fall of Man

Grubb maintains that he cannot accept the doctrine of 'Original Sin' "if it means that we can be held accountable for the sins of our ancestors".[102]

On the other hand, he accepts the arguments against a purely individualistic view of sin put forward by the Scottish theologian James Orr in his book *Sin as a problem of Today*[103] and in consequence declares his belief that:

> ...our ancestors have transmitted to us a nature which is to some extent handicapped in the moral struggle which we all have to wage; a nature which has in some measure chosen its freedom to chose the right. A strand of evil tendency has, if this belief represents the truth, been woven into the inmost fabric of our being. Our essential personality, including what we call our will, is partly disordered; and in consequence the history of our race is a discord and not a harmony. A racial tendency towards evil seems to provide a vera causa for the tragedy that human life presents, as a purely individual doctrine of sin does not.
> Yet I know of no real foundation for the dogma of 'TOTAL human depravity'. Were man's freedom wholly lost, were his nature completely alienated from goodness, it is impossible to see how there could be any Redemption - how, in fact, there would be anything left to redeeem.[104]

This quotation agrees with the core of conviction and the Quaker tradition in accepting a: "racial tendency towards evil". It also agrees with the Quaker tradition in rejecting the idea that we can be held responsible for the sins of our ancestors. Like the Eastern Orthodox tradition the Quaker tradition does not accept that Adam's descendants have inherited his guilt.[105]   The quotation disagrees with the core of conviction and the Quaker tradition in not tracing the human tendency towards evil back to the sin of Adam recorded in Genesis 3.

---

[102] ibid p.121

[103] J.Orr *Sin as a problem of Today* London: Hodder and Stoughton 1910 Chs.VII and VIII.

[104] Grubb *Christianity as Truth* pp.120-121

[105] See Barclay *Apology* Proposition 4 and Kallistos Ware *The Orthodox Way* pp.80-1

## SUMMARY

In this chapter I have examined six works which express the Liberal Quaker point of view. I draw four principal conclusions.

### Diversity

My first conclusion is that these writings show that Liberal Quakerism was not theologically uniform. There are clear differences between the theologies advocated by the five writers. Stephen accepts the traditional Quaker view that the Bible is: "the one common standard by which their teaching and practice may be judged". Graham holds that we have to judge the teaching of the Bible by the standard of our own spiritual enlightenment, and that Quakers have always felt free to disregard Biblical teaching when it was convenient for them to do so. Thompson sees the death of Christ simply as a: "foul murder". Stephen, Jones, and Grubb give it a much more positive and theological interpretation. Jones' idea that religion is based on God's essentially: "self-revealing and self-giving" nature is not found in the other four writers. Graham's belief that we are part of God as leaves are part of a tree, and Grubb's universalist interpretation of Christ's teaching about the Kingdom of God are likewise uniquely their own.

### Divergence from the core of conviction and the Quaker tradition

My second conclusion is that these three writings show that Liberal Quakerism differed substantially from both the core of conviction and the Quaker tradition. Despite their differences these six works have in common the fact that they diverge from the core of conviction and the Quaker tradition to such an extent that they disagree with them on matters central to Christian and Quaker belief.

*Quaker Strongholds* is, on the whole, theologically conservative, but it dissents from both the core of conviction and the Quaker tradition in its rejection of the verbal inspiration of the Bible.

*A Dynamic Faith* conflicts with both the core of conviction and the Quaker tradition on the issues of the basis of religion, the person of Christ, and the nature of Biblical inspiration.

*A Not impossible Religion* agrees with early and Quietist Quakerism in stressing the importance of first hand religious experience, but in so doing it disagrees with Evangelical Quakerism and the core of conviction.  It also disagrees with both the core of conviction and the Quaker tradition on the Fall, Miracles, Salvation, the Virgin Birth, the Resurrection, the person of Christ, and the Trinity.

*The Faith of a Quaker* differs from the core of conviction and the Quaker tradition on the basis of theology, the Trinity, Man's relationship with God, the person of Christ, the Resurrection, and the importance of the Bible for Christian practice.

Finally, *Christianity as Life* departs from the core of conviction and the Quaker tradition in what it says about Christ, the Kingdom of God, the Cross and the Resurrection;  and *Christianity as Truth* departs from them on Revelation, the Trinity, the meaning of the Incarnation, and the Fall of Man.

### A Christian and Quaker Form of Religion

My third conclusion is that, in spite of this divergence from the core of conviction and the Quaker tradition, Liberal Quakerism was still a distinctively Christian and Quaker form of religion.

The six writings are distinctively Christian in that they advocate a form of belief in God in which Christ has a central place;  in which He is seen as having a uniquely close relationship with God, and in which He is seen as the one who saves Mankind, or, as Graham puts it, makes Atonement.

These writings also contain distinctively Quaker ideas.  *Quaker Strongholds* and *The Faith of a Quaker* are books which explicitly expound and defend a Quaker interpretation of Christianity.  In *A Dynamic Faith* Jones seeks to show that the distinctive beliefs of the early Quakers can be seen to be based in the Bible.  Thompson's rejection of the Priesthood, sacraments, and creeds, and Grubb's interpretation of the nature and history of the early Church can be seen to reflect the distinctive Quaker views on worship and church order.

### External Influences on Liberal Quakerism

My final conclusion is that these writings reinforce the point made in the last chapter about the outside influences on Liberal Quakerism.  For example, Jones' understanding of the basis of religion is shaped by his study of mysticism in general, Graham's Christology is shaped by the thought of the Anglican writer

William Sanday and Grubb's view of sin is influenced by the Scottish Presbyterian writer James Orr. As I have said before, Liberal Quakerism was not isolated but was moulded by wider currents of religious thought.

### The Continuing Influence of Liberal Quakerism

Until the end of the 1950's the mainstream of British Quaker thought continued the pattern established by the writers reviewed in this chapter, in that it continued to put forward a form of religion that diverged from the core of conviction and the Quaker tradition, but was nevertheless still distinctively Christian and Quaker. Two examples will serve to illustrate the point.

Firstly, the Epistle sent out by London Yearly Meeting in 1932 declares that:

> What life may be and what Man may do in harmony with the will of God, have been made known to us in Jesus. In Him we know God and Man as nowhere else: He is the central fact of human history and experience. As he has been lifted up among us, we have learn anew from Him that there is no cheap or easy way through the world's troubles. The Cross shows us the greatness of the price. It means for us great ventures and, it may be, great sacrifices. We are upon an engagement very difficult. For in order to make possible a truly Christ like relation between men, our whole world will need to be remodelled. Jesus faced the darkness with the courage born of a constant renewal of His spirit in the life of God; so must we.
>
> The full meaning of Jesus Christ is to be found in the fact that in Him is life eternal. He lived in God and God in Him; and His life does not end on Calvary. So too our acts done in the will of God have the quality of eternal life; they are done not for time but for eternity. This conviction gives meaning and value to the tasks we undertake in the service of God and Man. For we become workers with God in His creative activity in the world.[106]

This statement diverges from the core of conviction and the Quaker tradition because it sees the Cross not as the place where Christ dealt with the barriers separating Man from God, but as the place where we understand the cost of building a better world, and because it does not describe Jesus as God. It is, however, distinctively Christian in presenting an understanding of God and human

---

[106] *London Yearly Meeting of the Society of Friends 1932* London: Friends House 1932 pp.288-9

life based on Christ and His Cross. Christ is the one who enables us to know God and Man as nowhere else, eternal life is to be found in Him, and His Cross shows us the way in which we must face the world's troubles.

Secondly, the Quaker Biblical scholar H.G.Wood, who was the first Edward Cadbury Professor of Theology at Birmingham University, declared in a pamphlet entitled *The Quaker Understanding of the Christian Faith*, published in 1955, that:

> God in Christ is reconciling the world to Himself. This is the essential truth of the divine mission of Jesus, apart from which we have no adequate gospel. The mission of Jesus is the divine adventure in search of His erring children. He will win men by love or not at all. In the Cross, God's deepest word is spoken, His last appeal is made. Here in the mystery of the Incarnation culminating in the Cross, is the source of that Spirit whose hope is to outlast all wrath and contention and whatsoever is contrary to itself. That of God in every man, in which we must believe, is the capacity, latent it may be not lost, to respond to the love of God who sent His Son to die for our sins. The gospel is not adequately presented in the general statement 'God is love'. The gospel is that God so loved that He gave His only son that whosoever believeth in Him should not perish but have life eternal. Herein is the revelation of the nature of God's love for us and the measure of the love we owe to one another. If it was thus that God loved us, we ought to love one another in the same manner.[107]

As his 1920 Swarthmore Lecture *Quakerism and the Future of the Church*[108] and his broadcast talks *Why did Christ die?*[109] make clear, Wood was a Liberal theologian. However, the passage I have quoted is distinctively Christian in that it uses traditional Biblical language, taken from 2 Corinthians 5:19, John 3:16, and 1 John 4:11 to emphasise that in the Cross of Christ we see revealed the nature of God's love for us, and, as a consequence, how we should love one another. It is also distinctively Quaker in that it links what it says about the love of God revealed on the Cross with two famous Quaker quotations. The words: _ "whose hope is to outlast all wrath and contention and whatever is contrary to

---

[107] H.G.Wood *The Quaker Understanding of the Christian Faith* London: FHSC 1955 p.12

[108] H.G.Wood *Quakerism and the Future of the Church* London: The Swarthmore Press 1920

[109] H.G.Wood *Why did Christ die?* London: Epworth Press 1953

itself" are taken from the dying words of James Nayler[110] and the words: 'That of God in every Man' are a reference to Fox's 1656 '.. exhortation to Friends in the Ministry.'[111] Among Quakers, Nayler's last words and Fox's exhortation have been among the best known and best loved of early Quaker statements.

Although Liberal Quakerism became dominant within the Society of Friends in this country after the Manchester Conference, Evangelical Quakerism did not die out completely, and Evangelical Quakers continued to defend their understanding of Quakerism well into this century. This is most clearly seen in the pages of the Journal *Friends' Witness to Scriptural Truth* which was the Evangelical equivalent of *The Friend* and was published between 1908 and 1942. The aim of this journal, as laid down in its first editorial, was:

> to set forth the truth as revealed in Holy Scripture and as held by the central body of the Society of Friends from its rise until the present time, especially keeping before us the testimony of the Bible and of our Society to three main truths, the Deity of Christ, His Atoning Sacrifice for Sin, and the Authority of the Holy Scriptures".[112]

In practice this meant a vigorous and repeated re-affirmation of traditional Evangelical thought. In an editorial on the 'Authority of Holy Scripture' published in August 1908 the infallibility of the Bible is re-emphasised:

> The question is repeatedly asked, 'Do you believe in an infallible Book?' The answer that we feel we must be given today is yes. For by this term we do not bind ourselves to every theory of verbal inspiration, but we do boldly and unflinchingly declare our readiness to accept as final and infallible any declaration or doctrine therein contained. It is sufficient for us if it be clearly stated there. It is not a question of building up whole theologies on a slight text, but of undeviating adherence to the doctrines of the New Testament of our Lord and Saviour Jesus Christ. If we can think it possible for God to reveal Himself to Man is it any less possible for Him to safeguard that revelation so that Man might know assuredly and unmistakably what it contains? If God revealed His will and

---

[110] See *Christian Faith and Practice in the experience of the Society of Friends* London: London Yearly Meeting 1972 Section 25

[111] Fox *Journal* pp.262-3

[112] *Friends' Witness to Scriptural Truth* vol. I No.1 First Month 1908 p.1

purposes to us In Jesus Christ (John 1:18), then is there not the greatest likelihood that the revelation He has given at so great a cost should be divinely guarded in its transmission to us through Apostles and Evangelists?

Nay, we can but believe that so great a declaration, so precious and important, given to us by one who is both omnipotent and omniscient, would be preserved for us in no uncertain forms. Let it once be granted that God revealed Himself to men by Jesus Christ, and it would be unthinkable that He should allow that revelation to be preserved in such a manner that error and misconception well nigh jeopardised its life.[113]

Alice Hodgkin, in an article entitled 'The Fourfold Vision of the Cross' published in June 1924 quotes the words of George Fox in support of the Evangelical Doctrine of 'Penal Substitution', the idea that Christ took our death upon Himself when He died on the Cross. Commenting on Christ's words 'My God, My God, why have you forsaken me?' she argues that these words have never been explained:

> ...more clearly than in the words of George Fox, the founder of our Society, in his reply to the question put to him by Priest Stevens in 1645 - 'why Christ cried out upon the Cross, My God, My God, why hast thou forsaken me?' 'And I told him' says George Fox 'At that time the sins of mankind were upon Him, and their iniquities and transgressions, with which He was wounded, which He was to bear, and to be offering for them, as He was man, but died not as He was God. And so in that He died for every man, He was an offering for the sins of the whole world. This I spoke, being at that time in a measure sensible of Christ's sufferings and what He went through.'
> Those in our Society today who reject the substitutionary work of Christ and His atoning sacrifice on Calvary, would do well to notice these words; though for us who believe the Bible, the words of Holy Scripture are all-sufficient, and of far higher authority than those of George Fox. It is remarkable that even before our Lord's death took place He Himself had given us its meaning in the clearest terms - 'This is My blood of the new testament which is shed for many for the remission of sins'. His precious blood shed for us is the ground of our salvation.[114]

---

[113]'The Authority of Holy Scripture' *Friends' Witness to Scriptural Truth* vol.I No.8 Eighth Month 1908 pp.85-6

[114] Alice Hodgkin 'The Fourfold vision of the Cross' *Friends' Witness to Scriptural Truth* vol. XVII No.6 Sixth Month 1924 p.61

It is interesting to note that she refers to Fox for the sake of the weaker brethren while firmly subordinating him to the authority of Scripture!

As a last example, an editorial entitled 'The Sin of Unbelief' which was published in October 1934 makes it clear that while Liberal Quakerism sought to meet the concerns of those who had difficulties with Christian faith, the Evangelical Quakers tended to take the view that such difficulties were manifestations of sinful and inexcusable unbelief.

> God has spoken. Men are without excuse. In Jesus Christ we behold Truth personified, lying, deceit, subterfuge, accommodation are as alien to His nature as darkness is to light, as vileness to purity. We are well assured by textual criticism that in the New Testament we have a true record of His words and teaching an an inspired picture of Himself.
> So patent are the facts and so conclusive is the evidence, that God holds guilty the man who wilfully rejects them. When God speaks, woe betide those who scoff, or quibble, or 'refuse Him that speaketh'. It is startling and solemn to learn that such people stand convicted of the sin of unbelief. And how widespread this is! It flares out from the pulpit and the press, as well as from the professorial chair. It has leavened the rank and file of our churches, as well as holding in the grip of death the masses who make no profession of religion.
> It is useless to plead 'honest doubt', for such melts instantly when confronted with the living and ascended Saviour. It finds its answer with doubting Thomas and can only exclaim 'My Lord and My God'.[115]

There are two points of particular interest about the views expressed in these statements. Firstly, they make clear that Evangelical Quakers continued to adhere to the core of conviction and the Quaker tradition. The beliefs about the Bible, the Cross, and the person of Christ expressed by them are all in line with the core of conviction and the Quaker tradition. For example, the "three main truths" which *Friends' Witness to Scriptural Truth* aimed to keep before its readers, "the Deity of Christ", "His Atoning Sacrifice for Sin", and "the Authority of the Holy Scriptures", are all truths which are emphasised in the core of conviction and the Quaker tradition. Secondly, they also make clear that Evangelical Quakerism

---

[115] 'The Sin of Unbelief' *Friends' Witness to Scriptural Truth* vol. XXVII No.10 Tenth Month 1934 p.109

made none of the concessions to 'modern thought' that were a feature of Quaker Liberalism. Evangelical Quakers kept on re-emphasising traditional beliefs in traditional language, and, as the last quotation indicates, they tended to see intellectual doubts and difficulties as manifestations of sin.

It is difficult to know how widespread such views were in British Quakerism as a whole since no figures appear to exist showing the proportion of Evangelicals in British Quakerism in this century. However, what we do know is that such views did not influence the development of the mainstream of British Quaker theology. The opinions expressed in *Friends' Witness to Scriptural Truth* were those of the past not of the future. Just as the Quietists became an uninfluential minority in the Quakerism of the nineteenth century so the Evangelicals in their turn became an uninfluential minority in the Quakerism of the twentieth.

# Chapter Four
## The Causes of Divergence

**The Early Radicals**

It was not only Evangelicals who were dissatisfied with the sort of Liberal Theology described in the last chapter. This theology was also criticized by those who thought not that it was too radical, but that it was not radical enough. Three examples illustrate this.

The first is a letter by Ben Vincent published in *The Friend* on the 3rd August 1928.[1] It responds to an anonymous article entitled 'A Statement of Faith' in the *Friends Quarterly Examiner* earlier in the same year.[2]

In the article, which sought to defend religious belief against scientific materialism, its author made appeal to the "doctrines of spiritually minded men in all ages".[3] In his letter Vincent argues that this appeal is unacceptable because faith cannot be based on an unquestioning acceptance of traditional doctrine but

---

[1] *The Friend* vol. LXVIII No. 31 August 3rd 1928 pp.708-9. By 1928 *The Friend* had ceased to be the mouthpiece for Evangelical Quakerism and had assumed its present character as the weekly journal for British Quakerism as a whole and the major forum for theological debate among Friends in this country.

[2] 'A Statement of Faith' *Friends Quarterly Examiner* vol. 62 1928 pp.229-38. The *Friends Quarterly Examiner*, now called *Friends Quarterly* was and is the heavyweight Quaker journal, containing articles that are longer and more substantial than those found in other Quaker periodicals.

[3] ibid p.231

must be "built up out of doubt".[4]  According to Vincent this questioning approach
to faith does not imply:

> a complete overthrow of the creed of our parents:  I think nothing
> could be more foolish than an attempt to build up an entirely new
> faith without profiting at all by the experience (viz trial
> experiments) of others; early Christianity itself, revolutionary as it
> was, did no such thing.  The new method of reasoning (I say new,
> but it is as old as reasoning itself) must be a test of belief, not sadly
> an origin for it.  There must not be, and I do not fear there is, any
> desire to throw over traditional beliefs just because they are
> traditional; my fear, in fact, is that just the opposite is the case, and
> that, paradox though it be, we desire overmuch to be orthodox
> Friends and Christians.[5]

He fears an excessive desire to be orthodox because such a desire leads to
an attempt to:

> _ force new meanings into old phrases and to say that we agree
> with what others MEAN, but not with what they SAY.  We try to
> deceive ourselves that we are not revolutionary at all.  This is the
> 'modernist' attitude, which tries to give a reasonable explanation of
> the miracles, for example, when a miracle is in its very nature
> inexplicable.  They say that when the Gospel writers said Jesus
> cured leprosy they meant that he cured ignorance or some such
> stuff; but the writers really meant what they said, and it is for us to
> believe it or not as a miracle.  An example ad hoc is our attitude to
> prayer.  Prayer is 'asking earnestly', 'begging a boon', 'an address to
> the deity' and this is the meaning it bears in English.  We cannot
> come up with a new definition of prayer and then say we believe in
> prayer in order to satisfy our desire to be orthodox.[6]

On the basis of a questioning approach to faith,    Vincent rejects the
existence of God and the concept of the immortality of soul:

> I have never found by experience, trial, experiment, the existence of
> attributes and personality without an outward manifestation.  As no
> such material being exists, I cannot believe in God.  I do not deny
> such an existence.  I only know that I have never known it.  Just as

---

[4] Vincent op.cit. p.708

[5] ibid p.708

[6] ibid p.708

I cannot perceive how any abstract thing can be without a material medium. I do not believe that love can exist without a physical lover. For the same reason I cannot believe in the immortality of the soul. As soon as the material body decays I believe its attributes are no more. I know a soul exists because I have experienced its existence; I know how it can change with the body and govern its movements and that they have a material influence on each other. But separate from each other I cannot conceive of them.[7]

Finally, Vincent declares that the "points of agreement" between Young Friends such as himself and Quakers with more traditional beliefs are that:

We all believe, I suppose, in the capacity of worship and self-expression in self-abnegation in every living being, the common capacity for holiness and love, the victory of love and its all satisfying power, the power of love that makes all war unnecessary and abominable, the belief that the story of the gospels presents us with an ideal expression of this love and holiness in a man, to be followed and adored.[8]

Vincent's belief that traditional doctrine needs to be questioned rather than just passively accepted is obviously compatible with Quaker Liberalism since this was itself born out of a questioning of Evangelical doctrine. However, Quaker Liberalism was concerned with precisely the sort of re-interpretation of traditional Christian language that Vincent criticizes. Grubb's *Christianity as Truth* is, for instance, entirely concerned with such a re-interpretation. Furthermore Liberal Quakers wished to retain faith in God and human immortality, and they would have regarded Vincent's "points of agreement" as an inadequate summary of basic Quaker belief because of its lack of any theological content. Vincent can thus be seen as having moved beyond the boundaries of Liberal Quaker Theology into a new and even more radical form of Quakerism.

My second example is a letter from Bertram and Irene Pickard published in *The Friend* of February 15th 1935. This letter too was responding to an earlier article, in this case an article entitled 'Quakerism and Christianity' written by John

---

[7] ibid p.709

[8] ibid p.709

A. Hughes and published in *The Friend* a fortnight earlier. This article argued that Quakerism was Christian in basis, and that:

> The central doctrine of Christianity is the incarnation, and not only the Christian theology, but also its ethic, is based on the conception of the Eternal God manifesting Himself in time in the person of Jesus Christ.[9]

The Pickards disagree with Hughes' article as a whole, and in particular they argue that the central Quaker belief, what they call "the essential Quaker heresy", that God's spirit is present in everyone, is incompatible with the idea of a unique revelation of God in Jesus Christ which Hughes had declared to lie at the heart of Christianity.

> The essential Quaker heresy - well brought out by J.A. Hughes - lay in claiming that 'each human being has a measure of the spirit of God as his light of life'. With courage and originality the early Friends rejected the false notion that the Word of God was limited to a single Church, or to a single Book, though they used to the full the riches of spiritual fellowship (the Quaker society) and spiritual records (the Scriptures).
> But they did not see (except in such flashes of light as Barclay's reference to Socrates and to the composition of the Church Universal cited by J.A.Hughes)[10] that their central discovery was equally incompatible with the central orthodox Christian conception of A SINGLE AND ALL SUFFICING revelation of God in history, namely in the person of Jesus Christ, and            supremely            in            his            death.
> It seems to us clear that the Quaker intuition that the incarnation was a continuing and developing historical process, of which the revelation of God in and through Jesus is only a part, is abundantly confirmed and illustrated by much of the new knowledge about the origins and development of Man (including studies in comparative religion and psychology), knowledge denied to the early Friends, and still more to the formulators of Christian doctrine.
> This view of Quakerism, we believe, far from diminishing the importance of the life and teaching of Jesus sets it in a perspective that alone makes it intelligible, whether intellectually or emotionally, to ordinary people outside the Churches.[11]

---

[9] *The Friend* vol. XCIII No.5 February 1st 1935 p.91

[10] ibid p.89

[11] *The Friend* vol. XCIII No.7 February 15th 1935 pp.150-1

Parts of the Pickard's argument are in line with the ideas of Liberal Quakerism. Their belief that the central tenet of Quakerism is confirmed and illuminated by recent anthropological knowledge is in line with the belief, expressed by the Liberals at the Manchester Conference, that Quakerism is in accord with modern thought.

However, as Punshon notes in *Portrait in Grey*:

> For all its freedom Liberalism was nonetheless rooted in the Bible with the claim, however expressed, that in the life of Jesus of Nazareth there was a unique and universally valid revelation of the divine nature".[12]

The Pickards reject this claim and in so doing they, like Vincent, move away from Liberal Quakerism.

My final example is again a letter in *The Friend*. On February 23rd 1951 Gerald Petrie writes:

> Half the population of the world has never heard the story of Jesus of Nazareth, his teaching, death, and resurrection. Of those who have heard it there are many who, after careful and even anxious thought and study, are unable to believe the story as historically accurate, or to place on it the interpretation accepted by most Christian Churches. Are the people of the first group denied, for no fault, something of God that is granted to Christians? And do those of the second group sin by their inability to believe something that is presumably repellent to their intelligence?
>
> It seems to me possible that we may be shutting our ears to a prophetic message from, for example, some agnostic, who, while humbly refusing to pretend to know something that he regards as outside the realm of human knowledge, yet holds with strong conviction his faith that there is the divine - that of God - in every man.
>
> It may be that Christianity is not enough and that some neighbour of ours travelling by a different route may be inspired by the light we also acknowledge to be in every man, to the prophetic message we seek, the message of UNITY in God for all men.[13]

By questioning the importance of faith in Jesus Christ, and suggesting that the prophetic message of unity in God for all men may be found outside rather than

---

[12] Punshon op.cit. p.259

[13] *The Friend* vol. 109 No.8 Feb 23rd 1951 p.160

inside Christianity, Petrie too steps outside the parameters of Liberal Quakerism. In accordance with the theology of the first Quakers, Liberal Quakerism, like Petrie, held that the light of God is present in every man, but it balanced this belief with a complementary emphasis on the importance of Jesus Christ which is lacking in his letter.

For instance, in her 1958 Swarthmore Lecture *The Concrete and the Universal* the Liberal Quaker writer Margaret Hobling follows the Anglican novelist and theologian Charles Williams in arguing that in order to find God while avoiding idolatry we must both affirm and reject the images through which God is revealed to us, and declares:

> There is a sense in which we have to follow the two ways of affirmation and rejection of images even with regard to the express Image of God, the Incarnate Word. We dare not affirm it in any narrow and exclusive sense which would prevent us from being open and receptive to the revelations of God given in other faiths which are 'in their degree' also images of God. We dare not affirm these images in any way that would impair the supremacy and centrality of the Incarnate Word.[14]

By "the Incarnate Word" Hobling means Jesus Christ, and so she is saying that we need to balance an openness to the revelation of God given through non-Christian faiths with a retention of the supremacy and centrality of Jesus Christ. It is this which Petrie does not do. Although he emphasises the need to be open to what may be said through those outside the Christian faith, he does not give equal emphasis to Christ's supremacy and centrality, and the consequent importance of having faith in Him.

---

[14] Margaret B. Hobling *The Concrete and the Universal* London: George Allen and Unwin 1958 p.57

These three examples of more radical Quaker theology have all been taken from letters in *The Friend*. Until the 1960s that is where such ideas are to be found. They express the beliefs of a radical fringe of British Quakerism, beliefs which were presumably also expressed in Meetings for Worship and other Quaker gatherings, but which are not to be found in the mainstream of British Quaker writing. For instance, no Swarthmore Lecture gives expression to them. In the 1960's however things began to change.

## The Modern Radicals

As Adrian Hastings notes, in the 1960's British society, like Western society as a whole, saw a questioning of:

_ the relevance (or capability for sheer survival) of long standing patterns of thought and institutions of all sorts in a time of intense and rather self-conscious modernisation.[15]

In the words of Keith Clements, during this decade:

Society was moving away from deference to assumed authority. It was an experimental culture. Kenneth Tynan was calling for the wholesale relaxation of censorship on stage and screen - and largely succeeded. In the 1962 Reith Lectures G.M.Carstairs was querying the traditional strictures of sexual morality and so was hailed as the archpriest of 'permissiveness'. Students became more highly politicized than ever, for as the Campaign for Nuclear Disarmament faded from the scene, the protest against the Vietnam War intensified from 1965 onwards, and in 1968, as elsewhere in Europe, student sit-ins and demonstrations marked the rejection of paternalistic authority. It was a society on the way to mass participation. Or so it felt. At least it was a society in which everything, in just about every sphere, from sex to drugs to music to violence to politics, was open to question.[16]

The prevailing atmosphere of questioning and change also affected the life and though of the churches. To quote Alec Vidler, during the 1960's the churches:

---

[15] Hastings op.cit.pp.580-81.

[16] Keith W. Clements *Lovers of Discord* London: SPCK 1988 p.145.

"were infected with the universal restlessness and passion for change and innovation".[17]

For example, in the wake of the Second Vatican Council, the Roman Catholic Church in this country began celebrating the Mass in English rather than in Latin from 1967 onwards and moved out of its traditional isolation to become involved in eceumenical activity with the other British churches. In addition, the authority of the church came to be called into question over the matter of birth control. The leading Catholic theologian Charles Davis left the church in 1966 because he believed the Pope was being dishonest on the issue and many Catholic priests and lay people refused to accept the Pope's ban on artificial methods of contraception in his encyclical *Humanae Vitae*.[18]

Another example of the questioning of accepted ideas within the churches were the criticisms of traditional theology put forward by a number of Anglican writers at the beginning of the 1960's.

In the previous decade Anglican theologians had tended to concentrate on matters of ministry, church order and sacraments and on how Christian truth might be more effectively communicated while more fundamental questions about the nature and validity of Christian belief and behaviour were largely ignored.[19] From 1962 onwards, hoever, the situation began to change.

In 1962 a group of Cambridge theologians led by Alec Vidler, then Dean of King's College, published a volume of essays called *Soundings* in an attempt to raise what they saw as the:

> Very important questions which theologians are now being called
> on to face, and which are not yet being faced with the necessary
> seriousness and determination.[20]

The essays raised critical questions about Christian doctrine, New Testament studies, Christian ethics, the philosophy of religion and the relation between

---

[17] Vidler op.cit.p.269.

[18] See Hastings op.cit. ch.34 for details.

[19] See A.R.Vidler *20th Century Defenders of the Faith* London: SCM 1965 pp.101-3.

[20] A.R.Vidler (ed) *Soundings* Cambridge: C.U.P. 1962 p.XI.

science and theology.    Particular controversy was caused by the essay by
H.A.Williams, Dean of Trinity College, on 'Theology and Self-Awareness'.
Drawing on the work of Sigmund Freud, Williams argued that the God portrayed
in the *Book of Common Prayer*, the traditional heart of Anglicanism:

> _ seems sometimes to be a merciless and egocentric tyrant,
> incapable of love and having to be manipulated or cajoled into
> receiving his children.[21]

and that because the supreme moral value is self-giving love, sexual relationships
outside marriage which embody this might be morally justifiable in spite of
traditional Christian teaching to the contrary.[22]

Shortly after *Soundings* was published Vidler became involved in a further
controversy after appearing on the BBC religious discussion programme *Meeting
Point* on the 4th November 1962.    During the programme Vidler launched a
vigorous attack on the Church of England for being too concerned with religion
rather than with helping people to live responsibly in their everyday lives, for being
too clergy dominated, and for suppressing critical thought and intellectual
integrity.    In response to a question on sexual morality he also declared that he
thought people in the church were far too dependent on moral laws understood as
rigid codes which had to be obeyed - a reply which was seen as advocating the
abandonment of moral laws altogether.[23]

The process of critical questioning continued in February 1963 when Vidler
and Williams and two other Anglican theologians, Donald Mackinnon and
J.S.Bezzant, gave a series of lectures in Cambridge under the auspices of the
Divinity faculty.    These lectures, which attracted audiences of about 1,500 and
were subsequently published, were on the subject of 'Fundamental Objections to
Christian Belief'.    In them the lecturers sought to present as clearly as possible the
leading difficulties facing Christian faith in the 1960's.    Mackinnon looked at

---

[21] ibid p.79.

[22] ibid pp.80-82.

[23] Clements op.cit. pp.162-168.

'Moral objections', Williams at 'Psychological objections', Vidler at 'Historical objections' and Bezzant at 'Intellectual objections'.[24]

Finally, in March 1963, the Bishop of Woolwich, John A.T.Robinson, published a book which provoked: "the most public, the most widespread and the most contentious theological controversy in twentieth century Britain."[25]   The book was called *Honest to God* and in it Robinson drew on the thoughts of the German Lutheran theologians Dietrich Bonhoeffer, Rudolf Bultmann and Paul Tillich in an attempt to construct a form of Christian theology that would bridge what Robinson saw as the:

> _ growing gulf between the traditional orthodox supernaturalism in which our faith has been framed and the categories which the 'lay' world (for want of a better term) finds meaningful today.[26]

In the new form of Christian theology put forward by Robinson, God was no longer to be seen as a supernatural being "out there" - a concept unacceptable to modern man - but as the underlying "ground of our being" witnessed to by the love encountered in personal relationships.  Christ was no longer to be seen as a supernatural being who had descended from heaven to become Man - another idea no longer acceptable - but as "the man for others" who was: "utterly open to, and united with, the ground of his being" because of his complete love for other people.  Worship and prayer no longer meant turning away from the world to be with God but responding in love to God's presence in other people.  Finally, Christian morality entailed expressing unconditional love rather than submitting to a set of prescriptive moral laws, so that: "nothing can of itself always be labelled as 'wrong'" including, for instance, divorce or sex before marriage.[27]

*Honest to God* was publicised in an article in *The Observer* dramatically entitled 'Our Image of God must Go' and it stimulated a widespread debate about

---

[24] A.R.Vidler (ed) *Objections to Christian Belief* London: Constable 1963.

[25] Clements op.cit. p.178.

[26] J.A.T.Robinson *Honest to God* London: S.C.M. 1963.

[27] ibid chs.3-6.

theology among theologians and non-theologians alike.[28]  As Clements notes, this debate continued for months and: "in retrospect *Honest to God* can be viewed as a crucial landmark in post-war religious thought in Britain" because

> Overnight people at all levels in the churches, or on the fringe of organised religion, realised that the agenda for discussion of belief was wide open.  Theology need no longer be on the other side of the fence from critical questioning, but was itself adopting the critical style.[29]

The examples of questioning and change in the British churches I have just given have been taken from the Roman Catholic and Anglican Churches. However, most, if not all, the churches were affected to a greater or lesser extent by the questioning mood of the 60's and as Vidler observes in *20th Century Defenders of the Faith*[30] the indication that the Quakers were affected as well came with the publication in 1963 of a work entitled *Towards a Quaker View of Sex*.[31]

This work was the report of an informal working party of twelve Quakers who had been trying to develop a Quaker approach to sexual ethics.  This work called for Quakers to take a positive view of human sexuality in both its hetero-sexual and homosexual forms.  It also rejected "almost completely" the belief shared by the Quakers with the Christian Church as a whole that sexual morality entailed obedience to a set of rules governing sexual behaviour.[32]  It argued instead that being moral did not mean accepting: "a formal morality, an observance of mores", but that a person's actions: "should come under searching scrutiny in the light that comes from the Gospels and the working of God within us".[33]

---

[28] See J.A.T.Robinson and D.L.Edwards *The Honest to God Debate* London: SCM 1963.

[29] Clements op.cit. p.178.

[30] Vidler *20th Century Defenders of the Faith* p.110.

[31] Alastair Heron (ed.) *Towards a Quaker View of Sex* London: Friends Home Service Committee 1963.

[32] ibid p.39.

[33] ibid p.41.

This radical non-prescriptive approach to sexual ethics, which was in striking agreement with the approach to ethics taken by Robinson in *Honest to God*[34] caused the same sort of furore as had greeted the publication of *A reasonable Faith* and *The Gospel of Divine Help* back in the 1880's.[35] However, just as their publication had signalled the growth of Quaker Liberalism so also *Towards a Quaker View of Sex* heralded the rise of Quaker radicalism and from the early 1960's onwards ideas more radical than those of Quaker Liberalism moved into the mainstream of British Quaker thought and writing. The theological questioning of the 1960's did not transform the beliefs and practices of the British churches in the ways hoped for by theologians such as Robinson. Nevertheless, the radical questioning of traditional beliefs has remained a prominent feature of British theology in the succeeding decades, finding expression in works such as *The Myth of God Incarnate* by John Hick and others, John Hick's *God has many names* and Don Cupitt's *Taking leave of God*, as well as in the continuing controversy surrounding the thought of the Bishop of Durham.[36] In a similar fashion the ideas of radical Quaker thinkers have become a prominent feature of British Quakerism. They are no longer confined to occasional appearances in the correspondence columns of *The Friend* but are to be found in a profusion of books, pamphlets, articles and Swarthmore Lectures.

As examples of this profusion I will look at four works by writers from the radical wing of British Quakerism. These four works are George Gorman's 1973 Swarthmore Lecture *The Amazing Fact of Quaker Worship*,[37] Lorna Marsden's

---

[34] See Robinson op.cit. ch.6.

[35] See *The Friend* vol.121 1963.

[36] John Hick (ed) *The Myth of God Incarnate* London: SCM 1977, John Hick *God has many names* London: SCM 1980 and Don Cupitt's *Taking leave of God* London: SCM 1980, T.Harrison *The Durham Phenomenon* London: D.L.T. 1985.

[37] George Gorman *The Amazing Fact of Quaker Worship* London: Friends Home Service Committee 1973.

essay 'The Quaker Christ',[38] Tim Miles's pamphlet *Towards Universalism*[39] and an article by Alec Lea entitled 'An immense salvation purpose'.[40]

### The Amazing Fact of Quaker Worship

In chapter three of this lecture Gorman, who was later to become the General Secretary of the Quaker Home Service Committee, poses the question: "Who or What do we worship?". He begins his answer by explaining that like other contemporary Friends he has difficulty using the sort of language traditionally employed by Quakers to describe their experience of Meeting for Worship. In his view, this difficulty:

> _ largely turns on the words we use to describe a fundamental experience shared by all Friends. We all trust in the conviction that life has meaning and purpose: the source of this trust is in the awareness of something always stirring in Man towards a creative transcendence. The difficulty that many of us feel in using God-language to describe this conviction is that it tends to imply an awareness of God as so obviously present in life in a manner that is not always true of our actual experience. God often seems to be so terribly absent.[41]

Despite this problem he remains:

> _ convinced that the depth of meaning expressed by the phrase 'communion with God' is a reality. It can also be known by many people who at first feel it cannot be theirs because the words do not convey to them anything that they are able to identify with their own                                                              experience.
> In order to help them as well as ourselves to reach this position a fresh look is required at the nature of religious faith through the insights now available to us. My approach to all this

---

[38] Lorna M. Marsden 'The Quaker Christ' in *The Prepared Heart* London: Quaker Home Service 1988.

[39] Tim Miles *Towards Universalism* Leicester: Quaker Universalist Group N.D.

[40] Alec Lea 'An immense salvation purpose' *Quaker Monthly*, vol.64 No.8 August 1985.

[41] Gorman op.cit. p.52

will be by way of a review of some of the reasons why people in the twentieth century have a particular problem about religious faith.[42]

Gorman begins this review by arguing that since the beginnings of Quakerism in the seventeenth century developments in human thought have reduced:"the inclination or apparent need for religious faith."[43] As a result:
"the majority of people in Britain are secular in their outlook, feeling no desire or need to believe in God."[44]  In order to account for this secular outlook in more detail he describes:

> _ two actual encounters I had with some young people, who seemed to me to represent all that is best in the younger generation.[45]

These young people had all rejected religious belief, and Gorman notes that:

> The rejection of a religious attitude by these young people seemed to turn on two main points.  The first that it is quite unnecessary and irrelevant to drag the concept of God in to life in order to provide it with a sense of meaning and purpose.  Such a sense, in so far as it exists, is provided by the business of living.  The second, that religion not only inhibits a full life, but also fails to fulfil its promises to provide real security when wanted.  Religious people are just as prone to fits of depression and despair as those who hold no religious faith.  Mixed in with these major objections is the embarrassing feeling that haunts intelligent people reared in a scientific age, that ideas worthy of acceptance should be subject to the possibility of verification. Religious ideas are notoriously difficult to verify in any objective manner.  The embarrassment of such people is heightened by the strong suspicion that religious feelings, and, especially the concept of God, are but the projections of man's desires, fears, guilts and needs.  However deeply Freud may have been misunderstood he had dealt a deathly blow to popular religion by his insight.[46]

---

[42] ibid p.52

[43] ibid p.54

[44] ibid p.55

[45] ibid p.55

[46] ibid p.57

Having explained why many people today find religious belief difficult, Gorman then goes on to expound an approach to religious experience which he thinks such people may find helpful. He begins this exposition by confessing that he has felt strongly the force of the arguments against religious belief, and that he might have abandoned religious belief altogether had he not encountered the Society of Friends, whose approach to religion he found attractive because they did not:

> hand you a complete spiritual package of faith, creeds and dogma, which one was asked to take whole, or leave entirely alone. For them religious experience didn't look much like what I thought to be religious at all. While the Society never disguised the fact that its corporate experience pointed to lofty ideas, and to a strong sense of the reality of God, Quakers nevertheless emphasised that the starting point of religious experience is always to be found in ordinary everyday experience.[47]

He quotes with approval the statement made by the Anglican theologian Alistair Kee in his book *The Way of Transcendence* "There is no direct experience of God only experiences which are interpreted in a religious manner",[48] and holds that it reflects the essence of the Quaker approach to religion:

> I am particularly drawn to Alistair Kee's statement, as to my mind it catches succinctly the essential approach made by Quakers, even though at first glance it appears to challenge them, to modify their long-held claim that in their life and experience they have direct and immediate experience of God. On reflection this will be seen to be human experience which Quakers have felt obliged to interpret in a religious manner.[49]

In support of this understanding of Quakerism Gorman argues that Quakers have always understood the Bible in this way:

> It has never been considered by them to be the Word of God, in which he has infallibly revealed his nature and purposes to men.

---

[47] ibid p.58

[48] ibid p.60  quoting Alistair Kee *The Way of Transcendence* London: Penguin 1971 p.18

[49] ibid. p.60

Rather the Scriptures have been seen as a most important body of
literature drawn together over a period of years.  It consists of
extremely honest accounts of human behaviour at its best and at its
worst, and is therefore a unique assembly of human experiences:
these have been interpreted by the biblical writers in such a way as
to disclose religious insights which are of the greatest value _. The
total impact of the Bible is to hold before men observations of
human experience which have been interpreted religiously and
disclose a dimension of unparalleled importance to which men have
given the name God.[50]

He next observes that:

In any Quaker Meeting for Worship a great and rich variety of
human experience will be available, focussed in the personalities of
those attending.[51]

In his view our experience of such personalities can be interpreted in a religious
way because:

For religious men, including Quakers, human personality can serve
as a vivid and powerful model for the concept of God, provided
always that like all analogies it is not pressed too far.  For God is
not to be thought of as an individual person, as you and I are
individuals, but rather as the ground of our being.[52]

The phrase 'ground of our being', which we have already come across in
Robinson's *Honest to God*, comes from the thought of Tillich, and implies that
God is not an individual being, but the reality underlying all individual beings and
keeping them in existence.

An aspect of our experience of human personality which Gorman sees as
especially significant is that of human love.  He declares that love is vitally
important since "we cannot exist as real people unless we are in some degree loved
and able to love."[53]  He also notes, however, that: "human love is a fragile thing

---

[50] ibid pp.61-2

[51] ibid p.63

[52] ibid p.65

[53] ibid p.65

and although it has within it the seeds of self-giving and self-sacrifice, it can go sour and fail us."[54]  It is when human love does fail us that:

> _ the life of Jesus and the way in which he met his death powerfully underline our conviction as to the ultimate power and creativeness of love.[55]

According to Gorman this is because:

> Friends, along with other Christians, have recognised that it was not only the truth, power and simplicity of his teaching that calls for their obedience.  In meeting his death with the words of forgiveness on his lips for those who executed him, Jesus disclosed a way of dealing with evil and released into the world a stream of loving and creative energy by which human wickedness can be transmuted. The death of Jesus did not end his contribution to Mankind, for all that was of deepest value in the life of Jesus continues to makes its impact on people who are open to the loving spirit in which he lived.
> In this sense every Quaker meeting gathers under the shadow of the cross;  not the shadow cast by an angry God seeking vengeance and retribution but of the God who is love.  For the whole purport of the teaching, life and death of Jesus is his unshaken conviction that God is love.  In one sense the execution of Jesus was a human act carried out by a society that did not comprehend his goodness.  He was a threat to the established orders of religion and politics and had to be eliminated by them. This terrible event only makes true sense when it is interpreted from a religious standpoint.  Then it discloses the truth that suffering, accepted as Jesus accepted it, can become a source of life and not of destruction.  For many Friends this is among the supreme signals for transcendence.[56]

Summing up his argument Gorman declares:

> I find it relatively easy to convince myself that the cumulative evidence of the religious interpretation of human experience and the many signals of transcendence that arise from it, all point to a

---

54 ibid p.67

55 ibid p.67

56 ibid pp.67-8

dimension that is beyond and to which one might properly ascribe the name God.[57]

Having summarised why he believes in God, he goes on to explain that all his thinking about God has been influenced by the concept of God's 'mediated immediacy' put forward by the Church of Scotland theologian John Baillie in his book *Our Knowledge of God*.[58] This is the idea that: "Men have no direct awareness of the presence of God that is mediated to them apart from their experience of the world."[59]

For Gorman this idea of Baillie's becomes clear:

> _ when one thinks about the question of guidance. I would hesitate to claim that I receive direct guidance from God - I do not hear a divine voice that tells me what to do. But I do have a sense that I am being drawn to take one course of action rather than another. The guidance, however, arises from a countless number of experiences, influences, attitudes and disciplines which I have accumulated over the years and upon which I have reflected. So certain types of action seem to be my natural response to particular circumstances. In them all the sense of the presence of God is real and immediate but not unmediated.[60]

Finally, Gorman concludes the chapter by explaining his understanding of the Holy Spirit. He quotes some words of H.A. Williams:

> The Spirit is ourselves in the depths of what we are. It is me at the profoundest level of my being, the level at which I can no longer distinguish between what is myself and what is greater than me. So, theologically, the Spirit is called God in me _. the place where God and me mingle indistinguishably.[61]

and contends that these words of Williams' point us to:

---

[57] ibid p.69

[58] John Baillie *Our Knowledge of God* Oxford: OUP 1939

[59]. Gorman op.cit. p.70

[60] ibid p.71

[61] ibid p.72  quoting  H.A.Williams *The true wilderness* Harmondsworth: Penguin 1968 pp.32-3

the deep still place at the centre of our being, where we are alone, and yet not alone, for we are compassed about and caught up in so great a cloud of witnesses. It is the most human of all human experiences, and at the same time the experience that cries aloud for religious interpretation. Today, and throughout its history, the Society of Friends has felt constrained to interpret this experience, always with flexibility and freedom, as an encounter with the spirit of love and truth and light, for which the only adequate name available is God.[62]

That is Gorman's account of who or what Quakers worship. Some parts of it follow the ideas of Liberal Quakerism. Gorman's emphasis on Quakerism as a non-dogmatic and experienced based religion echoes a similar emphasis in Liberal Quakerism. His desire to explain Quaker worship to those who have: "only a slight acquaintance with any religious ideas or possibly a strong resistance to them",[63] is in line with the apologetic concern of Liberal Quakerism. His assertion that Quakers have never seen the Bible as: "the word of God, in which he has infallibly revealed his nature and purposes to men" represents a reading back of the Liberal Quaker attitude to the Bible into earlier Quaker history. Lastly, his rejection of the idea of: "an angry God seeking vengeance and retribution" reflects the Liberal rejection of this picture of God.

However, there are also parts of Gorman's account which differ significantly from the theology of Liberal Quakerism.

Firstly, Liberal Quakerism had, as its basic belief, the idea that we **can** experience God directly. Thus in his 1956 Swarthmore Lecture *Quakers and the Religious Quest* Edgar Dunstan quotes Rufus Jones' definition of mysticism as the:

> type of religion which puts the emphasis on immediate awareness of relation with God, on direct and intimate consciousness of the Divine Presence

and comments that:

---

[62] ibid p.72

[63] ibid p.3

> This immediate awareness of God, known at times in measure by all men, should be the goal of all religious endeavour and aspiration.[64]

Gorman, on the other hand, follows Kee in arguing that we cannot have direct experience of God, only human experiences which we chose to interpret religiously.

Secondly, Liberal Quakerism saw the Bible as the record of God's progressive revelation of Himself to Mankind. As Meetings for Sufferings[65] put it in 1956:

> The Bible is the record of what God did with and for Israel and of what He has done for mankind through the discipline of Israel and the coming of Jesus Christ. The Old Testament relates the call of a nation to become a moral and spiritual example to all nations, the training of a people to be the bearers of God's truth and mercy to all peoples. It was the mission of Jesus 'to make the treasures of Israel available for mankind'. Throughout the story, from the call of Abraham to the coming of Jesus Christ and the gift of the Holy Spirit the divine initiative is manifest with unique intensity in a continuous and progressive revelation. As the record of this revelation the Scriptures become the primary and indispensable witness to the history and nature of salvation.[66]

Gorman, however, portrays the Bible not as the record of God's active self-revelation, but as a series of religious interpretations of human experience and behaviour. It is true that Gorman sees these interpretations as disclosing a dimension of life which men have called God, but he does not see this disclosure as being a result of God revealing Himself to us.

Thirdly, Liberal Quakerism saw the Cross as the place where God acted to bring the human race back to Himself. For instance, in his book *The Double Search* Rufus Jones describes the Cross in terms of God reaching across the chasm of sin separating Man from God:

---

[64] Edgar G. Dunstan *Quakers and the Religious Quest* London: George Allen and Unwin 1956 p.23

[65] The standing committee of London Yearly Meeting

[66] *Christian Faith and Practice* section 201

> What Man hoped to do, but could not, with his bleating lamb and
> timid dove, God Himself has done. He has reached across the
> chasm, taking on Himself the sacrifice and cost, to show the sinner
> that the only obstacle to peace and reconciliation is the sinner
> himself. 'This is love, not that we loved Him, but that He loved us',
> and this is sacrifice, not that we give our bulls and goats to please
> Him, but that He gives Himself to draw us.[67]

This view of the Cross contrasts with that put forward by Gorman. While Gorman
suggests that the Cross casts the shadow of the God who is love, the only
connection he makes between God's love and the Cross is Jesus' conviction that
God is love. Apart from this, the Cross is seen in purely human terms with no
suggestion of any divine activity or initiative.

Fourthly, behind the Liberal Quaker belief in God's self-revelation, and His
activity on the Cross lay the belief that God is to be seen in personal terms. In the
words of Robert Davis in *Studies in Christian Fundamentals*:

> The range of our experience is limited and the nature of God is far
> beyond anything that the mind of Man can conceive, but we claim
> that the God with whom we have to do cannot be less than personal
> and must be the kind of Being who can enter into personal
> relationship with men. When we say that God is love or that God is
> good, we assume in God the elements of personality, for love and
> goodness are qualities of personal character.[68]

Gorman's picture of God differs from this by being more ambiguous. For Gorman
personality is only a model for the nature of God, and a model which must not be
pressed too far since God is not an individual person but the ground of our being.
The extent to which the ground of our being is to be seen as personal is something
which is left unclear.

In summary, therefore, Gorman differs from Liberal Quakerism in denying
that we can have direct experience of God, in not seeing the Bible as a record of
God's self-revelation, in not depicting the Cross in terms of God's activity, and in
being ambiguous about whether God should be seen as personal. In his desire to
communicate with the non-religious Gorman reduces Quaker theology to talk

---

[67] Rufus M. Jones *The Double Search* London: Headley Bros. 1906 p.64

[68] *Studies in Christian Fundamentals* London: Friends' Home Service Committee 1943 p.23

about human experience and leaves no room for the initiative and activity of an un-ambiguously personal God.

### The Quaker Christ

In her essay 'The Quaker Christ', which is included in the anthology of her writings entitled *The Prepared Heart*, the prolific and influential Quaker writer Lorna Marsden declares:

> In modern times we have come to understand the universality of the power of myth, the persistence throughout human history of THE SAME MYTHOLOGICAL FORMS. We know that miraculous birth, the god that is slain and rises again, the division of the supreme deity into separate forms that are yet one, the importance of sacrifice, the potency of the ceremony of eating the body of the god - all these images, and more, that are related to the traditional Christian faith, are a part of the spiritual world of many cultures over thousands of years.
>
> This is the kind of thing that the Church has covered up, and this covering up has ended up by eroding the Church's credibility. What the Church has acknowledged and incorporated into its Pauline Christology is its accommodation to the concepts of Greek thought as well as Jewish tradition. That aside, it has failed to admit that the sources of its truth, the deep laid foundations of its legend, are to be found in the insights of the human imagination reaching back over many civilisations far into the past. These insights, born in the power house of the human unconscious, were not worked out in concepts but appeared as myths, and the truths of myth are assimilated and recognised at the deepest levels of the human mind.[69]

Marsden makes three points here. Firstly she contends that elements of traditional Christian belief such as the Virgin birth, Christ's death and resurrection, and the Trinitarian nature of God are not literally true, but are mythological images which are to be found in the religious life of many different cultures throughout human history. Secondly, she follows the Swiss Psycho-Analyst C.G. Jung in arguing that these mythological images represent insights of the human unconscious which have been expressed in mythological rather than conceptual

---

[69] Marsden op.cit. p.16

form, and which need to be accepted at the deepest level of the human mind.[70] Thirdly, she maintains that the Church has lost credibility because, instead of admitting these facts, it has tried to cover them up.

Having made these points she then writes:

> In the too externalised living of our times the rejection of myth has meant that religion as a whole has been largely thrown out, and where still pursued too often pursued without understanding. We who are Quakers should be saved from that mistake because of our inheritance. By a different route the early Quakers had also reached the point of discarding the outward observances and trappings of religion. But they were deeply held by the INNER experience, and in a day when the symbols of the experience were not questioned but totally received they did not reject the language of the Christian myth, but transformed it. They transformed it to such effect that though we do not use their language in the mode in which they used it, their spirit is preserved in us - or could be so preserved if we would only recognise it - because, fundamentally, their outlook meets the conditions of today. They were truly a prophetic people.[71]

That is to say, the current neglect of the inner realities of the spirit and the psyche (what Marsden calls the 'too externalised living of our times') has resulted in the rejection of myth. This rejection has led in turn either to the abandonment of religion on the ground that religious beliefs are mythological, or to the mistake of arguing that they are not mythological and defending them as literally true. Their Quaker heritage can, however, help Quakers to avoid this latter mistake. Like many people today the early Quakers abandoned the outward forms of religion, but they were gripped by its inner reality, and they re-used the language of the Christian myth to describe this reality in a way that is still relevant today even though we do not use language in the same way as they did.

Marsden illustrates this argument by noting:

> The early Quakers talked of 'the day of the Lord' and 'the Lamb's War', but this imagery was applied to the heart. This war was waged WITHIN them, and so was judgement. They saw the transformation of the world as coming about by the power of the

---

[70] See C.G.Jung *Psychology and Religion* Yale: Yale University Press 1938

[71] Marsden *The Prepared Heart* p.18

inner experience. Is not this the crying need of our own historical moment? The early Quaker intuition of God was existential. They were not primarily interested, as the Church has been, in an alleged supernatural event in history - (this too no longer arouses general interest today) - because they saw the world of experience as METAPHYSICALLY Christ centred, always and for all time. Their vision of Christ was not confined within the biblical record, but as an imprint on the soul of every human being who would receive him, named or unnamed. They assimilated what was paradoxical in such a vision by the strength of their untaught vision. Listen to James Nayler, on trial for blasphemy: 'If I cannot witness Christ nearer than Jerusalem I shall have no benefit by him, but I own no other Christ but that who witnessed a good confession before Pontius Pilate which Christ I witness in me now'. This was confusion to his examiners. To Nayler it was crystal clear.

What was this, in essentials, but a position tenable in our own terms today? Nayler, and the early Friends, saw behind and beyond the gospel figure the inner truth of which he is the symbol - the profound truth of which he is the symbol - the profound truth that Christ is ourselves, humanity. They did not INTELLECTUALLY elucidate this truth. They felt it on their pulses. In this way they not only preserved the mystery of Christ, its inextricable involvement in our western human destiny, but they also experienced the truth of Christ on the level of the eternal.[72]

Analysis of this complex statement shows that it contains four basic ideas.

1.      The early Quakers used the language of Christian eschatology - 'the day of the Lord' and 'the Lamb's war' - to describe the transformation of the world through the power of inner experience, and this is the sort of transformation needed today.

2.      Like many people today the early Quakers were not primarily interested in the Christ witnessed to by the Biblical record. They concentrated instead on the Christ present in the human soul.

3.      Although they did not express it intellectually, the early Quakers felt intuitively the truth that Christ is, in fact, ourselves.

4.      By understanding Him in this way the early Quakers preserved the significance of Christ for our Western culture, and experienced the truth about Him not as truth about a particular historical figure, but as eternal truth about the nature of human existence.

---

[72] ibid p.19

According to Marsden, the reason why the early Quaker view of Christ is still relevant today is that it:

> _. was not 'doctrine'. It was being 'in the life'. They used for this experience the only imagery available to them, the imagery of the gospel story. Earlier on, I tried to show how this imagery had its roots in universal human insights. Distorted and manipulated by the intellectual concepts of theology and the involved story of the Church, such insights become frozen into forms which time and history reject. We are living in such a period of rejection now. As always, rejection, which may be necessary in itself, has its aspects of blindness and can go too far. But the early Quakers themselves saw beyond 'notions' to a perennial truth - that the workings of God are incarnated in humanity, that we are inevitably and ineluctably the Children of God. There is nothing in modern experience which can deny this. It is not an intellectual formulation - it is a felt reality, a Presence in the Spirit of Man.[73]

Marsden is saying that the early Quaker view of Christ was not a matter of doctrine but of experience. More specifically, it was an experience of the perennial truth that God is at work in us and we are His children. Nothing in modern experience can deny this truth, and so it can survive the contemporary rejection of the particular forms in which the insights of the Gospel stories have been passed on by the Church.

Marsden concludes her essay by declaring that what the Quakers called the presence of God within:

> _ the Hindu calls Atman - that condition of the spirit that is one with Brahman - as the son is with the Father. These are words that convey what the gospel of John calls 'the word' _. They express the ineffable consciousness within humanity of its divine affinity. The vessel of this consciousness has been for the West the figure of Christ but it is one vessel the world over, in whatever name - and we fill it ourselves. It is not the elusive historical Jesus with which we are finally concerned, not the elaborate Christology of the Churches and the creeds. It is the reality of the inner human condition on which the mysterious figure of Christ opens the door.[74]

---

[73] ibid pp.19-20

[74] ibid p.21

In other words, Christ is just one of many symbols which express our awareness of being Children of God, and we are only interested in the historical Jesus or the Christ of the Creeds insofar as they symbolise this awareness.

As was the case with Gorman, Marsden's essay contains elements which are in accord with Liberal Quakerism. It continues the Liberal emphasis on the centrality of experience and shares the Liberal confidence that both Christianity and early Quakerism can be re-interpreted in a way that gives them contemporary relevance.

However, it also contains two elements which depart from Liberal thinking.

Firstly, as I have shown, Liberal Quakerism was centred on the person of Christ. As Grubb put it in his 1914 Swarthmore Lecture *The Historic and Inward Christ*:

> Our faith, then, as Christians and as Friends centres in a Person: a Person who has always been present in the souls of men, the revealer of God, though unrecognised or dimly apprehended; a Person who in the fulness of time took outward form in Judaea and Galilee, healing the bodies and the souls of men; who brought the age long process of revelation and redemption to its climax by laying down His life to save them; who through the very depth of humiliation and sacrifice revealed His exaltation in Glory; who ever lives, not in some far off heaven but in our midst, evermore to be the inward source of light and love, of power and joy, to those who are united with Him by faith and obedience.[75]

For Marsden, however, Quakerism is not centred on the person of Christ. He only symbolizes what is really important, which is our awareness of affinity with God.

Secondly, as noted earlier, Liberal Quakerism saw Christ as the supreme manifestation of God. If He was not the only way in which God was known He was certainly the central, climactic, and all important way. For Marsden, on the other hand, Christ is just one symbol among many others, the most important for us in the West, but certainly not absolutely the most important.

---

[75] Grubb *The Historic and Inward Christ* p.83

**Towards Universalism**

This idea that Christ is but one of many symbols, all of which have equal importance, is an example of 'universalism', the view that there are many equally valid forms of religion. Universalism is also the theme of my third example of radical theology, Miles' pamphlet *Towards Universalism*.

According to Miles, the purpose of his pamphlet is:

> _to give expression to the difficulties which some of us find over the claim that historical Christianity is the one true religion. For purposes of exposition I shall group these difficulties under two heads. In the first place, if we make this claim it is hard to see how we can avoid the charge of parochialism. Secondly, if the claim is valid, it follows that in order to be a Christian one must believe in certain HISTORICAL FACTS; and this requirement is uncomfortable since one's duty when faced with documents which purport to be historical must surely be to search for truth and not distort the evidence in the interests of some interpretation which has been specified in advance.[76]

Miles nowhere defines what he means by "historical Christianity". What he appears to mean, however, is a form of Christianity based on particular historical beliefs such as, for instance, the beliefs that Jesus existed and that He was the sort of person portrayed by the Gospels. This would explain why if this sort of Christianity is the only true religion: "one must believe in certain historical facts" in order to be a Christian.

Having explained the purpose of his pamphlet, Miles goes on to examine in turn each of his two sorts of difficulty.

He looks first at what he calls the "charge of parochialism". By this he means the accusation that belief in the unique truth of historical Christianity represents an unacceptable narrowing of one's religious outlook. As an example of such parochialism he quotes the words of the Swiss Reformed theologian Karl Barth in *Church Dogmatics* 1:2 : "the Christian religion is true because it pleased God who alone can be the judge in the matter, to affirm it to be the true religion."[77] In his view, these words "imply an exclusiveness which large numbers

---

[76] Miles op.cit. p.3

[77] Barth op.cit. p.350

of Friends, I am sure - and perhaps many members of other denominations - would find unacceptable."[78]    The reason why they would be found unacceptable is because they seem to express a narrow minded attitude and to imply the harsh view that: "anyone outside 'our' group - anyone not of 'our' particular religion - is necessarily excluded from salvation."[79]

Miles notes that in the early centuries of Christianity the Apologist Justin Martyr attempted to modify the "extreme form of exclusivity" advocated later by Barth by suggesting that:

> a person can still be a Christian even though he has in fact never heard of Jesus Christ.   In recent years such persons have been referred to as 'anonymous Christians': they may not actually use the NAME of Christ but they can still be his followers without knowing it.[80]

However Miles then rejects this theory of the 'anonymous Christian' because:

> _ there are three reasons why this view is not a satisfactory answer to the charge of parochialism.   In the first place it shows a lack of sensitivity since it is surely unpleasantly patronising to say to another person, 'you are a member of our exclusive group even though you do not realise the fact' _ Secondly, if the contention that there are 'anonymous Christians' is valid at all, it is hard to see why in that case there should not be 'anonymous Buddhists','anonymous Muslims' etc.; and, if so, we are back where we started, since there would be a number of different claims to primacy with no clear criteria for distinguishing between them.   Thirdly we should remember that, except in a small number of cases, people follow the religion of the country in which they were born and brought up; and it is surely uncomfortable to suppose that only those brought up in certain parts of the world have the chance to hear about the one and only true religion.[81]

For Miles, therefore, the charge of parochialism still sticks, and moreover,

---

[78] Miles op.cit. p.5

[79] ibid p.5

[80] ibid p.5 referring to Justin Martyr *Apology* 1:46 text in Justin Martyr *The Works* Oxford: Parker 1861

[81] ibid p.6

... with the increasing ease of travel from one part of the world to
another and - at least as far as Britain is concerned - the presence in
our schools of children from many different racial and religious
backgrounds the charge is not one that will simply disappear.  To
reiterate the 'certainties' of historical Christianity may meet the
needs of some individuals, but one must expect a growing number
of people for whom this will be insufficient.[82]

After considering the charge of parochialism,  Miles next looks at the
question of whether religious bodies may ask their members to accept particular
historical beliefs.  His answer to this question is "no".  As he sees it:

Religious bodies can justifiably require (or perhaps better, as in the
case of Friends, encourage) their members to ACT in certain ways,
for example by attending places of worship, and they can ask for
commitment to certain views about the human condition, for
example the view that there is 'that of God in every man' (provided
it is not given the status of a dogma);  but if they require belief in
particular historical matters they are no longer looking for a
religious commitment but for something else.  This can be shown if
one considers the case of a person who reads the gospels and the
relevant passages in Tacitus and Pliny and announces: 'Yes, you've
convinced me  - he (Jesus) WAS a historical figure'.  This is a
change of mind, certainly, but it is a change which has nothing to do
with religion_..  In brief, a religious body is entitled to make
religious demands, but it is inappropriate for it to ask its members
to accept any particular historical beliefs.[83]

According to Miles, the acceptance of historical Christianity as the one true
religion means the acceptance of certain historical facts.  However, as we have just
seen, he holds that religious bodies may not ask their members to accept particular
historical beliefs.  It follows, therefore, that for Miles religious bodies may not ask
their members to accept historical Christianity as the one true religion.

In summary, Miles puts forward two arguments against the claim that
historical Christianity is the only true religion.  Firstly, the claim is parochial and so
growing numbers of people will find it inadequate.  Secondly, religious bodies may
not ask their members to accept it because they  may not ask them to subscribe to
particular  historical beliefs.

---

[82] ibid p.7

[83] ibid pp.8-9

Miles therefore finds the claim that historical Christianity is the only true religion unacceptable. In its place he suggests the belief known as Universalism, which he defines as:   "the view that no religion has the final and exclusive revelation of truth."[84]  His argument for Universalism is:

> If our religious sensitivity is to grow, what we need, I suggest, is a series of images (or parables or myths) each of which can complement the others without necessarily implying exclusion. Thus if there is a message in the words 'God is love' this does not mean that there is no message in the words 'God is light'; and to argue on logical grounds that if God is love he cannot also be light would clearly be absurd.  In an earlier work,[85] I suggested that the challenge of 'ultimate' questions could usefully be met by the formula 'silence qualified by parables'.  In a sense (I argued) there is no option but silence in the face of such questions, as indeed has been pointed out by thinkers of many different religious traditions; but parables or myths may still have a significant message for us. At the time of writing I left it an open question as to whether a limited number of parables - in particular the central ones of the Christian tradition - were the correct or compelling ones.  I now believe that the claim that some parables are EXCLUSIVELY correct is divisive and unnecessary.[86]

Miles is arguing that  our talk about God, Man, and Man's place in the universe needs to be seen in terms of silence qualified by complementary rather than exclusive parables.  Although he does not explicitly say so, Miles presumably regards the theologies of the world's religions as consisting of such complementary parables, which is why none of them can claim to have an exclusive revelation of truth.

Having put forward this argument for Universalism he then maintains that part of the appeal of John's Gospel for Quakers:

> has arisen from the fact that it is the only one of the four gospels which comes near to being 'Universalist'.  If I have understood the writer correctly, the seemingly historical events which he describes provide only the setting for what is basically not an historical message at all, but a religious one.  In a sense the historical Jesus

---

[84] ibid p.3

[85] T.R.Miles *Religion and the Scientific Outlook* London: Allen and Unwin 1959

[86] Miles  *Towards Universalism*  p.14

fades into insignificance and a kind of 'Universal Christ' takes his place. This Christ is the logos; he is 'the true light which lighteth every man that cometh into the world'. There are many sayings too, - for example 'sayest thou this thing of thyself or did others tell it thee of me?' - which clearly have a universal significance and are intended to apply to any of us, not simply to be a record of this or that historical incident. Similarly the stories of the healing of the blind man and of the raising of Lazarus are not primarily historical records but relate to ourselves: it is we who (were) blind (and) now see' and it is we who in some sense (though it may not be clear in exactly what sense) cannot be touched by death. Although there are occasional passages which seem to imply exclusivity, for example 'No man cometh unto the Father but by me', the sense is surely of a universal Christ and does not imply 'Believe in a historical Jesus as opposed to a historical Buddha'.[87]

In Miles' view John's Gospel supports the points he has been making because its message is a religious rather than a historical one, concerned with a "universal Christ" rather than a "historical Jesus". He argues that this has been part of its appeal to Friends, thereby implying that the sort of universalism he is advocating has been attractive to those in the Quaker tradition.

Miles sums up his argument by declaring:

In effect, then, I am suggesting to Friends that they should move further in the direction of universalism by being open to images and parables of all kinds. I would emphasise that this is not to propose a novelty. It is rather to invite Friends to take account explicitly of ideas which are already implicit in their present practices. In particular it is no part of present practice to require applicants for membership to subscribe to any form of creed. If, however, it were to become policy that no one should be admitted to the Society if he does not interpret the gospel narrative in a particular way, this would be a retrograde step, and, indeed, tantamount to the imposition of a creed. In addition, if we take seriously the injunction to be 'open to new light from whatever quarter it may arise' it is hard to see how at the same time we can insist that the only     source     of     light     is     historical     Christianity.
A particular strength of Quakerism has been its ability to adapt to changing times without losing the insights which it has gained from the past. One of the striking changes that has taken place over the last century is that there is now vastly more opportunity for people with different backgrounds to meet and exchange ideas; and, this being so, it would be sad if those brought

---

[87] ibid p.15

up in Jewish, Buddhist, Moslem or other traditions - and indeed those with no religious upbringing of any kind were excluded from full participation in the affairs of the Society. I would suggest that further thought be given to ways of ensuring that such people are positively welcomed into the Society. No one is being asked to GIVE UP any other conviction: those who wish to retain traditional Christian beliefs are in no way being discouraged from doing so; and, indeed, for many people this may be the right and proper road to travel. I hope, however, that such people will be willing to worship ALONGSIDE those who - if they break the silence at all - might choose to use somewhat different forms of language.[88]

Miles is saying that the Society should thus cease to be a specifically Christian body and instead move to a universalist position.

Miles' argument in *Towards Universalism* can be seen to follow several of the ideas of Quaker Liberalism. Like Miles, Quaker Liberals rejected the idea that God is only at work through the Christian religion, and that those who are not part of the Christian religion are necessarily excluded from salvation.[89] Indeed, as we have seen, this idea was rejected by Quakers from the very outset of Quakerism in the 17th century. Like Miles, Quaker Liberals were unhappy with the idea that religious commitment meant subscription to a particular interpretation of history. One of the causes of their disagreement with Evangelicalism was the freedom they claimed to engage in historical study of the Bible unhindered by any traditional interpretations of it. Like Miles and in line with a continuous Quaker tradition, Quaker Liberals rejected the idea that Quakerism should have a creed, which is why they were unhappy about the 'Richmond Declaration' of 1887. Lastly, like Miles, Quaker Liberals thought that Quakerism should adapt itself to meet the changing circumstances of the contemporary world.

However, he also disagrees with Liberal Quakerism in two key areas.

Firstly, he seeks to sever faith from history, arguing that matters of history cannot be the objects of a religious commitment. This idea would have been news to Quaker Liberals, since at the heart of their religious commitment lay the belief that God had revealed Himself in the history of Israel, and then supremely through the historical personality of Jesus Christ. For them history mattered for faith. Like

---

[88] ibid pp.15-16

[89] See Hobling op.cit. passim

the early Quakers before them, Liberal Quakers had a religious commitment that held in balance a belief in both the immediate revelation of God in the soul, and the revelation of God in history witnessed to by the Bible. Miles dispenses with history and this balance is lost.

Secondly, he argues that Quakerism should become universalist rather than specifically Christian. This argument would not have been acceptable to the Quaker Liberals either. Although they rejected the idea that Christianity had a monopoly on religious truth, they held firmly to the belief that God had revealed Himself supremely through Christ and that Quakerism was unequivocally Christian in basis. For example, quoting John 15:1 & 4 and John 14:6, R. Duncan Fairn declares in his 1950 Swarthmore Lecture *Quakerism: A Faith for Ordinary Men*:

> Quakerism is Christian or it is nothing. 'I am the true vine, and my Father is the husbandman_. Abide in me, and I in you. As the branch cannot bear fruit of itself, except it abide in the vine; no more can ye, except ye abide in me'. 'I am the way, the truth and the life'. I make no apology for this reiteration because I dare not risk being misunderstood. Those who complain that this basically Christian foundation excludes them do but exclude themselves, good men and women though they may be.[90]

### An immense salvation purpose

My last example of radical theology, Lea's article 'An immense salvation purpose' was published in *Quaker Monthly* in August 1985. In this article Lea rejects the view that: "God exists independently of us humans", because:

> this view is founded on a conception of God that has been rendered obsolete by the discovery by Freud and Jung and their followers of the collective subconscious. God, with a capital G and the male gender, is only a personification of good and has now to be abandoned as not credible, just as Satan, the personification of evil, had to be abandoned two or three hundred years ago for the same reason.

According to Lea:

---

[90] R. Duncan Fairn *Quakerism: A Faith for Ordinary Men* London George Allen & Unwin 1950 p.20

The only way to glimpse a god of love today is to start from our own individual capacity for loving and to imagine what that would be like multiplied by the number of humans on this planet with all of whom we are in psychic contact through our subconscious selves. Why should not the loving power of the human race added together, all the four and a half billion individual capacities for loving fused together, actually comprise god? That would mean that god is derived from human love and human love is derived from god, the two indissolubly linked together and the truth that god is love really understood fully at last.[91]

Lea's argument here does have links with Liberal Quakerism in its attempt to develop a view of God compatible with contemporary thought. However his suggestion that the term 'god' should be used to describe the aggregate of human love goes beyond the thought of Liberal Quakerism, which agreed with the core of conviction and the Quaker tradition in insisting that God has an existence of His own which is other than, though intimately connected with, the existence of Mankind. For example, none of the six works I examined in the last chapter would make any sense if their talk about God was reduced to talk about human love.

Although the sort of radical theology I have illustrated has been an important strand in British Quaker Theology during the last thirty years it has by no means been the only one. There has also been a conservative strand of thinking expressed in more traditionally Christian terms. I shall once again use four examples to illustrate my point, taking them this time from writings by more conservative Quaker writers. The writings in question are Maurice Creasey's 1969 Swarthmore Lecture *Bearings or Friends and the New Reformation*[92] Lewis Benson's article 'George Fox's message *is* Relevant Today'[93] Gerald Priestland's 1982 Swarthmore Lecture *Reasonable Uncertainty - a Quaker approach to doctrine*[94] and John Punshon's book *Encounter with Silence*[95].

---

[91] Lea Art.cit. p.159. *Quaker Monthly* is a publication produced by Quaker Home Service designed to explain Quakerism to non-Quakers and those on the fringe of the Society of Friends.

[92] Maurice A. Creasey *Bearings or Friends and the New Reformation* London: Friends Home Service Committee 1969

[93] Lewis Benson 'George Fox's message *is* Relevant Today' in *The Quaker Vision* New Foundation Publications No.4 Gloucester: George Fox Fund 1979

[94] Gerald Priestland *Reasonable Uncertainty - a Quaker approach to doctrine* London: Quaker Home Service

**Bearings or Friends and the New Reformation**

In his 1969 Swarthmore Lecture Creasey, then the director of studies at Woodbrooke, uses the term 'the New Reformation' to refer to the theological ferment which took place during the 1960s, and which, in books such as Robinson's *Honest to God* and the American theologian Paul van Buren's *The Secular Meaning of the Gospel*,[96]

> opened up for discussion, often in a quite radical and uninhibited manner, every aspect of Christian - indeed, any theistic - faith, challenged practically every ethical principle and questioned every traditional form of the church's life, whether doctrinal, devotional, or institutional.[97]

Creasey's purpose is to enable Quakers to understand and respond to this ferment. He surveys the theology produced by this period of turbulence, assesses it critically, and then suggests how it should affect the present state and future development of the Society of Friends.

He sums up his understanding of how British Quakers should respond to the 'New Reformation' by stating that "the way forward for Quakerism is indicated by two convergent lines of evidence".[98] The first of these:

> _ involves our recognition of two facts. One is that the original thrust of Quakerism was towards the expression of a comprehensive interpretation of the nature, relationships and destiny of man as these are illuminated by the total fact of Jesus recognised as the Christ, the focal and definitive expression of what is ultimately real. In other words, it involves our recognition of the fact that original Quakerism was centred in Jesus Christ as the decisive revelation, in concrete, historical and personal terms, of God. This may be expressed in theological shorthand by saying that original Quakerism was Christo-centric. The second fact, intimately involved with this, is that original Quakerism was radical, for it was concerned to draw out from this Christ-centredness implications which were fresh and daring, and to apply these in

---

[95] John Punshon *Encounter with Silence* Richmond Indiana and London: Friends United Press and Quaker Home Service 1987

[96] Paul van Buren *The Secular Meaning of the Gospel* London: SCM 1963

[97] Creasey op.cit. p.1

[98] ibid p.64

uncompromising fashion to whole areas of life which had generally
been insulated from them by custom and conviction. These two
facts together justify us, I believe, in expressing the original vision
of Quakerism as a radical Christ-centredness or a Christ-centred
radicalism.[99]

The second:

> _ involves the recognition that these same phrases could be
> appropriately employed to describe the underlying, sometimes
> unconscious and often equivocally expressed thrust of what is
> positive in the new Reformation Movement. In other words, what
> gives this whole trend or tendency in contemporary religion and
> theology such unity and importance as it possesses is its recognition
> that the knowledge which is available to us of what is ultimately
> real and significant is to be defined and assessed in terms of what is
> given in the person of Jesus. Furthermore, this insight finds
> characteristic expression, not in attempts to construct large and
> comprehensive theological and philosophical systems, but in radical
> concern to challenge the existing social and political and economic
> order, to witness against oppression and to give practical and
> organised expression to compassion. It is closely allied, also, with
> radical criticism of many aspects of the inherited and traditional
> features of religion, both in doctrines and in institutions. In both
> respects, therefore, it reproduces several important features of the
> original Quaker attitude.[100]

Creasey is arguing that the way forward for Quakerism lies in the
recognition that both the original Quaker vision and what is positive in the New
Reformation Movement can be described as 'Christ-centred radicalism'.

This raises two questions: what precisely does Creasey mean by 'Christ-
centred radicalism'? and why is it important for Quakers to recognise that this term
can be used to describe both the original Quaker vision and what is positive in the
New Reformation Movement? His answer to the first question, which builds on
the findings of his Leeds PhD thesis on early Quaker Christology, is twofold.
Firstly he notes that:

> _ the phrase CHRIST-CENTRED RADICALISM brings together
> the two dimensions which, as Friends have rightly insisted, must

---

[99] ibid pp.64-5

[100] ibid pp.65-66

never be separated - the dimension of insight and faith and that of practical expression in life. Quakers are radicals in that they have always tried to get beneath appearances, to penetrate to the roots, and to propose remedies not for the symptoms but for the causes of human distress. But the inspiration and justification of this radical concern have always been derived from that understanding of the human condition and that resource of spiritual power for its remedying and redemption which are supremely expressed and embodied in Jesus Christ.[101]

Secondly, he goes on to argue that Friends are "radically Christ centred" because the understanding of God, Man and the Church put forward by the early Quakers were radically determined by their understanding of Jesus Christ. With regard to God they:

_ rightly reproached many of their contemporaries for employing conceptions of God which were practically uninfluenced by their beliefs concerning Christ. Most Puritans, for example, appeared to accept the idea of an inflexibly 'just' Father who required to be 'satisfied' by the self-sacrifice of a compassionate son. Friends insisted that what Christ was historically, God is eternally, that, as Paul knew, it is GOD who, in Christ, is reconciling the world to himself. In this, they were certainly true to the New Testament and to a central tradition of Christian theology.[102]

With regard to Christ they:

_ took with radical seriousness another central emphasis of the Christian tradition when, by their insistence that 'every man is enlightened by the divine light of Christ' they showed their determination to place at the centre of their conception of man not simply the 'first Adam' fallen degenerate and dead, but that of the 'last Adam', Jesus Christ. This, they said, is what Man essentially is in the presence of God. His actual state of alienation is a tragic fact, but it is to the divine resources for overcoming this state, in Christ, that they looked for their determinative conception of Man. In every man, therefore, they saw, not simply the actual, empirical facts of his present state, but also the Christ in him, the divine idea

---

[101] ibid p.67

[102] ibid pp.67-68

or image of Man which was in him struggling to be born, and to the 'answering' of which they directed all their energies.[103]

Lastly, with regard to the Church:

> The same concentration upon Christ was the inspiration of the early Quaker critique of the Church, its ministry, its worship and institutional forms.  Their starting point in relation to all these matters was expressed in the phrase 'Christ has come to teach his people himself'.  He alone is the Prophet to whose words we must attend; he is the sole Priest upon whose mediation we depend; his kingship neither requires nor brooks any structures of continuity or authority modelled upon those of earthly rule.[104]

Why then does Creasey think that the way forward for Quakers lies in recognising that Christ centred radicalism describes both early Quakerism and what is positive about the New Reformation?

Firstly, he argues that, since the seventeenth century, Quakerism has polarised between 'Christ-centred' Quakers who stand "firmly in the main orthodox Christian tradition emphasising the importance of such matters as conversion, evangelisation, and holiness"[105] and 'radical' Quakers who give priority to "individual and corporate action in the interests of such causes as civil rights, relief of sufferings, and protest movements of various kinds in the cause of peace and reconciliation".[106]  Seeing this polarisation as unfortunate, he then contends that recognition that early Quakerism was both 'Christ-centred' **and** 'radical' shows that:

> the two points around which Friends have for so long tended to rally are not the centres of two distinct, even if partially overlapping, circles, but are, so to speak, the two foci of an ellipse. The true shape of Quakerism can only be traced if it relates at every point to both.  The 'Christ-centred' Friend and the 'radical' Friend are to be seen as belonging together, each requiring the other for his own self-understanding, each preventing the other from

---

[103] ibid p.68

[104] ibid p.68

[105] ibid p.72

[106] ibid pp.72-3

becoming shallow or complacent and self-sufficient, each in creative
tension with the other.[107]

In other words 'Christ-centred radicalism' can act as a focus for Quaker unity.

Secondly, Creasey argues that the fact that both early Quakerism and the
positive side of the New Reformation can be seen as forms of 'Christ-centred
radicalism' provides a basis for dialogue between Quakers and those involved in
the New Reformation. As he puts it:

> those who have truly heard the message of early Friends and those
> who are open to the positive message of the New Reformation are
> 'on the same wavelength' and should be able to communicate
> without too much difficulty and to their mutual profit.[108]

Quakers would benefit from such dialogue because the New Reformation
would challenge them to face up to the vast spiritual and physical needs of the
world, and to take more seriously the facts that it is Jesus Christ who reveals God
to us, and that God can only be served through our service to the poor and needy
who are Christ's brethren. Conversely, it would also benefit the New Reformation
movement because the existence of the Society of Friends has important
implications for that movement. As Creasey sees it, the Society's existence:

> demonstrates the viability of a religious fellowship without the
> hierarchical, ecclesiastical and institutional features which are so
> prominent in the Roman, Orthodox and main-line Protestant
> Churches and which, to many people today, seem such hindrances
> to those Churches' ability to relate themselves creatively to one
> another and to the wider world. It exhibits the possibility, under
> modern conditions, of the combination of profoundly religious
> concern with genuine intellectual openness and freedom, of a
> refusal to recognise any ultimate division between the sacred and
> the secular. It shows, too, that a high degree of ethical
> sensitiveness and responsibility can exist in the almost complete
> absence of a legalistic or prescriptive moral code.[109]

---

[107] ibid pp.78-9

[108] ibid p.66

[109] ibid p.81

The issues mentioned here are all ones which Creasey has already identified in chapter one of his lecture as being important to those involved in the New Reformation. What he is saying, therefore, is that if Quakers need to learn from the New Reformation movement they also have things to teach it on matters which it finds important.

In the introduction to his lecture Creasey acknowledges the influence on him of his predecessor at Woodbrooke, H.G. Wood:

> To him I feel I owe any insight I may have into the meaning of Christian faith and discipleship as these have been known among Friends. Through him, also, I have come to feel a deep concern that the truth as Friends have known it may be ever more vitally related to whatever has proved its truth in the experience of men everywhere and also to the ongoing apprehension by the Christian fellowship as a whole of the truth as it is in Jesus.[110]

This intellectual debt to Wood shows itself in the fact that Creasey's lecture stands squarely in the tradition of Quaker Liberalism which Wood represented. Like the Quaker Liberals, Creasey seeks to reinterpret Quakerism in line with the development of modern thought, in this case the development of theological thought in the 1960's which he refers to as 'the New Reformation'. Again like them, he believes that when properly understood Quakerism has a message which is relevant to those who are questioning traditional forms of Christian thought and practice, in this case those involved in the New Reformation. Lastly, like them, and unlike Marsden or Miles, he sees God as supremely revealed in the historical figure of Jesus Christ. For him, Jesus Christ is still at the centre of theology.

It should be noted, however, that although Creasey follows the Liberal tradition in seeing Christ as the supreme revealer of God, he does not describe Christ as divine. Instead he quotes John Robinson's statement: "Jesus while not claiming to be God personally, nevertheless does claim to bring God completely"[111] and declares that John Macquarrie says what needs to be said about Christology "most memorably":

---

[110] ibid p.3

[111] Robinson  op.cit. p.73

> when he speaks of the event of Jesus Christ as 'symbol' and as
> 'focus'. It focuses, he says, 'the presence and activity which are
> indeed everywhere, but of which we remain unaware until such a
> focusing occurs, and the 'mystery hidden for ages' is made
> 'manifest'. Jesus Christ then is the focus where the mystery of
> Being is disclosed.[112]

When Macquarrie mentions 'Being' he is talking about God, so if we put these two quotations together what Creasey appears to be saying is that Christ is not God personally, but does bring God to us by being a symbol or focus through which God's universal presence is disclosed. This interpretation of what Creasey is saying is supported by reference to his pamphlet *A Christian Affirmation* in which he writes:

> I have spoken of the vocation of Jesus to be the Christ in terms of
> 'embodiment' and 'response'. The word embodiment stresses the
> expressive action of God as holy Being, which reached in Jesus, as I
> believe, its fullest manifestation in human terms as a life of totally
> self-giving love. 'Response' emphasises the claim that this becomes
> possible not simply by overwhelming divine power but through
> unforced human obedience and faith and trust. In Jesus the double
> search, of God for a willing, faithful, and comprehending agent, and
> of Man for the God whose purpose calls for and justifies Man's
> total self-offering, met in a mutual fulfilment.[113]

In this quotation Jesus is not described as divine but is seen as the man through whom, as "a willing, faithful, and comprehending agent", God was most fully manifested in human terms, and this is, I think, the Christology which underlies what Creasey says about Christ in his Swarthmore Lecture.

### George Fox's Vision is Relevant Today

Lewis Benson's article 'George Fox's Message *is* Relevant Today' was originally published in *Friends Quarterly* in October 1974 and then reprinted in a collection of his works entitled *The Quaker Vision* published in 1979.

---

[112] Creasey *Bearings* pp.69-70 quoting John Macquarrie *Principles of Christian Theology* 1st ed London: SCM 1966 p.249

[113] M.A.Creasey *A Christian Affirmation* London: Friends Home Service Committee 1969 p.6

Benson was an American Quaker. The justification for the inclusion of his work in this thesis is the same as that for the inclusion of the work of Rufus Jones, namely that Benson's work, like Jones's, has influenced the development of British Quaker thought. He was an authority on the thought of George Fox, and his interpretation of Fox's message was the inspiration behind the founding in 1979 of 'The New Foundation Fellowship', a group within British Quakerism which sees the renewal of Quakerism as coming about through greater understanding and acceptance of Fox's teaching.[114]

In his article, which was originally published to mark the 350th anniversary of Fox's birth, Benson first of all summarises Fox's original message as follows:

> Fox believed that the Christianity of his day was irrelevant because it had lost touch with the basic problem of man. The problem of man in the Old Testament is how to know what God's will is for us and how to respond to it in obedience. This is what the law and the prophets are all about. But in his seeking years Fox was confronted with a form of Christianity that defined man's basic problem as the problem of guilt. This is a part of the problem of man and Christ is the answer to it. But, Fox maintained, it is not the whole problem. He argued that this doctrine had separated salvation by Christ from God's call to righteousness in the Old Testament. He was led to these convictions through a personal quest for the power that is greater than the power of temptation. In his early years he consulted reputable religious leaders who told him that such power exists but the Christian does not have access to it until he reaches heaven. He called these counsellors 'miserable comforters' and he sought and found a better answer. In the New Testament he found the apostolic witness to Christ as the Moses-like Prophet who is to be heard 'in all things' and who turns all men from their iniquities.[115] He was soon travelling up and down the country proclaiming 'This prophet, Christ, has come' and wrote evangelistic epistles addressed to many heads of states and 'to most parts of the world' telling them 'how God had come to teach his people himself by his Son'.
>     Fox's gospel message was an intentional challenge to the Christianity of his day. He puts the issue squarely to the Churches' leaders when he asks them '_ is it not for you to preach to all people, Christ Jesus the new covenant, how that in it and by it shall all be taught of God from the greatest to the least? and is not this gospel? but instead _ do you not preach that men must have sin the

---

[114] See Godwin Arnold 'The New Foundation Fellowship' *Quaker Monthly* vol.61:4  April 1982 pp.69-71

[115] See Deut. 18:15 and Acts 3:22-23

term of their lives? and so are preachers of sin and not of Christ who came to take away sin, and to destroy the works of the devil and to make men perfect.[116]

According to Benson, this teaching:

> _ had its greatest appeal for those men and women who were struggling with the basic human problem: how can I know what is right and what is wrong? and how can I do the right and resist the temptation to do wrong? For such people Fox had good news. He taught them that Christ is the living prophet in the midst of his people teaching them what is right and what is wrong and giving them the power to do the right and resist the wrong.
>        The 'teacher to whom Fox was turning people was the teacher of God's PEOPLE. Christ is not only able to deliver the individual from moral confusion and impotence, but he can lead his PEOPLE to the knowledge of the righteousness of God so that they learn together, obey together, and suffer together. Those who were convinced by Fox's message and who became 'settled and established' on Christ their 'teacher and saviour and rock and foundation ' became gathered into a new kind of Christian community which had the character of a Church of the Cross.[117]

Benson is saying that Fox taught that Christ not only answers the basic problem of individuals by giving them the knowledge and power to do what is right, but also leads His people to a corporate knowledge of the righteousness demanded by God that results in their learning, obeying, and suffering together. Furthermore those who accepted Fox's teaching came to form a new type of Christian community which was a "Church of the Cross", by which Benson means a church which is willing to suffer as a corporate body for the sake of obedience to God.[118]

Benson concludes his article by arguing that Fox's message can still meet the needs of people today:

> This is an age in which the decline of moral standards and moral behaviour have undermined the foundations of mutual trust on

---

[116] Benson op.cit.pp.12-13

[117] ibid pp.13-14

[118] See Lewis Benson *Catholic Quakerism* Philadelphia: Book and Publications Committee Philadelphia Yearly Meeting pp.38-42

which society rests. The old social institutions are in a precarious
state and many are in ruins. For many young people today the only
course open seems to be to try to live a meaningful life without
moral absolutes or inherited social institutions.

The need for moral assurance and moral strength and the
need to experience primary community in a fellowship ruled by God
are not needs that were peculiar to the men of the 17th century.
These needs are felt today with as much urgency as they were in
Fox's day. The Bible bears witness to the God who made all things
and who calls men to righteousness and community. Fox's great
discovery is that God has given us a 'way' by which we can answer
this call for righteousness and be gathered into a community ruled
by him. Christ is this 'new and living way'.[119]

In his book *Catholic Quakerism*, in which he develops his ideas in more detail,
Benson acknowledges his debt to the "encouragement and stimulating criticism of
Maurice A. Creasey".[120] If one compares the article by Benson which I have just
summarised with Creasey's Swarthmore lecture one can see three points of
similarity.

Firstly, both Benson and Creasey look back to the early days of Quakerism
for their theological inspiration. It should be noted, though, that while Creasey
looks back to the whole of early Quakerism Benson tends to concentrate on the
thought of Fox.

Secondly, both stress that the early Quaker message was centred on Christ.
This leads Benson in another of his articles, entitled 'Universal Dimension in the
thought of George Fox', to reject the universalism advocated by Marsden and
Miles on the grounds that, while Fox was quite clear that God speaks to all men,
he was also clear that the way he does so is by speaking through Christ.[121]

Thirdly, both agree with Quaker Liberalism that, when it is properly
understood, the early Quaker message is still relevant to people today.

However, there are also two differences between Benson's article and
Creasey's lecture which point to major differences between the work of these men
as a whole.

---

[119] Benson 'George Fox's Message is Relevant for Today' p.15

[120] Benson *Catholic Quakerism* Foreword

[121] Benson 'Universal Dimension in the Thought of George Fox' in *The Quaker Vision* pp.39-47

Creasey follows Liberal Quakerism in seeking to re-interpret the message
of early Quakerism, by, for instance, using the language of John Macquarrie to
express the importance of Christ.    Benson, on the other hand, makes no
comparable attempt to re-interpret and re-express Fox's thought, or to update what
Fox has to say. His reason for not doing so is that:

> In these times of rapid and constant change nothing seems to stay
> relevant for very long. Today's 'Idea whose time has come' is
> tomorrow's 'Idea whose time has passed'.  If we think of relevance
> in religion as bringing our religion 'up to date' we soon find
> ourselves on a treadmill.  Moreover this kind of 'relevant' religion
> does not necessarily give men greater moral character or lead them
> to true community or make them feel they are a part of a great
> work of God in history.  Religion that is perfectly attuned to the
> spirit of its own time can be just as incapable of channelling the
> power of God to men as religion that is hopelessly fettered by
> mindless attachment to some outmoded historical form of religion.
> George Fox was a man of the 17th century and we cannot
> make him into something else.  In past generations Fox has been
> represented as a quietist, a conservative, an evangelical protestant,
> a liberal, a modernist, a humanist, etc. etc.  By making Fox in their
> own image Friends have created a whole series of George Fox's and
> each one seemed to have special 'relevance' in the age in which it
> was created.  But Fox can never really be made relevant today in
> the sense that we discover him to be a 20th century man like
> ourselves.   The relevance of George Fox for today lies in his
> message. His MESSAGE has something to say to us today because
> he is telling us something about Christ that is related to the
> condition of men and women today.[122]

The second difference between Creasey and Benson lies in the issues to
which they address themselves.   In Creasey's case the New Reformation sets an
agenda for discussion to which he then responds.  For Benson, what Fox said in
the 17th century determines the issues tackled in his article.

What is true in the case of this one article is, I think, true of Benson's work
as a whole and also of the work of the New Foundation Fellowship.  Benson and
the New Foundation Fellowship which he inspired are concerned to expound the
distinctive message preached by Fox, and to show its relevance for today.  This is a
perfectly legitimate task, but it is one that is limited in scope.  It is limited because

---

[122] Benson 'George Fox's Message is Relevant for Today' pp.14-15

it excludes discussion of those areas of Fox's thought which were not distinctive, such as his views of the Tri-unity of God, or the inspiration of the Bible, or the fallenness of Man. It also excludes discussion of those issues which are of concern today but which were of no concern to Fox, such as how to speak of God in a secular age, how psychology has affected our view of man, or how historical criticism has altered our view of the Bible.

## Reasonable Uncertainty

In the introduction to his Swarthmore Lecture *Reasonable Uncertainty* Gerald Priestland, the former religious affairs correspondent at the BBC, states that it arose out of his Radio 4 series *Priestland's Progress*, which was a layman's guide to Christian doctrine, and that its purpose is "to retrace some of my steps on that 'Progress' to look more deeply into my own reactions and to face - as a Christian as well as a Quaker - the implications of Christian doctrine as I see it".[123]

Priestland begins its argument by contending that there is a battle going on to save the Christian Church from the forces of "religious reaction" and "atheistic materialism"[124]. He argues that Quakers should join this battle to save the Church because they need its existence for three reasons:

–      To "keep alive" the Biblical stories about God through its teaching, preaching, and celebration of them;

–      To act as a check upon the religious beliefs and insights of individuals through the exercise of the "discipline and authority" provided by its corporate tradition;

–      To "remind us that a faith - particularly the Christian faith - is not something we can practice in isolation from other people.[125]

For these three reasons Quakers: "need the Church and need to recognise and demonstrate that we are part of it".[126]

---

[123] Priestland op.cit. p.3

[124] ibid pp. 15-16

[125] ibid pp.16-22

[126] ibid p.23

Priestland then examines the function of the Church's doctrine, an aspect of the Church with which Quakers have traditionally been unhappy. He explains the function of doctrine in two ways. He declares that it is really about: "the secure packaging of information so that it can be transmitted".[127]

For instance, the Church's Creeds are the attempts of previous generations of Christians to pass on their understanding of truth intact to future generations. He also argues that, while doctrines do not give us the absolute and complete truth about God, they do give us a framework within which to conduct our own personal exploration of Him:

> One of the drawbacks of Quakerism in its ultra-contemporary form is that it offers very little to push against. That, I think, is one of the most important functions of doctrine. It gives the enquirer some framework to climb in, the reformer something to challenge, the debater something to debate. In the world of science it is necessary to engage the established body of knowledge in dialogue in its own language if you want to prove your new discoveries.
>
> To put it another way: doctrine provides the explorer of God with a set of tools and techniques with which he can tackle the mountain-face. If he declines to use them he cuts himself off from a wealth of experience and forces himself to start from scratch. In one sense he must: for his own experience is irreplaceable. But it is arrogant to pretend no one has ever been your way before and that there is nothing to be learnt from them.[128]

Priestland describes a traditionalist Roman Catholic rally he attended in London, and urges Quakers to try to understand the ultra-conservative Catholic beliefs expressed at it; suggesting that while Quakers have not been called to take the Catholic path it may be right for others. His reason for this suggestion is that:

> If God had wished us to be of a single faith, He could surely have arranged it. The fact that He did not indicates to me His delicate appreciation of our varying conditions.[129]

Having made this point Priestland then qualifies it by stating:

---

[127] ibid p.25

[128] ibid pp.27-8

[129] ibid p.35

What I am quite sure of is that He would think little of us for failing
to pursue Him to the limits of our intuition, failing to develop our
spiritual equipment to meet our changing environment.[130]

The standard objection to this sort of development is that it is unnecessary
because, while our environment may change, God Himself does not. Priestland
meets this objection by going on to argue that God does in fact change. As he sees
it, not only does God appear to change as human beings look at Him in different
ways, like a mountain viewed from different angles, but He may actually be:

_ changing in response to our changes, our needs, our capacity,
even to the demands we make upon Him. SOME things about God
may not change. I suspect there are truths about Him that are
eternal, His creatorship, His fatherhood (or, if you prefer it,
Parenthood), His love. But His expression of Himself, as Mankind
has understood it, has not always had the same emphasis (to say the
least). The God understood by the folk poets of Genesis is not the
same as the God of Jeremiah, who is not the same as the God of
St.John or St.Paul. There may be traces of one in the other, but a
mighty change has taken place.[131]

Priestland then declares:

It seems to me that one of the most dynamic elements in religion -
particularly in the Jewish-Christian understanding of God - lies in
the concept of two-way response.[132]

He means by this that not only does God respond to the religious activities of
Mankind, but He also takes the initiative and calls us in a way that demands our
response to Him.

Priestland next applies this idea to the doctrine of Creation, stating "the
doctrine of Creation, as I read it, involves a continuous and continuing activity in
which Mankind is - and always has been - invited to share".[133] Putting the same
thing more specifically, Priestland further notes:

---

[130] ibid p.35

[131] ibid p.38

[132] ibid p.39

[133] ibid p.40

I have found general agreement among theologians that God is
ONLY active in history through the agency of human cooperation:
not through miraculous interventions that brush Mankind aside.
His natural order may present us with unexpected things -
crossroads, decision points - but we then have to respond, and if we
do so in tune with His will, the outcome is creative.[134]

If God's creative activity is, as Priestland argues, dependent upon our
response, this implies a certain weakness in God in that He cannot do all that He
might wish.  Having looked at the doctrine of creation, Priestland then turns to
consider the idea of God's weakness in more detail, making three points.

Firstly, the story of Adam and Eve tells us that God: "has weakened
Himself by giving us - like Adam and Eve the freedom to reject Him"[135] and sin is
our exercise of this freedom.

Secondly, the fact that "God has weakened Himself by constructing not an
arbitrary Universe which He manipulates at whim but a Universe of natural laws
which He Himself must observe"[136] rules out His miraculous intervention in the
world, and is the theological explanation for the occurrence of natural disasters,
which are simply outworkings of natural law which  He is powerless to prevent.

Finally, on the Cross:

God was so weak that, His love being rejected, He could do
nothing but hang there saying 'I am like this - I am like you'.  He
could do nothing but forgive, which is love, a form of love
undeserved by those upon whom forgiveness is bestowed.[137]

According to Priestland, when the love shown by God on the Cross is responded
to: "it then becomes the mightiest power in the Universe: comforting, healing,
pacifying and resurrecting",[138] but He is still dependent upon us to give His love
this power because: "we, Mankind, stand between God and His power to be active

---

[134] ibid pp.40-41

[135] ibid p.43

[136] ibid p.43

[137] ibid p.44

[138] ibid p.44

through us. It is not our power, but His; yet we have the free will to frustrate it."[139]

Following his exploration of Divine weakness, Priestland next examines the question of religious authority. He asks what use it is to claim authority for our doctrines and returns a two-fold answer.

> First, it gives us a certain solidarity with holy people of the past and enables us to enter into their insights. There is a certain arrogance in pretending that no generation till ours had a valid religious experience. Next, by availing ourselves of their insight and experience and accepting - if only provisionally - its formulations, we gain access to its language: we can use it AS IF it were true. This may seem a hypocritical way to seek God, but it is in fact a humble one. If we insist upon complete certainty that a formulation is true we shall make no progress at all, for it is God we are talking about and we cannot possibly encompass Him or any part of Him with human language. The best we can do is to take some instrument forged by people we have reason to trust and use it AS IF it were reliable, up to the point where it ceases to be so. At that point we have to think again, perhaps even ask ourselves whether we need go any further or whether the provisional will, in fact, do.[140]

In this section of his lecture Priestland also considers the authority of the Bible and writes:

> Fox would have said that the scriptures themselves were lifeless unless they were received by the Spirit within the heart of the reader; and it seems to me that the remarkable endurance of the Bible - what makes it 'the Word of God' - is that there was so much of the Spirit in its writing that it constantly evokes the Spirit in its reading. But in every age, according to human circumstances, it is different things that are drawn up from the depths of scripture to be reborn. Jesus Himself treated it selectively. And (goodness knows!) so do the fundamentalists. But there is a world of difference between allowing life to play freely upon the Bible - illuminating a passage here and a passage there - and seeking to impose the Bible flatly upon life. All Scripture has its authority, its authenticity, for the particular circumstances in which it was written, and some of these circumstances abide permanently in the human condition. But

---

[139] ibid p.44

[140] ibid pp.48-9

> others change dramatically, and to ignore that is, in fact, to ignore
> the creative activity of God.[141]

He makes three points in this statement. Firstly, building on the thought of Fox, he
contends that what makes the Bible 'the Word of God' is that it constantly evokes
the Spirit when it is read. Secondly, he maintains that what is drawn out of the
Bible differs according to the changing circumstances of each succeeding age.
Thirdly, and here he is attacking the ultra-conservative Protestants whom he
describes as 'fundamentalists', he argues that it is a mistake to try to impose the
Bible upon contemporary life in a way that fails to acknowledge that parts of the
Bible may no longer be authoritative because the particular circumstances for
which they were authoritative have now drastically changed as a result of God's
creative activity.

In the final part of his lecture Priestland considers the doctrine of the
Incarnation. After explaining that this doctrine means the belief that Jesus: "was
and still is God",[142] he notes that:

> The notion that God should have taken flesh in the shape of a first
> century Galilean carpenter's son immediately raises the Scandal of
> Particularity: the stumbling-block, that is, of the question 'Why this
> particular person, place and time rather than any other, or several
> others?' Apart from anything else, it seems unfair on those who
> have missed the Christian bus, through no fault of their own, by
> being at the wrong place or in the wrong time.[143]

Having outlined the nature of the "Scandal of Particularity", he then
responds to it. Firstly, he answers the question: "Why this particular person, place
and time rather than any other or several others?" by observing:

> _ if there was to be an Incarnation, it was bound to be particular.
> The choice of time, place and circumstances were _ rather clever.
> What would not have been clever is a series of Incarnations

---

[141] ibid p.51

[142] ibid p.51

[143] ibid p.54

scattered about the globe, each bound to develop into a competitive regional cult.[144]

Priestland does not explain why the details of the Incarnation were "rather clever" but he does return to the point that Incarnation was: "bound to be particular" later in his lecture, declaring:

> _ the essence of the human condition is its particularity. We are all individuals in a particular place and time, and God would not have been fully human if He, too, had not been once-for-all in the same way.[145]

Secondly, he rejects the idea that the particularity of the Incarnation means the damnation of all non- Christians, and suggests that Jesus' apparently exclusive statement in John 14:6 "I am the way, the truth and the life. No Man comes to the Father except by Me" really means: "The way, the truth and the life are all that I stand for. Anyone who seeks them sincerely is on his way to my Father".[146]

After responding to the "Scandal of Particularity", Priestland sets out how he thinks Quakers might understand the meaning of the doctrine of the Incarnation:

> They may also be able to see, in the person of Christ, a sacrament of unequalled power, a sign of unmerited love that demands love in response and this becomes in itself an act of worship. It seems to me that it is this quality of being worshipped, of having been worshipped, or worshipfulness that endows Christ with much of his divinity. It is almost as if Jesus was God because we say so. Once, I found myself writing 'If Jesus was not God - He is now'. In the same mysterious way it also occurred to me that in Jesus God was saying 'I am like THIS. Indeed, I am so like this that as far as you will ever I AM this.[147]

Priestland concludes his lecture by considering how Christ's life, death, and resurrection bring about our salvation. He also finds unacceptable the traditional

---

[144] ibid p.54

[145] ibid p.58

[146] ibid p.57

[147] ibid p.59

Evangelical idea that Christ's death saved us by paying the penalty for our sins.  As
an alternative he puts forward the view that in Christ we have a "salvation signal":

> For all I know, it is not impossible that some 'salvation signal', a
> sign of how God was and how man could be reconciled with Him
> through suffering, forgiveness and resurrection, was sent to us
> before Jesus. It is not impossible that there were garbled or
> unrecognised signals, signals that were incomplete because the
> atmospheric conditions were not favourable to reception.  It may be
> that this was a signal God had always been sending to us, but that
> for the first time, in Christ, it was received in its true form;  picked
> up on a human receiver accurately tuned in to the divine
> wavelength.    I must apologise if I seem to be exploiting a
> convenient modern metaphor, but it does present me with a way of
> understanding what the doctrine of unique salvation is trying to say.
> By hanging between God and Man, eternal life and inevitable death,
> Jesus saves us from the breakdown of communications: and in that
> exchange, we have almost as great a part to play as God Himself.
> God recognises Himself in Christ, and we recognise ourselves.[148]

Priestland's Swarthmore lecture differs in two major respects from the one
given by Creasey in 1969.  It does not touch on the specific theological issues of
the 1960's with which Creasey's lecture is concerned, and it derives its theological
inspiration less from the distinctive theology of early Quakerism than from the
doctrinal tradition of the Christian Church as a whole as encountered by Priestland
during the making of 'Priestland's Progress'.  These differences notwithstanding,
Priestland's lecture is like Creasey's in that it too stands in the tradition of Quaker
Liberalism.  This can be seen both in what it affirms and in what it denies.

Priestland's lecture follows the Liberal Quaker tradition by affirming a
theology which is explicitly Christian, and which upholds basic elements of the
Christian faith, such as belief in a personal creator God, in the Incarnation and in
salvation through Christ, while at the same time re-stating them in contemporary
language and re-interpreting them in line with modern thought.  Just as the Quaker
Liberal Edward Grubb sought to re-state and re-interpret traditional Christian
belief in the 1920's in his *Christianity as Truth*, so Priestland seeks to do the same
thing in the 1980's.

---

[148] ibid pp.63-4

His lecture also follows the tradition of Quaker Liberalism by rejecting the beliefs, found in the core of conviction and the Quaker tradition, that the whole Bible has binding authority, and that, on the Cross, Christ paid the penalty for our sins. In his view parts of the Bible have now lost their authority due to the change in human circumstances since they were written, and the idea that Christ's death paid the price for our sins involves an "utterly barbarous" view of God. These two beliefs are firmly embedded in the core of conviction and the Quaker tradition. By proposing a form of Christian faith which excludes them, Priestland is endorsing the Liberal departure from both the core of conviction and the Quaker tradition.

Quaker Liberalism took a middle path between on the one hand unreservedly accepting the interpretations of Christianity, advocated by the core of conviction and the Quaker tradition, and on the other rejecting traditional Christian beliefs altogether. It is this middle course which Priestland also follows.

There is, however, one area of his lecture in which he departs from this Liberal Via Media. This is his treatment of the relationship between Christianity and the non-Christian religions. He holds that the various religions which exist in the world represent the means which God has found: "_ of speaking to many different cultures in the ways appropriate to them."[149] He also holds that, just as Quakers should accept their membership of the Christian Church, so also: "_the Christian Church should accept its membership of the wider family of faiths."[150]
The only advantage Priestland sees the Christian Church having within this 'wider family' is that: "_ it has a far greater potential for adaptation to local conditions and far greater freedom of theology than any of its sister faiths."[151]

This view of the relationship between Christianity and other faiths would have been unacceptable to Quaker Liberals. In accordance with the core of conviction and the Quaker tradition, they held that Christianity has a uniquely privileged position among the religions of the world, not simply because it is the most adaptable and possesses the largest amount of theological freedom, but because its knowledge of the revelation of God in Jesus Christ means that it has a

---

[149] ibid p.56

[150] ibid p.22

[151] ibid p.56

greater knowledge of the truth about God than any other religion. On this issue Priestland is closer to the Universalism of Marsden and Miles than he is to the Liberal tradition.

### Encounter with Silence

In this book Punshon seeks to explain the distinctive nature of Quakerism within a specifically Christian frame of reference. For example, chapter thirteen, 'Celebration and Sacrifice', compares the silent worship of Quakerism with the celebration of Holy Communion in other Christian Churches. This Christian frame of reference means that, in the context of contemporary Quakerism, Punshon's work is a conservative one. It is of particular interest because, in spite of this basic conservatism, it contains all three ways of thinking that have been present in British Quakerism this century; the Evangelical, the Liberal, and the Radical. Three extracts illustrate this.

The first extract describes how, after years of going to Quaker Meetings for Worship, Punshon  became a committed Christian following the death of his father.

> I took down the New Testament and read nearly all of it, it seemed, on and on. Actually I must have chosen the familiar parts, but for the first time ever I heard what it was saying. Instead of using my secular philosophy and attitudes to explain (or explain away) what was there, I began to take it as the meaning of life and interpret all other things by it. It was coherent, consistent, intelligible. That night I came to know that as Christ was resurrected, so should my father live. For the very first time, I had life in me.
> I found that my father's death had caused me unreservedly to commit my life to Christ. Before then I would never have used that kind of vocabulary, to do so would have been to lose twenty years of liberal cool. The measure of my conversion is that this no longer matters to me. But if I had not the search, the finding would not be what it is. When I compare the prodigal son with his elder brother, I reflect that the seed grew best where the soil of hard experience was richest and deepest. Once more, what had happened to me was given shape and form by my silent devotions. Over the years I had been growing into the person I now was, by the grace of God. In a lexicon, the Greek work Metanoia is used in a variety of senses: a change of thought or feeling; to make a change of principle and practise. Each of the above things happened to me. I date my conversion from the act of repentance I made that night. The unreality of death changed my whole attitude

*word ?*

to life.  Since then I have come to realise fully the need to call upon
Christ to save me.  But one never comes to that experience cold, I
believe.  In retrospect I see that in the years of still waiting, when
God came to me incognito, as it were, God was using my religious
exercises to bring me to this point, which I myself would never
have foreseen.  And when I arrived, I was able to recognise the
truth of what was revealed to me, and the rightness of the path by
which I had come.[152]

Although Punshon declares that the classical model for what happened to
him is the conversion of Francis of Assisi,[153] what happened to him after his
father's death and subsequently can also be seen as a classic example of an
Evangelical conversion experience.  At the heart of the Evangelical piety, which
was shared by Evangelical Quakers with Evangelicals in general, lay the idea of an
individual coming to understand the Biblical message and, as a result, being led to
a conversion experience marked by repentance, commitment of one's life to Christ,
and a realisation of the need to be saved by Him.  It is this process which is
described by Punshon, and he is even prepared to use the Evangelical term "being
born again" as a label for it.[154]

My second extract from Punshon describes the Quaker attitude to the
Bible:

The substance of history _ can be seen as the conflict between
actions taken under divine guidance and those which negligently or
deliberately frustrate the divine purpose.  Every part of human
history will display the same features, but it is classically
exemplified in the Bible.  This is why, for most of their own history,
the Quakers have asserted that the authority of scripture arises not
because it is an inspired writing, but because it is a record of
AUTHORITATIVE EVENTS which are themselves the sources of
revelation.  This is half the story.  Friends would go on to assert
that this lesson can only be learned if one sees the record with the
eyes of faith.  The Bible is a living document to the extent that one
comes to it with the same inspiration as those who wrote it.  There
is no escape from the commitment of faith.  Those who hear the
gospel and respond to God under the leadings of the Holy Spirit

---

[152] Punshon *Encounter with Silence* pp.15-16

[153] ibid p.16

[154] ibid p.17

will receive their revelation, for they will have taken sides in history.[155]

The ideas that there is a conflict in history between those actions which are guided by God and those which frustrate His purpose, that this conflict is classically exemplified in the Bible, and that the Bible can only be properly understood when it is read with faith under the Holy Spirit's guidance, are basic to Quakerism and would have been acceptable to Early, Quietist, Evangelical, and Liberal Quakers alike. What makes this extract distinctively Liberal is its location of the Bible's authority not in its verbal inspiration, but in its recording: "authoritative events" through which revelation occurs. In spite of Punshon's declaration that Quakers have held this view of the Bible "for most of their own history", it is in fact typically Liberal in its attempt to retain the traditional Christian belief in the authority of the Bible while re-interpreting it in a way that dispenses with the idea of its verbal inspiration.

My last extract concerns Christian witness to those of other faiths. Punshon declares:

> If, truly, Christ Jesus and the Father are one, there is not one person on this planet who, invoking the deity by whatever name they know, is not calling on the God whom Christians worship in Christ. Here is the Quaker doctrine of the light, approached in another way. The pearl, the mustard seed, the light is planted in all people and is a sufficient guide to life if heeded in humility and sincerity. This is why the unprogrammed meeting, barren of images, innocent of words, is a place where those of true faith can come together to worship.
> Here we approach the kernel of relations between the faiths. There is a kind of witness to Christ among the nations which requires treachery. This particular call to conversion is destructive of family, upbringing, language, customs, tradition, and lively faith in God. It knows little of fulfilment and seeks an outward conformity with the letter.
> There is another witness which places the challenge of the gospel before the world, not the written record of it. The Christ within all is no different from the Christ of history - except that he is alive and often incognito. The challenge of the gospel is to turn and change, to embrace self-denial, simplicity, and servanthood, to hear the call to obedience and righteousness. Wherever this call is

---

[155] ibid pp.119-20

heard, under whatever name, there is a confirmation of the passion
and resurrection of Christ, and there is salvation.[156]

Although the starting point of this extract is the orthodox Biblical assertion
that: "Christ and the Father are one",[157] the argument that Punshon develops from
this basis is a radical one.  In accordance with Quaker tradition, Liberal Quakers
held that, although there is a witness to God in the hearts of all Men that is
sufficient to bring them to salvation, this witness nevertheless needs to be
supplemented by knowledge of the historical Jesus Christ if people are to know the
full truth about God.[158]  Punshon goes beyond this Liberal position by contending
that Christians should only present the **ethical** challenge of the gospel to those of
other faiths.  This seems to imply that knowledge of the gospel witness to the
historical Jesus is superfluous.

In summary, although *Encounter with Silence* is on the whole a
conservative work by the standards of contemporary British Quakerism, it
nonetheless contains all three strands of thought which have been present in British
Quakerism this century;  the Evangelical, reflected in Punshon's account of his
conversion, the Liberal, reflected in his treatment of the Bible, and the Radical,
reflected in his view of Christian witness to those of other faiths.

## Summary and Conclusions

In this Chapter I have shown that during the period when the Society of
Friends in this country was dominated by Quaker Liberalism a minority of British
Quakers advocated a more radical theology.  I have also argued that in the 1960's
British Quakers, like the members of other Churches, were affected by the
intellectual turmoil of the day and that from that time onwards radical ideas
entered into the mainstream of British Quaker thinking where they have co-existed
with more conservative points of view.

---

[156] ibid p.56

[157] John 10:30

[158] See H.T.Hodgkin's 1916 Swarthmore lecture *The Missionary Spirit and the Present
Opportunity* London: Headley Bros. 1916.

This co-existence of radical and more conservative beliefs has meant that recent British Quaker theology has been marked by a twofold diversity.

In the first place, the ideas put forward by those with radical views have naturally differed from the ideas put forward by those who are more conservative. For example, if we compare Marsden's essay 'The Quaker Christ' with Benson's article 'George Fox's message is relevant today' we can see that Marsden's understanding of the current significance of early Quaker teacher is very different from Benson's. Likewise, if we compare the Swarthmore Lectures by Gorman and Priestland we can see that Priestland takes a much more positive view of the contemporary relevance of traditional religious language than does Gorman.

In the second place, the radical and conservative wings of British Quakerism themselves contain a great diversity of theological ideas. For instance, both Gorman and Lea can be seen to be on the radical wing of British Quakerism yet they disagree with each other in that Gorman still believes in a God who exists outside of Man, whereas for Lea talk about God is simply a way of talking about the aggregate of human love. Both Creasey and Benson are part of the conservative wing of current Quaker thought, but Creasey differs from Benson in that he seeks to re-interpret and up-date the theology put forward by the early Quakers while Benson does not.

There are five factors which have contributed to this great diversity between and within the radical and conservative wings of British Quakerism.

Firstly, as I have noted, the prominence of Quaker radicalism over the past thirty years reflects the fact that radical questioning of traditional Christian beliefs has been a prominent feature of theology in general during this period. For example, theologians have questioned whether it is still meaningful to talk about the objective existence of God,[159] whether it is still helpful to see Jesus as the incarnate Son of God[160] and whether Christianity can still be seen as superior to all other religions[161], and just as the Quaker Liberals reflected the Victorian questioning of Christian beliefs so the Quaker radicals have reflected this more

---

[159] See Don Cupitt *Taking leave of God*

[160] See John Hick (ed) *The Myth of God Incarnate*

[161] See John Hick *God has many names*

recent questioning. Thus, as we have seen in this chapter, Lea rejects belief in the objective existence of God, Marsden rejects traditional views of the person of Christ in favour of the idea that He is a symbol of Man's inherent affinity with God, and Miles holds that all religions are to be seen as equally valid.

Secondly, the diversity within British Quakerism has also been caused by the influence exerted by a variety of non-Quaker thinkers and theologians. For instance, Gorman is influenced by Kee, Tillich, Baillie and Williams, Marsden is influenced by Jung, and Creasey is influenced by Macquarrie. Each of these different influences have taken the Quakers involved in different directions and the result has been theological diversity.

Thirdly, different Quaker thinkers have drawn inspiration from different aspects of the Quaker tradition. Thus Marsden looks to the way in which the early Quakers re-used the language of the Christian myth, Creasey looks to their 'Christ-centred radicalism' and Benson focuses on Fox's teaching on Christ's ability to bring people to a corporate obedience to the will of God. Like the different uses made of the Quaker tradition by the Evangelicals and Liberals at the end of the last century this use of Quaker tradition has once again led to diversity.

Fourthly, Quakers have accepted as axiomatic the twin Liberal beliefs that it is proper to re-interpret Quakerism to fit in with contemporary developments in thought and that there should be freedom for Quakers to develop their own beliefs without being censured by the Society of Friends for so doing. For example, as we have seen, Miles declares that: "A particular strength of Quakerism is its ability to adapt to changing times" while Gorman states in his book *Introducing Quakers* that:   "_ the Society of Friends encourages, and is enriched by, the variety of approach to religious faith made by its members." and that:

> The Society has never required its members to conform to a particular view about Jesus, holding that the only valid test of a Christian is whether he lives in the spirit of Christlike love, and not what he says he believes.[162]

The acceptance of these two beliefs has encouraged diversity in that it has meant that people have felt free to engage in theological exploration and to re-

---

[162] George Gorman *Introducing Quakers* London: Friends Home Service Committee 1974 p.18.

interpret Quakerism without feeling the need to defer to any kind of Quaker orthodoxy.

Finally, the diversity of contemporary Quakerism has been contributed to by the existence within British Quakerism of what are known as 'interest groups'. Punshon defines these as: "associations of Friends with particular interests or concerns which they wish to pursue as part of their religious life."[163] Some of these groups, such as the 'Friends Historical Society' or the 'Quaker Fellowship of the Arts' are not concerned with specifically theological issues; others are. Examples of these are the 'New Foundation Fellowship', the 'Quaker Universalist Group', and the 'Open Letter Movement'.

The 'New Foundation Fellowship' sees the renewal of Quakerism as coming about through acceptance of Fox's original message. The 'Quaker Universalist Group' argues that all religions lead to a truth that is greater than any of them and campaigns for the Society of Friends to be officially open to those of all faiths and none rather than being specifically Christian.[164] The 'Open Letter Movement', so called because it was launched with an open letter in *The Friend* in 1976, seeks to promote open-minded study of the contemporary meaning and application of Quaker ideas, and acts as a kind of radical Quaker 'think tank'.[165] Such groups contribute to British Quakerism's theological diversity by developing and promoting their own particular viewpoints by holding meetings to discuss their ideas and producing literature to publicise them. Examples I have noted are Miles' *Towards Universalism* and Benson's 'George Fox's message is relevant today' which were published by the Quaker Universalist Group and the New Foundation Fellowship respectively.

It could also be argued that the diversity of modern Quakerism is a sign of the failure of these interest groups. As I explained in Chapter Two, the movement from Evangelical to Liberal domination of British Quakerism was caused by an organised group of Quaker Liberals managing to persuade the majority of British

---

[163] Punshon *Portrait in Grey* p.261

[164] See Arthur Peacock 'The Quaker Universalist Group' *Quaker Monthly* vol.61:5 May 1982 pp.95-6

[165] See Richard Allen et al 'The Open Letter Movement' *Quaker Monthly* vol.60:10 October 1981 pp.200-1

Quakers to accept their view of Quakerism. No interest group in recent years has managed to emulate their success and as a result no generally agreed model of what Quakerism should be has emerged to act as a check on Quaker diversity.

In this chapter I have surveyed the diversity of recent Quaker thought and suggested some reasons for the existence of this diversity. I have not yet compared the contemporary Quaker theology with the beliefs of the core of conviction and the teaching of the early Quakers. The extracts from Quaker writings from the last thirty years which I have considered in this chapter do not given an adequate coverage of the five topics of Revelation, God, Christ, Man and Salvation which I have selected as a basis for comparison. For example, only Priestland addresses the idea of the fallenness of Man and none of the others considers directly the belief that the wicked will suffer eternal damnation. Therefore in my next chapter I shall extend my picture of recent Quaker theology by examining what a wider sample of Quaker writings from the last thirty years has had to say on these topics.

## Chapter Five
## A Clash of Traditions

In this chapter I shall compare contemporary Quaker theology with the beliefs of the core of conviction and the teaching of the early Quakers. In order to do this I shall examine what a representative sample of recent Quaker writers has had to say about the subjects of Revelation, God, Christ, Man and Salvation, which I have chosen as the basis for comparison. At the end of the chapter I shall argue that this examination shows that in spite of its diversity contemporary Quaker theology as a whole has diverged from the core of conviction and the teaching of the early Quakers and that this divergence can be traced back to the continuing influence of Liberal Quakerism and to the questioning of traditional Christian beliefs by non-Quaker theologians.

### Revelation

The first thing to note about the treatment of this subject by British Quaker writers over the past thirty years is that, like British Quakerism as a whole, it has been marked by great diversity. To illustrate this I shall quote from five Quaker writers who have written about revelation during the time in question and who have all come to different conclusions.

Betty Soper in a letter published in *The Friend* on October 17th 1975 writes about how, for her, Jesus Christ has become the revelation of God.

> I find that Jesus has become for me the 'speaking likeness' of God, uniquely the living word whom God speaks to Men, that he meets me and calls me to relationship with him.[1]

Maurice Creasey writes in *A Christian Affirmation*[2] about how he obtains a partial knowledge of God through experience of himself and the world about him, and how this partial knowledge of God is completed in the manifestation of God in Jesus Christ.

First of all he notes that:

> ...nothing in my own experience of myself and my world is self-explanatory or unambiguous. In whatever direction I move out in thought from my own experience I encounter mystery, and, like the dove in the Genesis story of the Flood, can find no rest.

Reflection upon this "mystery" leads him to the belief that: "the physical .... is part of a larger environment to which I am learning to relate myself." Echoing the terminology employed by Macquarrie in *Principles of Christian Theology*,[3] Creasey calls this "larger environment": "Being itself, the incomprehensible source from which all finite beings proceed, the power by which they are all sustained." He sees it as "a part of what I mean when I say the word 'God'", and declares that in Jesus it has been revealed in paradigmatic fashion, contending that:

> ...in Jesus of Nazareth there has in fact occurred a manifestation of the character and purpose of God as holy Being such that, if we begin to be grasped by its meaning, we will discover that it interprets, corrects or confirms our responses to all other manifestations

and stating that:

> ...for me, Jesus is of universal significance, not because it is only in him that the truth of Being has found expression, but because he has opened my eyes, as in fact no one else has done, to discern the

---

[1] *The Friend* October 17th 1975 vol.133 No.42 p.1129

[2] Creasey *A Christian Affirmation* pp.4 and 6

[3] Macquarrie *Principles of Christian Theology* revd.ed. ch.5

truth of Being where, but for him, I would have misunderstood or
failed to recognise it.

Writing in language influenced by Harry Williams' *The True Wilderness*[4],
Gorman describes in *Introducing Quakers*[5] how God can be known in an
encounter in the depths of our being.

> From time to time ... something happens for good or ill, which
> causes us to think and meditate profoundly about our very
> existence. Then we are driven into the depths of our being where
> we are vividly aware of ourselves as unique and individual persons.
>   We struggle to find words to describe that of which we are
> aware, and they evade us, because no words are fully adequate to
> express a state that defies definition. Perhaps the words 'life', 'spirit'
> and 'consciousness' are among those that come most readily to our
> aid, but even they fail to disclose the full sense of our identity as
> living beings. Our first reaction to our interior journey may well be
> one of anxiety, or even of terror, as we sense our insignificance,
> finitude and loneliness. But as we allow ourselves to be calmed by
> the stillness at the centre of our being, we can find a deeper
> awareness of our rootedness to other people. We know that it is
> from this deep place that our insights into the real meaning of life
> arise, and that the power to live it is found. In this kind of dynamic,
> vital experience we realise that we have discovered a new level of
> existence, in which our spirit is fused with spirit itself in a creative
> encounter. Religious men of all ages have spoken of this
> experience as an encounter with God.

In an article entitled 'Agents of God' published in *The Friend* on February
20th 1981  R.Eric Holtumm writes that we come to a direct knowledge of God
through a "spiritual environment" acting upon the human subconscious:

> in times of insight we realise that we live in a spiritual environment
> as well as the material one of which our bodies are parts. That
> spiritual environment provides all that we can directly know about
> God, though God is presented to us also indirectly through the
> whole of creation, especially through human individuals whom we
> meet or whose words we read,

---

[4] Williams op.cit.

[5] Gorman *Introducing Quakers* pp.13-14

and goes on to write that "it seems to me that our spiritual environment which we call God, acts upon the subconscious parts of our minds, in which there must be a spiritual element."[6]

George Boobyer, Professor of Biblical studies at the University of Newcastle, writes in an article in *The Friend* on April 25th 1986 entitled 'Bible, Creeds, and Quakerism' that his equivalent to the internal monitor of Quaker tradition is:

> ...a compound of knowledge, experience and belief gathered through many sources, though much indebted to the Bible and Jesus. It is the outcome of a search for truth aided by what is, I hope, divine guidance as available through meditation, prayer, and worship. In its content and method of acquisition it differs from the light within of the first Friends (Quakers) in giving a greater place to human reason. It assumes that religious light which is truly light must, as far as possible, draw upon all relevant sources.[7]

Part of the diversity reflected in the work of these writers has been caused by a disagreement about the place of Jesus Christ in revelation. During the last thirty years there has been an almost continuous debate within British Quakerism about whether, and, if so, to what extent, Jesus Christ is central to revelation. This debate has not reached any generally accepted conclusion.

Some British Quaker writers have argued that the revelation of God in Jesus Christ is the only way in which human beings may come to a knowledge of God.

For example, in an article entitled 'It's time to Quake' published in *The Friend* on December 12th 1976, which reflects her encounter with the Charismatic Renewal Movement, Sheila Hendley writes:

> it would be a very cruel situation if God had just left us to search around in the dark for clues to his existence, with only the tools that Man had invented himself - such as science and psychology - to help him. But I offer this article because I know that God has not left us in the darkness. He sent his light Christ. What could be clearer? Christ said 'I am the way, the truth, and the life. No one

---

[6] *The Friend* vol.139 No.8 February 20th 1981 p.205

[7] *The Friend* vol.144 No.17 April 25th 1986 p.518

comes to the Father but by me.' The importance of Christ is crucial For through Christ we gain a personal relationship with God, who is also the infinite God of the Universe. Without Christ as our focus everything is out of perspective. Remember God's words to George Fox: 'There is one, even Christ Jesus, that can speak to thy condition.'[8]

On the other hand, writers on the radical wing of British Quakerism have argued that there is a universal revelation of God to the human race that has no necessary connection with Jesus Christ.

As an example, in an article entitled 'Finding a name for it' published in *The Friend* on December 12th 1969 Ralph Hetherington, who delivered the Swarthmore Lecture in 1975, accepts the idea known as 'cultural relativism' which holds that our beliefs are culturally determined[9] and argues that religious experiences:

> ...do not come to us with conveniently labelled signposts to a creed or dogma, they are not labelled God or Atman or Universal Mind or Allah or Cosmic Love. It is we who, on the basis of our training and culture provide the name on the label. But it is the experience that matters and not the name we give to it. Some would go further and insist that it is the behaviour that ensues from such experiences which give them their validity.
> Since the majority of Friends have been reared in a Christian culture they have learned to associate names like God, Christ, Jesus, Holy Spirit with their religious experiences, and therefore insist that they need Jesus. Of course they do, since this is the name they have learned to use. I am not saying that Jesus is only a name, but I am saying that Jesus is one of several possible names we could use in trying to talk about religious experience. God has a multitude of names and it would be absurd and patently untrue to assert that he reserves his grace for those who call him by a particular one.[10]

During the last thirty years there have also been British Quakers who have followed the tradition of Quaker Liberalism and have argued for the intermediate

---

[8] *The Friend* vol.134 No.51 December 12th 1976 p.1469

[9] For details of this idea see D.E.Nineham *The use and abuse of the Bible* London: S.P.C.K. 1976.

[10] *The Friend* vol.127 No.50 December 12th 1969 p.1525

position that there is a universal revelation of God to all human beings, but that this revelation finds its highest and clearest expression in Jesus Christ.

For example, L.Hugh Doncaster writes in his 1963 Swarthmore Lecture *That of God in every Man*[11] that there is a universal revelation of God which: "is known personally and inwardly and presently by each one of us" but states that this revelation:

> is the light of Christ. He makes its character and content plain. In him it shines supremely, so that his character is its character, and that which we see only faintly in one another, and ourselves we see shining clearly in him.

He further writes in the same lecture that: "To all men the light is given in measure, but in Christ it shines fully so that he is the light of the world".[12]

Another disagreement has been about the place of the Bible in the revelation of God to the human race. This, however, has not been a disagreement about the nature of the Bible. British Quakers have generally agreed with the Quaker Liberals in seeing the Bible as a fallible record of human religious experience. As George Gorman writes in *Introducing Quakers* there is "wide acceptance among modern Quakers" of the idea that the Bible should be seen as:

> a remarkable collection of writings covering the history and experience of countless, ordinary, fallible men and women, as individuals and in community, through a span of many hundreds of years. Among them have been people who had a great capacity to reflect upon the inwardness of this experience, and to interpret it to their fellows in such a way as to command respect for their insights, and interpretation of events and experiences which made sense to them, as disclosing a meaning and purpose that called for response in behaviour and action. These insights were of course expressed in the thought forms and assumptions of the day.
>      In this way a religious attitude and pattern of values were gradually developed. The authority of the Bible does not rest on an external and infallible guarantee of its truth, but on its ability to arouse the response and trust of Man: to speak to their condition by its innate truthfulness. As Dr.Sanday, a famous biblical scholar has said in his Bampton lectures, 'the test of inspiration is the

---

[11] L.Hugh Doncaster *That of God in every Man* London: George Allen and Unwin 1963 p.42

[12] ibid p.8

capacity to inspire.' So powerful has the influence of biblical literature been on the minds and lives of men, that for those who have responded to its insights it has seemed to disclose to them a knowledge of such fundamental importance that they have felt compelled to describe it as knowledge of God: indeed many have spoken of a self-revelation or disclosure of God.[13]

British Quakers in general have also agreed with Liberal Quakerism in rejecting the Evangelical belief in the supreme authority of Scripture. Instead they have returned to the early Quaker position that the supreme authority in matters of religion is not the Bible but the Spirit which inspired the Bible and still speaks to us through it.

As the Quakers' 'Committee on Christian Relationships' put it in a booklet *To Lima with love,*[14] which was the Quaker response to the Lima document on Baptism, Eucharist and Ministry produced by the World Council of Churches:

The same Spirit which inspired the writers of the Bible is the Spirit which gives us understanding of it: it is this which is important to us rather than the literal words of scripture. Hence, while quotations from the Bible may illuminate a truth for us, we would not use them to prove a truth.

The disagreement about the status of the Bible has instead been concerned with what importance the Bible still retains given that its authority is subordinate to that of the direct guidance of the Spirit.

A number of British Quaker writers have seen the Bible as having great importance as a subordinate authority.

For example, Doncaster writes in his pamphlet *The Quaker Message: a Personal Affirmation* that while the Bible is not the "final authority" for Quakers it is nevertheless "fundamentally important" to them because it is:

a unique record of religious experience showing the development over more than a thousand years of insights which nourished the faith of Jews, Christians and Moslems. The Bible (Old Testament) also nourished the experience of Jesus and provided the framework of thought in which he expressed himself. It is the historical record

---

[13] George Gorman *Introducing Quakers* pp.22-3

[14] *To Lima with love* London: Quaker Home Service 1987 p.7

of all that we know of his life and character, his teaching, the
impact he made upon his contemporaries.  It tells us of the way in
which the first two generations of his followers understood and
misunderstood him, and how they organised the group life of the
early Church.  It provides a solid base in history, set in a time and
place of which we know quite a lot from other sources, for that
which has proved itself relevant and contemporary in every
subsequent generation.  To cut ourselves off from the biblical roots
of our faith would be to open the way for airy fairy speculations
and hunches, unchecked by the objective reality of a historical
person set in a developing culture and giving birth to a new world
faith.[15]

On the other hand, more radical Quakers have seen the Bible as having
much less importance as a secondary rule than is given to it by Doncaster.

For instance, Gerald Richards asks in a letter published in *The Friend* on
March 4th 1977:

Would it not be .... sensible to bring up to date the account of the
activity of the Spirit since the time of Pentecost and Paul? ... isn't it
time we had a Quaker Bible giving an account of the continuity as a
continually unfolding process - a book more bespoken to the needs
of enquirers who ask the way in our present generation?  To me the
testimonies of Friends, and others before them, which sprang from
the life and teaching of Jesus of Nazareth and the work of the
apostles are no less important than the Bible revealed as it stands ...
A Quaker Bible should be an open-ended book, not a closed one.
We should spend less time re-hashing Truth past, and give more
attention to interpreting Truth present.[16]

### God

British Quaker writers have shown just as much diversity in their treatment
of God as they have in their treatment of revelation.  As Geoffrey Hubbard
observes in his book *Quaker by Convincement*, Quakers "are unable to agree
about the nature of the manifested God"[17]

---

[15] L. Hugh Doncaster, *The Quaker Message: a Personal Affirmation*, Wallingford, Pennsylvania:
Pendle Hill Publications 1972 p.10

[16] *The Friend* vol.139 No.9 March 4th 1977 p.256.

[17] Geoffrey Hubbard, *Quaker by Convincement* London: Quaker Home Service 1974 p.80

To illustrate Hubbard's contention I shall again quote from the works of British Quaker writers who give widely differing answers to questions of who, or what, God is.

In her 1964 Swarthmore Lecture *Tradition and Experience* Richenda C. Scott engages with the views expressed the previous year by John Robinson in *Honest to God* and defends the idea that there is personality in God and that God is both transcendent and immanent. She writes that:

> when we come to discern the action of God upon us, and the possibility of communication with Him ... we are plunged into a personal relationship with something not ourselves, but which includes the element of personality - the personality not OF God, which may lead us again into anthropomorphism, but personality IN God. As we apprehend something of the majesty and wonder and incomprehensibility of the infinite and absolute we find, paradoxically, that this is someone, something, near and close. I use the term someone with hesitation because to many it seems at once to conjure up some divine potentate, creating the world by his mere command, aloof from strife and suffering - a supreme being, who is nevertheless an object like other objects, which God as the unconditional can never be. What I mean by 'someone' is the personal element at the heart of reality, with whom we can have relationship, which includes purpose and will and love and grace that seeks and responds to the love and truth in the human being. At the risk of being accused of suggesting God as 'out there' or 'up there', I would suggest that this creative love and purpose is not exhausted by the universe we know, is infinitely beyond as well as within the world. But He IS in it, in all the agony of creation and creative effort, in the long, terrible patience of natural evolution, in the struggling human being and the tragedy and comedy of human life.[18]

In an article entitled 'The Personality of God' published in *The Friend* on January 13th 1967, Edward James comes close to the Monism of the Advaita Vedanta school of Hinduism in his advocacy of the pantheist position that the creation and God are one. He writes that: "creation" is "God himself in visible form" and that:

---

[18] Richenda C. Scott *Tradition and Experience* London: George Allen and Unwin 1964 pp.46-7.

> God is not separate from but is himself the creation eternally
> evolving from a spiritual conception, born into the swaddling
> clothes of matter to grow into a mature conscious life.[19]

James's affinity with Eastern thought is typical of many contemporary
British Quakers, especially of those on British Quakerism's Universalist wing.

In an article entitled 'Basic Quakerism 1969', published in *The Friend* on
November 14th 1969 Beatrice Saxon Snell writes that God is a "self-
communicating reality" of "power, love and wisdom".

> Friends are aware of a reality, to which most of them give the name
> of 'God' which is apprehended by them as Being, Power, or Spirit
> according to temperament or circumstance (sometimes as one out
> of the three, sometimes as two out of the three, and sometimes as
> all three at once). It is a reality of power, love and wisdom, and it
> is therefore a self-communicating reality, for power, love and
> wisdom cannot exist without objects. Its function in relation to
> human beings is cherishing, enabling, and guiding.[20]

Alec Lea, in an article 'Through the Cobweb Curtain', in *The Friend* on
January 4th 1985, argues that God must be seen as an impersonal spirit of love.

> The conception of God as an all-powerful being behind or above
> the physical world, and continually interfering with it on behalf of
> humans who pray and worship is simply not credible any more.
> God has to become an 'it' a spirit of love which can only work
> through humans, which has no other dwelling place than them, and
> which is probably blind.[21]

Finally, in an article entitled 'The Allegory of God', which was published in *Quaker
Monthly* in December 1986, Alan York agrees with the idea put forward by
Ludwig Feuerbach, and more recently by Don Cupitt, that talk about God is really
talk about the human condition.[22]

---

[19] *The Friend* vol.125 No.2 January 13th 1967 p.38

[20] *The Friend* vol.127 No.48 November 14th 1969 p.1406

[21] *The Friend* vol.143 No.I January 4th 1985 p.5

[22] See L.A.Feuerbach *The Essence of Christianity* Tr. Mary Ann Evans, London: J.Chapman
1853 and Cupitt *Taking Leave of God* p.239

> We might see the whole of our thought about God and Man - the whole of our story about the Creator and Creature - as itself an allegory. The allegory is about the nature of Man and his world, it is our way of telling to ourselves the story of Man's developing perception of what is fundamental to his life, and how it should be lived.

He suggests later on in the same article that "we... have invented God" for the purpose of this allegory.[23]

Amongst this variety of opinions there have been some who have wanted to continue to see God in traditional Trinitarian terms.

For instance, Richenda C. Scott writes in her booklet *Rejections and Discoveries*:

> ....The Trinity, that fatal word, which can petrify most Quaker audiences into frigid horror, or rouse them to a passion of rejection. I have often wondered why, for the doctrine of the Trinity is only the attempt to express, as poetry or symbol, the fullness of God's revelation in Christ and of his relationship to the world. The careful choice of words which are yet too frail to hold the concert of meaning, may be too static in concept for the present age, yet the truths they attempt to embody remain, and there is nothing in them to frighten or repel the Quaker. They are, basically, truths of our experience. It was George Fox speaking on behalf of the Quakers of 1682, who made the always impossible attempt to state the inner richness and complexity of the Christian knowledge of God in the following terms:
> 'We believe 1st that there is one God and Father of whom are all things. 2ndly That there is one Lord Jesus Christ, by whom all things were made, who was glorified with the Father before the world began, who is God over all, beloved for ever. That there is one Holy Spirit, the promise of the Father and the Son, and leader and sanctifier and comforter of his people. And we further believe, as the Holy Scriptures soundly and sufficiently express, that these three are one, even the Father, the Word, and the Spirit' ('Something in Answer to all who falsely say the Quakers are no Christians').[24]

---

[23] *Quaker Monthly* vol.65:12 December 1986 p.239.

[24] Richenda C.Scott *Rejections and Discoveries* London: Friends Home Service Committee 1965 p.1

However, echoing the doubts about Trinitarian theology expressed by Quaker Liberals such as Thompson, Graham and Grubb, British Quaker thought about God during the past thirty years has generally been non-Trinitarian. Of the fifty six writers whose works I have studied to determine how they have treated the subject of God, only four have put forward a definitely Trinitarian understanding of God. Furthermore, only one Swarthmore lecturer in the last thirty years has put forward a Trinitarian view.[25] Also, none of the works written to explain Quakerism and Quaker beliefs to those outside the Society of Friends (works such as Gorman's *Introducing Quakers*, Hubbard's *Quaker by Convincement*, or Harold Loukes' *The Quaker Contribution*[26]) has put forward a Trinitarian view of God. The diversity of thought about God which the writers have displayed has been within a generally non-Trinitarian approach.

British Quaker writers have normally taken a Unitarian view of God, seeing Him as a simple rather than as a Triune unity. For instance, when Joyce Blake writes that:

> God is not a mere notion or philosophical abstraction, nor a product of man's minds; nor a power indifferent to man, but in a real sense a spirit than can reach out to Men, be felt by Men as a loving, caring, guiding, strengthening presence[27]

or when Hubbard describes God as a:

> spiritual, non-material force or entity which may or may not have a separate existence away from the material man, but which dwells indeed in the inmost heart of every man.[28]

or when John Lampen, Swarthmore Lecturer in 1987, in his book *Twenty Questions about Jesus*[29] talks about God as "the quality of rightness" which is "something inherent in the world" and which is "an active principle to which we

---

[25] Doncaster on p.75 of his 1963 Swarthmore lecture *That of God in Every Man*

[26] Harold Loukes, *The Quaker Contribution* London: SCM Press 1965

[27] *The Friend* vol.125 No.43 October 27th 1967 pp.1134-5 Article 'I believe'.

[28] Hubbard op.cit. p.31

[29] John Lampen *Twenty Questions about Jesus*, London: Quaker Home Service 1985 p.89

can relate in the most intimately personal way", they are writing about God in Unitarian terms typical of British Quaker writers over the last thirty years. It should be noted, however, that Quaker Unitarianism differs from that of the Unitarian Churches in that it is generally mystical rather than intellectual or rationalist in basis.

During this period there have been Quaker writers such as Thomas Green in his article on 'The Holy Spirit' published in *Quaker Monthly* in July 1964,[30] or Loukes in *The Quaker Contribution*, or Peter North in his article 'Walking in the light' published in *Quaker Monthly* in June 1975,[31] who have written about the Holy Spirit as well as simply writing about God. But it is unclear whether they are putting forward a binitarian theology since they do not speculate about whether or not the Holy Spirit has a distinct existence within the Godhead.

## Christ

Not surprisingly, British Quaker writers have disagreed as profoundly about Christ as they have about revelation or God.

As Lampen notes in *Twenty Questions about Jesus*:

> For some members of your [Quaker] Meeting, he [Jesus Christ] may be a wise teacher, in the mould of Socrates; for others one of the first 'enlightened human beings, like the Buddha; for others, 'Very God', the Second Person of the Trinity, our Saviour; while a few are hostile to him, because they honestly find his influence on history disastrous, or the talk of 'redeeming us by his precious blood' morally repugnant, or the concept of 'the only begotten son of the Father' unacceptably sexist. There may even be someone who has toyed with the idea that Jesus was a spaceman - or an intoxicating mushroom.[32]

To illustrate this great range of opinion about Jesus Christ I shall quote from the works of six British Quaker writers.

Saxon Snell argues in an article 'Humble learners in the School of Christ' in *The Friend* on June 11th 1965 that:

---

[30] *Quaker Monthly* vol.43 No.7 July 1964 p.101

[31] *Quaker Monthly* vol.54 No.6 June 1975 pp.117-8

[32] John Lampen *Twenty Questions about Jesus* p.1.

Jesus himself appears to have thought of himself as the REPRESENTATIVE of God to man - he showed us what God is like in human terms. He was the vehicle of a supremely important revelation to Man of God's nature and spirit.

She further defines Jesus in the same article as: "the man through whom the Christ-Spirit was fully manifested".[33]

Donald Court, in an article entitled 'A Scientific age and a declining Church - What has a Friend to Say?' published in *The Friend* on September 24th 1965 describes Jesus in evolutionary terms:

If I may use an analogy from evolutionary theory, Jesus was a highly developed example of a new species of Man - spirit directed and not instinct driven Man. Paul sensed this when he described him as 'the firstborn of a great brotherhood'. To talk of his divinity has no meaning for me, because in my thinking there is no break where God ends and Man begins. I believe that Jesus has a highly significant place in the evolution of mankind, but I don't consider that necessarily he is the final word in Man's development. It seems to me that the Church's insistence on his uniqueness has made it more difficult for men and women to follow him, and has lessened the significance of countless other lives lived in his Spirit.[34]

In *Friends Quarterly* for July 1976 Lorna M. Marsden states in an article entitled 'Fox's Word of Life', in terms influenced by the work of Jung, that Christ is a symbol of the integration of the human personality:

We, who no longer see Christ as a supernatural visitant, do see him as an image of what we are called to be, as, potentially, WHAT WE ARE ... We now recognise in him a particular form of an archetype deeply embedded in the human spirit, another expression of the ancient puer aeternus, and a perfect symbol of that integration of the human personality that is sought by modern depth psychology.[35]

John C. Lawton explains in a letter published in 'The Friend' on November 19th 1976 that he sees Jesus Christ in Buddhist terms:

---

[33]*The Friend* vol.123 No.24 June 11th 1965 p.694

[34] *The Friend* vol.123 No.34 September 24th 1965 p.1143

[35] *Friends Quarterly* vol.19 No.7 July 1976 p.296

> When I moved into Quakerism, I also moved towards Mahayana
> Buddhism and, as a result, I now regard Jesus the Christ as a great
> exemplar and incarnation of the Bodhisattva principle of
> compassion, and, as such, a son of Man who realised oneness with
> the Father.[36]

In an article reflecting Hindu thought entitled 'Jesus as the Universal Self'
published in *The Friend* on September 5th 1980, Robert Bell asks whether it is not
possible to see Jesus as the "Universal self" rather than as "divine". He asks us to
consider what would be the result:

> ....supposing all the evidence that is commonly used to support the
> claim that Jesus is divine were used, as it can be, to prove
> something else? All the scriptural quotations, for instance, that are
> used to support this astonishing claim can be made to bear another
> meaning. It could be that what Jesus is really saying is not "I am
> God", but "I am the universal self. I have in me the true deep self
> that all men have, for it is universal". He then further invites
> "anyone who cares to do so, to re-read the Gospels from this
> different angle seeing Jesus as the universal self made flesh. In this
> sense he is me, he is you, he is God. This is why, when he speaks,
> the heart quakes.
>        And he speaks everywhere. In the Hindu scriptures we hear
> his authentic voice. Having attained to Brahman, the sage (Christ?)
> declared, "I am life, my glory is like the mountain peak ... I have
> attained the freedom of the self ... I am immortal, imperishable"
> (Taittiriya Upanishad).[37]

Lastly, as we saw in the previous chapter, in his Swarthmore lecture
Priestland defends the doctrine of the incarnation by explaining Christ's divinity in
terms of His being a "sacramental sign" of God's grace. That is to say, he suggests
that Christ may be seen as a visible sign of God's unmerited love for us when we
respond to Him with worship.

Amidst all these different views about Christ four points stand out.

Firstly, whereas in the theology of Liberal Quakerism Christ was still seen
as someone of unique importance, for many contemporary Quakers this is no
longer the case. This was seen in the last chapter in the theology of Marsden and

---

[36] *The Friend* vol.134 No.47 November 19th 1976 p.1360

[37] *The Friend* vol.138 No.36 September 5th 1980 p.1111-2

Miles and earlier in this chapter in connection with the subject of Revelation. It is further emphasised in four of the extracts just considered. Court considers that Christ is not necessarily the final word in human development and that the Church's insistence on His uniqueness was a mistake. Marsden sees Him as only a symbol of the integration of human personality. Lawton sees Him simply as an example of the Buddhist principle of compassion and Bell as a manifestation of the universal self possessed by all men.

Secondly, only a minority of British Quaker writers have followed Priestland and Quaker Liberals such as Jones, Graham and Grubb in accepting the traditional Christian belief that God was incarnate in Christ. Of seventy two writers on the subject of Christ whose works I have examined only seven have explicitly talked about Jesus Christ as God. Furthermore, in the last thirty years only two Swarthmore lecturers, Priestland and Doncaster in his 1963 Swarthmore lecture *God in Every Man*[38], have described Christ as God incarnate.

Instead the divergence of opinion among Quaker writers has been almost entirely about how to understand Jesus Christ as a Man.

Thirdly, many British Quaker writers have been either sceptical or agnostic about the historicity of the miracle stories in the Gospels, especially those about Christ's virgin birth and bodily resurrection.

For example, Court, in his article 'A scientific age and a declining Church - what has a Friend to say?' quoted earlier in this chapter, writes: "I regard Jesus as a man, and I find no place in my belief for his allegedly unnatural birth, for miracles, or for a physical resurrection".[39]

Like Graham and Grubb, those British Quaker writers who have been sceptical or agnostic about the historicity of the Gospel accounts of Christ's bodily resurrection have sought to provide alternative explanations of what happened at the first Easter. The variety of ways in which they have sought to do this is illustrated by Holttum, Gorman and Peacock.

Holttum writes in a letter which was published in *The Friend* on January 26th 1968:

---

[38] Doncaster *God in Every Man* pp.76-81

[39] Court Art.cit. p.1143

What is quite certain is that after the death of Jesus the disciples received extremely vivid evidence that his presence was, in some way, still with them;  and it was upon that assurance that they began to establish a Christian community. Most of us believe that the spiritual nature of every person who dies somehow continues a spiritual existence;  and to me, no other kind of continual existence can be claimed for the spirit that was in Jesus.[40]

Gorman, on the other hand, writes in *Introducing Quakers* that most Quakers:

would agree that the essential meaning behind the story of the first Easter is that death could not destroy all that was of real value in the earthly life of Jesus.  The love experienced by his disciples could not be taken from them by his death, because they recognised that it was of an infinite and eternal quality.  In fact, it was only after his death that they came to understand and to appreciate fully the deep meaning of his life and to be set free by it.[41]

Peacock writes in an article entitled 'The Christhood of all Mankind' published in *The Friend* on July 11th 1975:

The fundamental myths of Christianity present, in symbolic form, a series of philosophical statements about the meaning of human life and "Christ's resurrection and ascent into heaven" represent the "soaring of the imagination on eagles wings" in "a new vision of cosmic rebirth".[42]

While many British Quakers have been either sceptical or agnostic about the stories of miraculous events in the Gospels, there have also been some who have wanted to defend the  miraculous elements of the Gospel stories.

Ernest Hall, in an article entitled 'Where are we going?' published in *The Friend* on May 12th 1972, writes "I believe in the conquest of the moon because I have heard of it from witnesses whom I trust.  I believe in the resurrection of Jesus Christ for the same reason".[43]

---

[40] *The Friend* vol.126 No.4 January 26th 1968 p.110

[41] Gorman *Introducing Quakers* p.20

[42] *The Friend* vol.133 No.28 July 11th 1975 p.783

[43] *The Friend* vol.130 No.19 May 12th 1972 p.576

In a letter published in *The Friend* on March 7th 1975 which endorses the New-Orthodox critique of Liberal Protestantism, John Punshon notes that:

> Liberal Protestantism wanted to make Christianity intelligible to a public acquainted with the philosophy of progress and political liberalism, natural science and evolutionary theory. There was no room for the supernatural in this scheme so the Jesus - Christ dichotomy was developed. Jesus' ethics and commanding personality could be understood in naturalistic terms and presented to a sceptical world. His miracles, his eschatology, his transfiguration, his resurrection were supernatural, useful as symbols perhaps, but inessential.
>
> Modern criticism and research shows that this programme is impossible of fulfilment. Jesus' ethics stand with his eschatology and his parables with his proclamation of the Kingdom. The miracles are not credulous accretions but belong to the earliest strata of the synoptic tradition. The New Testament is not a systematic presentation of the facts of Jesus's life, but a response to the fact of the resurrection, an attempt to make the incredible intelligible.[44]

The fourth point arising from the writings about Christ is that there have been a number of British Quaker writers during the period under review who have argued that Christ was limited and imperfect either in knowledge or in character.

Thus, W. Arnold Hall writes in a letter published in *The Friend* on April 24th 1970:

> Jesus, called Christ, is not a synonym for God: he was a child of his theological times and (as such) articulated some untenable eschatological and providential opinions, as Albert Schweitzer (in 1891) and Bishop Robinson (in the 1960s) have respectively indicated.[45]

Thus also, Lampen argues in *Twenty Questions about Jesus* that if we see Jesus as the human Son of Man rather than the Divine Son of God we can recognize his limitations.

---

[44] *The Friend* vol.133 No.10 March 7th 1975 p.246

[45] *The Friend* vol.128 No.17 April 24th 1970 p.493

The Son of God must be sinless; but we can admit that the Son of Man could be dispirited, angry, unfair towards his opponents. The Son of God could never have looked at a girl with a lustful eye; the Son of Man may have had to struggle with the impulse himself, before he could pronounce it an abuse of womanhood. His friendship with Mary Magdalene, or John Bar-Zebedee, may have had a strong sexual component. The Son of God could foresee all that would happen to him, the suffering and the glory; the Son of Man, even at the end, could be tempted to fight his way out of a tight spot - and we can admire all the more the triumphant way he put the temptation behind him.[46]

## Man

When examining how Quaker writers have treated the subject of Human Nature the first observation is that they demonstrate as wide a diversity of understandings of Man's nature and situation as of how revelation occurs, of who, or what, God is, and of the identity and significance of Jesus Christ.

To illustrate this I shall again quote from the works of British Quaker writers from this period.

In her Lecture *Tradition and Experience*[47] Richenda C. Scott presents a view of Man that brings together the insights of Psychology and the theology of George Fox, the Apostle Paul and Paul Tillich.

She begins by noting that:

George Fox stated that the first function of the light is to show man his state and condition while living in separation from God. According to some modern psychologists this sense of being sundered even from other human beings is at the root of many neuroses, and first occurs when the child realizes itself as distinct from the mother who feeds it. The realization brings a sense of insecurity with its resultant anxiety and fears. These cling about the adult human being until he can achieve a mature relationship with his fellow which is independent, responsible and perceptive, but is neither the loss of self by complete identification with another, nor the domination of another by using him simply to subserve one's own needs.

---

[46] Lampen op.cit. p.70

[47] Richenda C. Scott *Tradition and Experience* pp.57-59

She then further notes that because Man is "not merely a creature of the temporal world" but "has a foothold also in the eternal and infinite" it follows that:

...he can never rest wholly satisfied within the limits of the temporal. Unrecognized, frequently unknown, beneath the crowding desires of his mundane life, whose attainment brings no lasting satisfaction, is the yearning for a fuller, greater life, of whose limitless beauty and possibility we all catch glimpses and flashes transient but penetrating. So we are divided creatures of warring impulses, restive and torn in two. In this state of conflict we are powerless to become what we should be and long to be. As Paul realized all too bitterly, we cannot do the good we want to do, and constantly do the evil we deplore. A gulf has been opened up between Man and God because of Man's failure to find and receive his true self as the gift of God. That gift may pass to us through different hands, including human love and friendship or the skill and patience of the psychologist. However it comes it means that we have to take the gift of grace and learn to live in the light of the eternal. Until that happens man either adopts an attitude of aggressive self-assertion against God, snatching at knowledge like Adam, that he may become as God and prove his complete independence; or he relapses into an infantile state, whining at God to meet his wishes, to shield him from the storms of life, trying to shift all the responsibilities of his existence and choices on to a divine dictator and provider. Pride and failure of nerve, the choice of evil or the refusal to face the facts of reality, aggressive self-centredness with its greedy demands, or self-doubt so deep that it dare not trust the light within - these are among the ultimate sins which breed all the rest and divide man from his true being and potentialities, and so from God. Paul Tillich claims that the separation itself is the root sin, the cause of the divided self and its frustrations.

In his article 'A Scientific Age and a Declining Church - What has a Friend to say?', Court puts forward the idea that Man possesses conscious reason, an immensely powerful but dimly understood darker side, and a third element which he calls spirit.

Rejecting moral dualism, I believe that when we understand them sufficiently all parts of human personality will work together for good. And so my third foundation is reverence for Man. But although I find no place for primitive concepts like original sin .... yet, through the insight of poets and novelists, the development of analytic psychology and the study of mental illness, we are beginning to know that in addition to our conscious reason we have an immensely powerful, dimly understood element in our nature which produces painful tensions within us and is capable of leading even to self-destruction .... one of the most important lessons I have to learn is to try to understand this darker side, and to accept it in myself and in other people.

To stop here would leave me no more than a humanist, and I am in fact very close to the sincere humanist. But Christianity insists that there is a third dimension in man's nature, and I do too. Not for me an extra which comes in at baptism or confirmation; but as natural a part as body or mind. Our Quaker language uses a variety of names - 'that of God', 'the seed', 'the inward light' - but I prefer simply to call this faculty spirit. And, as with body and mind, when we understand how it works it begins to produce its own health in us. The qualities of spirit are 'love, joy, peace, patience, kindness, generosity, fidelity, tolerance and self-control' (Gal.v.22 J.B.Philips' translation). At this point I am a Christian humanist, identified with and seeking the welfare of all men.[48]

Eric F. Bowman combines the Biblical stories of the Prodigal Son and the Creation of Man in an article entitled 'Humanism and Quakerism: co-existence or conflict?' published in *The Friend* on January 5th 1968 in which he states that:

Man may be evil but he is also good; he is not 'hopelessly lost' in Barth's phrase. The prodigal son did return to his father of his own free will, on his own steam, so to speak. We must start, not from condemnation of Man, but from faith in him. Our answer is therefore not secular humanism but Christian humanism. We have the faith that there is the divine in Man: that, as the Book of Genesis puts it, when God created Man he breathed into him - not just life; the bodily life that begins at birth and ends with death - but 'pneuma', a portion given to Man of God's own divinity; God made Man 'in his own image'.[49]

Gwen Hogan argues in an article entitled 'Miserable Sinners' in *The Friend* on April 22nd 1977 that innocence, which she defines as "wholeness", is a state which we only enjoy in childhood and that therefore:

Sin - being divided against ourselves - is the normal condition of human adults on their long journey from innocence to salvation; so normal in fact that we can forget about it for long stretches, just as

---

[48] *The Friend* vol.123 No.39 September 24th 1965 p.1142

[49] *The Friend* vol.126 No.1 January 5th 1968 p.21

we forget morality in the joy of vigorous living. We don't have to
be consciously miserable all the time![50]

In *Reasonable Uncertainty* Priestland re-interprets the stories of the
Creation and Fall in Genesis in accordance with the thoughts of Paul, of Fox, and
of the theologians he encountered whilst making 'Priestland's Progress' and puts
forward the two ideas that God is incarnate in the best human beings as they co-
operate with Him in the work of creation, and that human beings have been given
the freedom to either accept or reject God's will for them.

Priestland puts forward the first of these ideas when he writes that:

> The doctrine of Creation, as I read it, involves a continuous and
> continuing activity in which Mankind is - and always has been -
> invited to share.
>      We see this from the start, in that earliest myth of creation,
> wherein Man and Woman are given dominion over every living
> thing, and over every tree and fruit and seed. And it is confirmed
> again in God's covenant with Noah. Mankind is appointed steward
> over God's estate to work with Him in the continuous flow of
> creation ... I would say that God's creating Man 'in His own image'
> implies something more: it tells us that the seed of the Incarnation
> ... of God being involved and expressed in human flesh ... was there
> from the start. We shall have to look further into Incarnation in due
> course, but it seems to me that St. Paul's linking of the first and
> second Adam (something which George Fox brought together in
> his astonishing vision of Paradise)[51] points to that conclusion.
>      Just as Adam stands for all men, and at his best is doing the
> will of God, so all men and women at their best are doing the work
> of creation. Thus God is active in history, incarnate in the best of
> our kind. I have found general agreement among theologians that
> God is ONLY active in history through the agency of human co-
> operation: not through miraculous interventions that brush mankind
> aside. His natural order may present us with unexpected things –
> crossroads, decision points – but we then have to respond, and if
> we do so in tune with His will, the outcome is creative.[52]

He presents the second idea when he writes:

---

[50] *The Friend* vol.135 No.16 April 22nd 1977 p.445

[51] The reference is to a vision received by Fox in 1648 in which he identified Paul's idea of
becoming like Christ with the idea of returning to the state which Adam was in before the Fall -
see Fox *Journal* p.32.

[52] Priestland op.cit. pp.40-41

The story of the choice of Adam and Eve to disobey God and help themselves to the power of moral decision symbolises God's gift to us of Free Will. I am not suggesting that our will is totally free, in the sense that we might have no social historical or genetic bias working upon us. But it is free enough for us to know what it is, and to be responsible for our actions. All our decisions could have been made for us: we could have been programmed to do nothing but the best, to be nothing but God's puppets. He could have made us so entirely obedient to His will that we never conflicted with one another, never took risks, never ran into any kind of danger. But if you reflect upon that you will find that it amounts to saying that God could have made us not to be men and women at all. And He could have made us so completely aware of His will that – while we might have feared Him - we could never have loved Him of our own free choice. But love, to be loved, cannot be coerced. It must be freely given. And that has to bring with it the freedom to withhold, to reject.[53]

My next observation is that British Quaker writers have interpreted the idea of the 'Fall' of Man from a variety of standpoints.

Some have taken a traditional view of the Fall and seen it as an historical event. For example, Donald Harvey writes in a letter published in *The Friend* of January 14th 1977:

The first human beings were without sin. Sins are actions contrary to the will of God, so Adam and Eve did God's will until they decided to try something different, and since they had free will they were able to choose. This departure from God's will had disastrous effects. Mankind was ejected from the paradise of Eden and death came into the world to destroy each individual in time to present them from becoming devils.[54]

The majority, however, have followed the Quaker Liberals in rejecting the historicity of the early chapters of Genesis and in consequence have not viewed the Fall in historical terms. Instead they have given a number of different non-historical interpretations. Four writers will illustrate this point.

---

[53] ibid pp.42-43

[54] *The Friend* vol.135 No.2 January 14th 1977 p.396

Firstly, Peacock argues in a letter published in *The Friend* on April 2nd 1976, in which he draws on the psychology of Freud, that the Fall should be recognised as:

> ...a ubiquitous cosmic principle, as necessary to the existence of the universe as creation itself. Freud acknowledges the essential function of these two principles in the make-up of every individual when he conceived the polarity of EROS and THANATOS, the life instinct and the death instinct.[55]

In a letter published in the same issue of *The Friend* Saxon Snell refers neither to Freud nor the Medieval Church, but argues for the continued relevance of the Fall story on the basis of a common sense approach to human experience:

> Far from being non-existent, outdated and irrelevant to modern life, the Fall and the redemption are timeless and still with us. Human beings are still guilty, guilty, not 'mistaken', though sin is always a mistake - of any or all of the following:
>
> GREED. There were plenty of other fruits in the garden, and this has a certain relevance to the considerations which our vegetarian friends have lately been laying upon us.
>
> IMPATIENCE. 'A fruit to be desired to make one wise'. But wisdom comes only through grace and experience. We live in an age of attempted short cuts; ranging from 'convenience foods' to war.
>
> WILLINGNESS TO ACCEPT INNUENDO WITHOUT PROOF. The mass media would not indulge in this form of character assassination if there were not demand for it.
>
> DISHONESTY. Eve's willingness to accept a specious justification of what she knew to be wrong. The excuses people make to themselves for smoking, drinking, speeding and sexual indulgence without due precautions
>
> LACK OF INTEGRITY. Adam letting his affection for Eve trap him into wrongdoing. Do we of the nineteen seventies find it less hard to say 'no' to someone we love?
>
> LACK OF LOVE, following, as it does so often, on lack of integrity. One facet of this is the ugly names people give to those they fear or dislike 'fuzz', 'niggers', 'commies', 'do-gooders'.
>
> COWARDICE. The pair of them hiding from the Presence. But the presence modern Man shuns is only too often himself.
>
> PRURIENCE – being ashamed or afraid of one's own body. We have substituted for this obsession a constant titillation – see any railway bookstall.                                    (I have

---

[55] *The Friend* vol.134 No.14 April 2nd 1976 pp.374

said nothing of the traditional 'dis-obedience'. Disobedience is not nowadays considered a fault: it is 'natural', with which our forefathers would have agreed. And therefore not wrong – a conclusion that would have shocked them to the marrow)[56]

In an article entitled 'The Fall – History and Myth' published in *The Friend* on April 30th 1976 Mary Mitchelson argues that the story of the Fall is impossible as history, and ambiguous and morally objectionable as myth.[57] She contends that the story of the Fall is impossible as history because

it is not only that, for example, fossil bones prove that non-human creatures suffered from arthritis long before there were men to bring such a punishment down on them, but a moment's thought will show that death is as integral a part of life as birth. Quite literally, where there is death, there's hope. A world in which nothing died is inconceivable.

She declares that the story of the Fall is ambiguous because:

As has been pointed out, even the medieval church regarded it as 'Felix culpa', a fortunate sin, for if Adam's sin resulted in mankind attaining a whole new dimension of thought - the ability to distinguish between good and evil, the possibilities of moral choice - he is obviously a benefactor in the spiritual sense greater than Prometheus himself.

Lastly, she maintains that the story of the Fall is objectionable for two reasons.

In the first place it implies that there is something wrong with nature and with Man. This is not the case. Everything that happens in nature is the work of the creative energy of God and the egoism of the new born baby is not a sign of original sin but is a state which is necessary for the baby's survival and which it can eventually be encouraged to grow out of.

In the second place the idea that there is something wrong with nature and with Man implies that there is something wrong with God's creative activity. This is also not the case. God knows perfectly well what He is doing and requires our co-operation rather than our criticism.

---

[56] ibid. p.375

[57] *The Friend* vol.134 No.18 April 30th 1976 p.485

The anonymous author of the chapter entitled 'Encountering Eve' in the 1984 Swarthmore Lecture *Bringing the Invisible into the light - some Quaker Feminists speak of their experience* seeks to rehabilitate Eve by re-reading the story of Eve's eating the forbidden fruit in extremely positive terms:

> Until Eve's encounter with the serpent, the humans had been curiously cardboard images who acted in a largely unseeing, unthinking manner. They give no indication that they recognise the goodness of the creation in which they find themselves. Nor do they thank God for it. After Eve's encounter with the serpent, however, she looks upon the tree, delights in it and desires its fruit. This is the first time any feelings are expressed by the humans in the creation narrative. As Eve looks at the tree, suddenly, we find a human being becoming conscious of creation, alive to it, moved by it and by the promise it offers.
> I am not willing to blame Eve for eating the apple, neither am I willing to call it, unequivocally, a disobedient act. Eve recognised the tree as beautiful and she wanted to partake of the fruit. She was additionally motivated by the dimmest thought that, through eating this fruit, she could also participate in divinity.[58]

My next point is that modern Quaker writers have followed the Quaker Liberals in rejecting the idea that since the Fall human beings have been tainted and depraved by original sin.[59] The following examples will make the point clear.

Bernard Canter, the editor of *The Friend*, writes in an editorial entitled 'Life and Eternal Life' on November 13th 1964:

> A fallen race? tainted with Satan, even in the very womb? oh no; let all such blasphemies be cast away. Man's force comes from God; God is the ground of Man's being and the tide that pounds through it.[60]

---

[58] Quaker Women's Group *Bringing the invisible into the light* London: Quaker Home Service 1984 p.31

[59] A classic example of the Liberal rejection of this idea is Grubb's claim on p.99 of *Authority and the Light Within* that: "The doctrine of total human depravity had its sole foundation in a literal interpretation of certain texts of Scripture; it is contradicted by all our experience of life, and also by the plain teaching of the Master Himself ... We cannot possibly admit that Man, as Man, is hopelessly corrupt and dark."

[60] *The Friend* vol.122 No.46 November 13th 1964 p.1354

Cyril Harrison writes in an article called 'Propagating Quakerism' in *The Friend* on February 15th 1974 that:

> Few indeed of us would regard our fellow men as 'miserable sinners' utterly depraved and 'lost' or as 'brands to be plucked from the burning'. These concepts do not fit in with the authentic view of the nature of Man, or his psycho-spiritual constitution.[61]

Adam Curle, Professor of Peace Studies at Bradford University and Swarthmore Lecturer in 1981, in his article 'What do Friends Really Mean?' in *The Friend* on September 17th, 1982[62] describes the Augustinian idea that:

> After the fall we were separated from God, marked with an ineradicable stain of sin which could only be cleansed by divine grace following the mediation of Jesus who, through his sacrifice on the cross, took upon himself the sins of the world

as being: "very alien to my idea of Quakerism", and argues that "we should not allow our disgust at evil to distort our perception of reality, hypnotising us into accepting our 'innate depravity'."

**Salvation**

As may be expected, British Quaker writers have diverged widely on the subject of Salvation. Again I shall illustrate with representative quotations.

Richard Foat writes in an article entitled 'Unless one is Born Anew' published in *The Friend* on March 8th 1968, that when:

> a man receives and believes in Jesus, he is given the power to become a Child of God, born anew of God, born of the Spirit. And unless he is born anew he cannot see the kingdom of God nor can he enter it. Once-born of the flesh, he remains in the flesh; reborn of the Spirit, he adds a new dimension to his life, and that is, potentially, the beginning of his fulfilment.
> So we have first to seek and find Jesus in the Bible, to believe in him with our minds and receive him in our hearts. This is a predominantly intellectual exercise, even the receiving into our

---

[61] *The Friend* vol.132 No.7 February 15th 1974 p.158

[62] *The Friend* vol.140 No.38 September 17th 1982 pp.1167

hearts being largely dependent on the assent of our minds. When we receive his teaching and believe in it, we naturally turn to him - that is, we repent - yielding ourselves to his redemptive, creative power. And when we have acquired such humility, Jesus can come into our lives, he dwelling in us and we in him and this is the rebirth in the spirit .... even after rebirth we still have our free will, to choose what use we make of our new spiritual potential. God makes himself available, to the uttermost limit of enabling us to become perfect as he himself is perfect. For as H.A.Williams puts it, Christians believe in God's love, 'but if they believed in it fully with the totality of their being, they would be perfect'.[63]

In a letter published in *The Friend* on November 6th 1970 Joseph R.Sandy argues that the modern synonym for salvation is survival:

religion is the only exercise for which Man is really fitted, the only way in which Man can survive.(Survival is the modern synonym for salvation; it has nothing to do with the soul or the next world)[64]

In her article entitled 'Our Corporate Commitment to Christ' published in *The Friend* on November 13th 1970 Damaris Parker Rhodes, Swarthmore Lecturer in 1977, declares that salvation means the restoration of Man's ability to live instinctively.

Alienation from instinct and from nature (the Fall) has gone side by side with the development of reason and morality, causing Man to lose touch with the deeper sources of his life. This makes him neurotic. It is possible to restore him to the ability to live instinctively, not by crushing out instinct but by spiritualising it and so releasing new potentiality for creative purposes (This is salvation).
    Reason cannot achieve this integration by itself, though an effort of the will is needed. Symbols assist in it, and it is necessary now to realise that these symbols are not real in the sense that bread and butter are real but are tools for realisation. Reality probably cannot be reached without such tools. Words like 'loving Father', 'God', 'Creator', 'Redeemer', are of this type. Faith is necessary to relearn how to trust that part of oneself from which healing and wholeness and creativity come (People take pills for every headache, plan every moment, and allow nothing to happen of its own accord, just because they do not any longer trust life to bring

---

[63] *The Friend* vol.126 No.10 March 8th 1968 p.269

[64] *The Friend* vol.128 No.45 November 6th 1970 p.1338

forth        healing          and        abundant          life).
Those who invite life and embrace it trustingly, giving
themselves wholeheartedly to others in love and friendliness, will
find themselves eaten up in the process; but in losing themselves in
unselfishness and outgoing action they discover their own
meaning.[65]

Hendley writes in her article 'Its time to Quake', to which I have already
referred, that: "God is offering you his plan of salvation today; Christ" and that
she had come to realise that: ".... through the cross Christ had died for my sins
because God knew that on my own I would never be worthy of eternal life".[66]

In an article entitled 'Thinking of Salvation' published in *The Friend* on
August 14th 1981 Annie M.C.Elliott depicts God's saving activity in
conservationist terms, saying that God:

saves us as we save milk bottle tops or paper, so that we might be
used in a new role. I always find it easier to avoid abstract nouns,
so abandoning the word 'salvation', I think instead of the verb 'to
save'. Certainly, the interpretation given by others is there: we
speak of being saved from disaster, death itself, and pray to God,
'Our help, our salvation' that we may be delivered from evil. Yet,
leaving out this aspect for the moment, I turn to the other, everyday
meanings of the word. We 'save' stamps or dried flowers for
instance to make a precious collection; we 'save' paper or milk
bottle tops for recycling, in order to make some new material or
manufactured object; we 'save' money so as to buy something we
really want, or just in case we might need it at some later time.
It seems that God is the supreme saver and ecologist: he
saves us as we save stamps, to make a collection of concerned
people; he saves us as we save milk bottle tops or paper, so that
we might be used in a new role; nothing is wasted, neither people
norevents..
This, for me, goes a long way towards my beginning to
understand the problem of suffering and the death of Christ, not
'willed' by a jealous God (in whom I refuse to believe) but used by
him to 'save' the rest of us that we too may be used in the setting up
of the Kingdom of Heaven.[67]

---

[65] *The Friend* vol.128 No.46 November 13th 1970 pp.1349-1350.

[66] *The Friend* vol.134 No.51 December 17th 1976 p.1469

[67] *The Friend* vol.141 No.11 March 18th 1983 p.317

In her booklet *Credo*, in which she seeks to re-express traditional Christian ideas so as to make them acceptable to those who have rejected fundamentalism, Joyce Neill understands salvation in terms of being safe.

> Salvation is a stumbling block to many, especially if 'being saved' is described as a sudden revelation which is quite outside the experience of many people. I have found this concept much easier to accept by using the related word 'safe' rather than saved. Not safe in the sense that nothing unpleasant or dangerous can happen, but in the knowledge that God - the Holy Spirit - Spiritual Power - is always there to support and sustain us through whatever may happen; we are safe because this power will enable us to cope. Then even hymns like 'Safe in the Arms of Jesus' become acceptable in one sense - we are safe and supported by the example and faith shown in the life of Jesus, and the metaphor of arms is, after all, a very old one: 'underneath are the everlasting arms'.[68]

The second point about the Quaker writers' treatment of salvation is that over recent years many of them have followed the example of Quaker Liberals such as Richardson and John Wilhelm Rowntree in rejecting the Evangelical beliefs that on the Cross Christ was punished for our sins, or offered Himself as a sacrifice for them, on the grounds that such beliefs are morally and theologically unacceptable. They have also rejected the other traditional beliefs that on the Cross Christ made satisfaction for our sins or ransomed us out of the power of the Devil.

The following quotations typify this rejection.

In her article 'Atonement and Redemption', published in *Quaker Monthly* in May 1965, Saxon Snell rejects the view that Christ's death was a sacrifice for our sins because "what kind of God would demand that the innocent should give his life for the guilty?", the view that Christ's death was the punishment for our sins because it "makes the Father of our Lord Jesus Christ a monster of injustice", the view that Christ's death was a ransom paid to the Devil because it "puts the devil on a bargaining equality with God", and the view that Christ's death made

---

[68] Joyce Neill *Credo* London: Quaker Home Service 1986 p.13

satisfaction for our sins because "Jesus did not represent God to us as an outraged dignitary, but as a loving father".[69]

Priestland writes in *Reasonable Uncertainty* that:

> I still meet clergy who insist that all of us, even the most evidently virtuous are so totally depraved that we deserve .... annihilation, and would indeed receive it at the hands of a just God were it not for the fact that Christ has 'paid the price for our sins - undergone the punishment in our place - sacrificed Himself for the world'. To me, that proposes a God who is unspeakably barbarous, but I am told that this is because I am presuming to judge Him in human terms, for after all he is responsible for our humanity and would be condemning His own work if He did otherwise. I suspect the savage view of God derived from an age when relatively little was understood of cause and effect, and a great many events must have seemed either miracles or divine punishments.[70]

Lampen writes in *Twenty Questions about Jesus* that two theories of the meaning of Christ's death emerged as the Church began to ask questions about what His death achieved.

The first theory held that on the Cross Christ set us free by paying the Devil the debt of eternal punishment which we owed him as the price for our sins. Lampen rejects this theory because:

> Theologically, it fails to justify the role and power (equal to God's) attributed to the devil; logically, it doesn't explain how Jesus' brief encounter with death is equivalent - not to our deaths, since we still die - but to everyone's fate in 'the world to come'.[71]

The second theory held that infinite recompense or 'satisfaction' is required because of the affront to God's holiness caused by our sins and that on the Cross Christ's death offered this recompense. Lampen rejects this theory also for five reasons. (1) It contradicts Jesus' description of God as a "loving and freely forgiving Father". (2) It is "morally unsatisfactory" to argue that innocent suffering can act as a recompense for sin. (3) It is "impersonal" because it depicts

---

[69] *Quaker Monthly* vol.44 No.5 May 1965 p.68

[70] Priestland op.cit. pp.60-61

[71] Lampen op.cit. pp.59-60

our salvation as a "legal deal" between the Father and the Son and does not take account either of the life and work of the historical Jesus or the moral strivings of individual human beings.  (4) It is "not clear what has changed" since Christian tradition still insists that people will be rewarded or punished as a result of their individual behaviour.  (5) It is "incomplete" because it does not take account of those who have had no opportunity to have faith in Jesus.[72]

It is true that in  *Quaker by Convincement* Hubbard indicates that some British Quakers do take the view that the Cross:   "shows the Son of God dying that we might be saved, bearing our sin and redeeming us by his sacrifice"[73] yet I have not found this understanding of the cross put forward by any British Quaker writer in the last thirty years.  It is also true that Hendley writes, as has been noted, that "through the cross Christ had died for my sins", but it is impossible to say whether or not she would accept any of the traditional theories of how Christ's death on the cross was an objective act of atonement.

The final point which should be noted is that almost no British Quaker writers over the last three decades have put forward the traditional Christian belief that at the last judgement there will be a separation between the saved and the damned, with the saved going to heaven and the damned going to hell.  I have only found two writers  who have put forward a belief in the possibility of people going to hell: Thomas Green in an article entitled 'Studies in Christian Belief 4 - Eternal Life' published in *Quaker Monthly* in August 1964,[74] and an anonymous Quaker in an article entitled 'Diversity of Belief United in Worship'  published in *Quaker Monthly* in January 1975.[75]

There are, I think, three reasons why almost no modern writers have accepted the idea of a separation between the saved and the damned at the last judgement.

Firstly, British Quakers are generally loath to be dogmatic about the nature of life after death.  As Gorman notes in *Introducing Quakers*:

---

[72] ibid p.60

[73] Hubbard op.cit. p.83

[74] *Quaker Monthly* vol.43 No.8 August 1964 pp. 121-122

[75] *Quaker Monthly* vol.54: 1 January 1975 pp.9-10

> There are Friends who are convinced that there is an after-life, and
> there are those who are convinced that there is not. All Friends feel
> that it is more important to get on with living this life, and seek to
> improve the conditions of man in this world than to engage in
> speculation about the next.[76]

Secondly, belief in a separation between the saved and the damned has seen
heaven and hell as reward or punishment for conduct in this life and British
Quakers are generally unhappy about the idea of the next life being a reward or
punishment for conduct in this one. To quote Gorman again:

> The hope of life after death has never been considered as a reward
> for virtue, nor as a compensation for adversity. Neither has the fear
> of damnation been used as a threat to induce godly living. Such
> ideas are wholly repugnant to Quakers.[77]

Or, as Hubbard writes in *Quaker by Convincement*:

One thing is quite certain. Quakers today would not ever offer the next life
as either reward or punishment or consolation for the life on earth.[78]

Thirdly, in response to the Victorian questioning of the morality of the idea
of eternal punishment, Liberal Quakers turned away from this idea. As we have
seen, Worsdell argues in *The Gospel of Divine Help* that there was a possibility of
salvation for those who died impenitent, and in *Christianity as Life* Grubb
interpreted Jesus' teaching about the Kingdom of God as meaning that in the end
all Men would repent and be saved. In similar fashion Wood declares in
*Quakerism and the Future of the Church* that: "we do not and we cannot preach
again the old doctrines of hell fire and eternal punishment".[79] In recent years a
number of Quaker writers have followed this Liberal lead and have argued that in
the end all will find salvation.

For example, Jesse Payne writes in an article entitled 'I Believe' published in
*Quaker Monthly* in December 1968 that:

---

[76] Gorman *Introducing Quakers* p.371

[77] ibid p.37

[78] Hubbard op.cit. p.104

[79] Wood *Quakerism and the Future of the Church* p.24

Because choice is an essential element in human personality I
accept the possibility of eternal punishment which would be eternal
separation from God, but paradoxically I cannot believe that a
single human soul could continue to choose separation for ever. If
not in the world as we know it, then in the future life, even the
coldest and most unloving person would be unable finally to resist
the abiding love of God.[80]

As a further example, Harrison states in an article entitled 'Love
Immeasurable' published in *The Friend* on April 30th 1971 that:

If 'God is a consuming fire', then he is a consuming fire of love,
devoid of all wrath, all vengeance, all penal exactions; whose
judgments are all judgments of love, and whose mercy is implicit in
his love. It is now almost impossible to understand the harshness
which once sustained the belief in hell and eternal punishment,
condemning countless millions of men to everlasting damnation for
their human frailties, for being born in a heathen country, or for
refusing to accept a penal orthodoxy. Modern genetics and
psychology, as well as sober common sense, have long since
discredited a belief which is the survival of a medieval phobia.[81]

## Conclusions

I draw four main conclusions from this sample of Quaker writings.

The first and most obvious conclusion is that there has been nothing
approaching a concensus of opinion on any of the topics in question. I have
explored the reasons for such diversity at the end of the last chapter and there is no
need to comment further here.

The second conclusion is that in spite of this diversity their thinking has on
the whole departed from the core of conviction and the teaching of the early
Quakers.

On the subject of Revelation the early Quakers agreed with the core of
conviction that Jesus Christ gives us the definitive revelation of God and, in spite
of their subordination of the Bible to the Internal Monitor, the early Quakers also
agreed with the core of conviction in seeing the Bible as a God given and therefore

---

[80] *Quaker Monthly* vol.47 No.12 December 1968 p.66

[81] *The Friend* vol.129 No.18 April 30th 1971 p.493

definitive rule of faith and practice.  While some recent Quaker writers have agreed that Jesus Christ and the Bible do have a definitive role in revealing God to us, British Quaker theology as a whole has not been committed to this idea and has, instead, encompassed a variety of opinions about how revelation occurs and about the importance of Christ and the Bible in revealing God to us.

On the subject of God the early Quakers agreed with the core of conviction that God has an independent existence apart from Man and that He is to be understood in Trinitarian terms.  As is shown by the extracts from James, Lea and York given in this chapter, a number of recent Quaker writers have challenged the idea of the independent existence of God.  Furthermore, the majority of British Quaker writers have taken a Unitarian rather than a Trinitarian view of God.

The early Quakers, in spite of their unorthodox Christology, agreed with the core of conviction in believing that Christ was God as well as Man and in accepting at face value the miraculous elements in the Gospel stories.  As I have argued in this chapter, only a minority of recent British Quaker writers have seen Christ as God incarnate and indeed many of them have not even seen Him as having unique importance as a human being.  In addition, many of them have been sceptical or agnostic about the historicity of the miracle stories in the Gospels, particularly the stories of Christ's virgin birth and bodily resurrection, and a number have rejected belief in Christ's moral and intellectual perfection.

The early Quakers agreed with the core of conviction in believing that, as a result of the Fall, Mankind has been tainted and depraved by original sin.  In contrast, as I have shown in this chapter, British Quaker writers over the past thirty years have generally rejected the idea that there ever was a historical Fall of Man and have also rejected the idea that Man is tainted and depraved by original sin.

Lastly, on the subject of Salvation, the first Quakers followed the core of conviction in using the traditional picture of Christ's being a sacrifice offered to God for the sin of the world and in accepting the idea that there would be a separation between the saved and the damned at the last judgement.  Recent British Quaker writers, on the other hand, have been unhappy with the idea and indeed with all the traditional images used to express the significance of the Cross. Furthermore, they have not generally affirmed the belief that in the next life there will be a separation between the saved and the damned with the damned going to Hell.

The third conclusion is that the reason for many of these disagreements between the thinking of modern Quakers and the beliefs contained in the core of conviction and the teaching of the early Quakers is the influence of the Liberal Quaker tradition. As I have indicated, the fact that Quakers see the Bible as a record of human religious experience rather than as the infallible Word of God, their tendency to Unitarian views of God, the attempts made by some of them to re-interpret the resurrection stories, their rejection of belief in a historical Fall and in the consequent depravity of Man, their general rejection of traditional interpretations of the death of Christ and the assertion by a number of them that in the end all will be saved, all reflect ideas put forward by Liberal Quaker writers at the end of the last century and at the beginning of this.

The reflection of such ideas is not necessarily due to the works of these writers having been widely read by British Quakers over the past thirty years. I have found no evidence that this has been the case, even though these works are undoubtedly still read by some Quakers. On the other hand it is not simply due to coincidence. The explanation is, instead, that when Liberalism became dominant within British Quakerism in the early years of this century such ideas entered the mainstream of British Quaker thinking and have continued to shape Quaker theology ever since.

The fourth conclusion is that the influence of Quaker Liberalism is also indirectly responsible for British Quaker writers over the last thirty years disagreeing with the core of conviction and the teaching of the early Quakers in ways that go beyond Quaker Liberalism. The questioning or rejection of ideas such as the centrality of Christ and the Bible in revelation, the independent existence of God, the Divinity of Christ, His unique religious significance and His intellectual and moral perfection, all features of British Quaker theology in recent years, represent disagreements with the core of conviction and early Quaker teaching which are not to be found in Quaker Liberalism. Nevertheless, they are indebted to two aspects of the Liberal tradition.

Firstly, as I noted at the end of the last chapter, Quaker Liberalism established a tradition of intellectual tolerance which has allowed radical Quaker thinkers the freedom to develop their own ideas.

Secondly, one of the key principles of Liberal Quakerism has been the belief that Quaker theology needs to adapt to fit in with the development of contemporary thought. Radical Quaker thinkers have felt that the application of this principle has demanded a greater departure from the beliefs of the core of conviction and from the early Quaker tradition than was undertaken by the Liberals, and this has led them to go beyond Liberalism in the ways I have described.

At the end of the last chapter I explained that the ideas of the Quaker radicals reflected the questioning of traditional Christian beliefs by non-Quaker theologians.

In respect of the topics I have examined in this chapter this is true in two ways.

Firstly, the thinking of Quaker radicals has been directly influenced by the work of non-Quakers. For example, Miles' view in *Towards Universalism* that insistence on the unique importance of Christ is parochial is influenced by the work of John Hick[82], and Neill's view in her booklet *Credo* that Jesus is to be seen simply as a "holy man with exceptional gifts and insights" is influenced by the books of the Jewish New Testament scholar Geza Vermes.[83]

Secondly, the questioning of traditional Christian beliefs by Quaker radicals has reflected similar questioning by non-Quakers not because of direct influence but simply because both are responding to the same challenges to the Christian tradition.

The Quaker radicals' questioning of the importance of the Bible reflects the fact that all theologions, whether Quaker or non-Quaker, have been faced with the challenge of trying to work out the status of the Bible in a world in which, as

---

[82] See Miles op.cit. pp.4-6 quoting John Hick 'Towards a philosophy of religious pluralism' in *Faith and Freedom* 34:3:102 1981 pp.139-56 and *Christ in a Universe of Faiths* Leicester: Quaker Universalist Group N.D.

[83] See Neill op.cit.p.7 referring to Geza Vermes *Jesus the Jew* London: S.C.M. 1983, *The Dead Sea Scrolls* London: S.C.M. 1982 and *Jesus and the World of Judaism* London: S.C.M. 1983.

James Barr notes in his book *The Bible in the Modern World*, people are now asking:

> Why the Bible? Why should a group of ancient books have this dominant status? If a group of ancient books, then why this group of ancient books? And why in any case should anyone suppose that any objective external authority, in the shape of a group of books, or any other shape, exist at all?[84]

Their questioning of the independent existence of God reflects the fact that all theologians have had to try to find a picture of God that is meaningful in a world in which, to quote Langdon Gilkey:

> Almost every dominant motif and movement in modernity - its expanding scientific inquiry, its emphasis on what is natural, experienced and verifiable, its persistent search for the greater well-being of human beings in this world, its increasing emphasis on autonomy and on present satisfaction - has progressively challenged the concept of God and unsettled both its significance and certainty.[85]

Lastly, their questioning of traditional views of Christ reflects the fact that all theologians have had to come to terms with the challenge to such views posed by issues such as the criticial investigation of the New Testament and early Christian thought, the fact that the language of traditional Christology often seems unintelligible, the impact of a greater awareness of the non-Christian religions and the fact that a number of feminist theologians now claim that the Christian emphasis on 'God the Son' reflects and reinforces a male bias in theology.[86]

---

[84] James Barr *The Bible in the Modern World* London: S.C.M. 1973 p.36.

[85] Langdon Gilkey 'God' in Peter Hodgson and Robert King (eds) *Christian Theology* London: S.P.C.K. 1983 p.62.

[86] For a useful survey of such issues see John Bowden *Jesus – The Unanswered Questions* London: S.C.M. 1988.

# Chapter Six
# A Contemporary Statement

In the last two chapters I have shown how developments in British Quaker theology since 1895 have resulted, over the last thirty years, in a theology which is marked both by diversity and by a general divergence from the core of conviction and the teaching of the early Quakers. In this chapter I shall show how Scott's Swarthmore Lecture epitomizes recent British Quaker theology by accurately reflecting both these trends.

### Divergence

In her 1980 Swarthmore Lecture, Scott reflects the ways in which contemporary British Quakerism has diverged from the core of conviction and the teaching of the early Quakers in her treatment of the topics of Revelation, God, Christ, Man and Salvation.

### Revelation

As we have seen, the core of conviction and early Quaker teaching both gave a central and definitive place in the revelation of God to Jesus Christ and the Bible. Scott, by contrast, reflects the position taken by a number of radical British Quakers in recent years by rejecting this idea.

In her view, God is made known to us through a potentially infinite series of mental constructs which she calls: "God's models" and which are: "signs or symbols which lead us to various aspects of God's being".[1]  These models can be understood in two ways.  On the one hand they can be seen as "the ways of revelation, how God is self-revealed to us" and on the other they are also  "the ways of experience, how God is met, known, understood and interpreted in human life".[2]

Scott includes Jesus Christ and the Bible among "God's models".  She declares that if we see Christ as a model for God we can see that this model "...reveals God as reaching out to humanity, as working 'to seek and to save the lost'.  It reveals the unexpected qualities of God, the upsetting of human values and order".[3]  She sees this as a valuable model because by revealing:  "the involvement of God with the criminal, the suffering, the oppressed, with all that is unlovely in human life".[4]  It provides  "...a sure ground of hope, a strong basis for community and an invitation to abandon certainty and to live with risk".[5]

She also argues that the Bible has value as a model for God because it links us to religious experience of Biblical characters such as Abraham, Elijah and Ruth and:

> As we share the important moments of their lives, the dimensions of our experience are opened up.  We learn from their discoveries and mistakes and join in the search for permanent values, for 'the true religion which doth never change' and for the spirit from which they come.  We are more assured of that spirit constantly at work and of the variety of ways in which the divine is known.[6]

However, Scott does not regard either Christ or the Bible as definitive models of God.  She includes Christ as only one among a number of models of revelation which she discusses, the others being: "the universe and the natural world", "the community", "history", "the scriptures" and "worship".[7]  She also sees

---

[1] Scott op.cit.p.63

[2] ibid p.63.

[3] ibid p.70 referring to Lk 19:10

[4] ibid p.70

[5] ibid p.70

[6] ibid p.68 referring to George Fox, Epistle 171 (1659)

[7] ibid p.64.

the Bible as only a sub-set of "the scriptures" since this model is used by her to encompass: "the sacred and significant writings of all faiths".[8]

The reason she does not give a central place to either Christ or the Bible is twofold.

Firstly, she uses Christ as only one of a number of revelatory models because she believes that it is very important to recognise that: "there are a number of models of the truth" which are equally valid.[9] Recognising this, according to Scott, has four valuable consquences.
It means:

> We are saying ... no one form of words, no one concept, no one belief or set of beliefs can possibly contain or describe the whole of God's truth. And this is true to Quaker experience.[10]

It means:

> ...we become open to growth and development as we recognise that our intellectual views are provisional and not unchallenged. We realise there are choices.[11]

It means:

> ...our freedom is preserved by other people's freedom. Wherever one belief gains a monopoly position in a state it seems to seek to uphold itself by persecution. When we look at the sad history of mankind, and unfortunately the sad present, we see so many examples of attempts to crush minorities. The freedom to be different is very precious and very fragile.[12]

Lastly, the freedom to choose between models "...preserves our free will and integrity towards God. It is consistent with a concept of God as wishing us to enter freely into relationship".[13]

---

[8] ibid p.67

[9] ibid p.19

[10] ibid p.19

[11] ibid p.19

[12] ibid pp.19-20

[13] ibid p.20

Secondly, she puts the Bible on the same level as the sacred books of the non-Christian religions because, in line with what we have seen to be the attitude of a number of contemporary Quakers and theologians of other denominations, she holds that we must give equal importance to these religions alongside Christianity:

> We are learning the value of other faiths and in meeting and knowing Jews, Sikhs, Muslims, Hindus, in seeing their courage and devotion, we are discovering in a much more personal way that we must respect the light given to others and look for unity with them.[14]

## God

On the subject of God, Scott diverges from the core of conviction and the teaching of the early Quakers because, in line with the Liberal Quaker tradition and the majority of contemporary British Quaker writers, she declines to take a Trinitarian view of God.

She acknowledges that the Trinitarian model of God does have some advantages because:

> In trying to incorporate our different experiences of God it includes relationship in God and so sees in divinity some of the personal qualities we value in humanity. And it allows within one model for both the transcend-ence of God and for our knowledge through revelation and experience.[15]

Despite these positive aspects of the Trinitarian model she nevertheless rejects belief in the Trinity for five reasons.

Firstly, she seems to identify the Athanasian creed as the traditional doctrine of the Trinity and she declares that the words of this creed:

> ...are not exact terms and when the creed was being formulated were taken to have different meanings by different groups. Indeed,

---

[14] ibid p.11

[15] ibid p.50

I strongly suspect that the formulation is successful only as long as no one asks too closely what it means.[16]

Secondly, she complains that although the creed:

...relates Christ and God in godhead it leaves unsolved their relationship in Manhood. There is still no satisfactory way of explaining how the human Jesus could also be the incarnate God.[17]

Thirdly, she claims that the doctrine of the Trinity: "has caused many splits in the Christian Church".[18] As examples she cites the power struggles associated with the Arian controversy in the fourth century, the excommunication of the Monophysite Churches in the fifth century, and the split between the Latin and Byzantine Churches in the eleventh century, partly caused by their dispute over the addition of the filioque clause to the Nicene-Constantinoplian Creed.

Fourthly, she further suggests that the doctrine has also caused a split between Christians and those of other religions. As evidence she says that: "over the centuries the charge that Jesus killed God has led to horrific consequences" and that: "Muslims find it difficult to see how the Trinity can be reconciled with monotheism".[19] Scott views the charge that the doctrine of the Trinity divides Christians from those of other faiths as important because she accepts the idea put forward by Hick in *The Myth of God Incarnate* that:

...we are being called today to attain a global religious vision which is aware of the unity of all mankind before God and which at the same time makes sense of the divinity of God's ways within the various streams of human life.[20]

---

[16] ibid pp.49-50

[17] ibid p.50

[18] ibid p.50

[19] ibid p.51

[20] ibid p.51 quoting Hick (ed) *The Myth of God Incarnate* p.180

By causing division between Christianity and other faiths the doctrine of the Trinity obviously makes the attainment of this vision more difficult.

Fifthly, she contends that the doctrine limits God:

> It gives the impression that God can be understood and described. But 'the nature of God is incommensurable with human ways of thought'. We come always to the point where words fail, where definitions are inadequate, where omnia exeunt in mysterium.[21]

In place of a Trinitarian view of God Scott suggests three linguistic models: God as noun, God as adjective and God as verb.

She argues that the use of the word God as a *noun*: "emphasises above all God's transcendence and difference from us"[22] and refers to: "the creator God of whom we use words such as majesty, power, glory, eternal, infinite, ineffable".[23]

By contrast the use of the word God as an *adjective* points us to: "the immanent aspect of God, the divine to be found in all creation and in all people".[24]

In her view:

> ...we need both of these models to balance each other, the outer and the inner, the transcendent and the immanent, the terror and the tenderness, the glory and the vision. But even this is not sufficient to describe our experience of God. For this we need to add the third model, God as *verb*.[25]

She notes that: "one verb that is frequently used of God is Being, sometimes extended by Becoming",[26] and in line with her desire to seek unity with those of other faiths she refuses to exclude this way of speaking about God because it:

---

[21] ibid p.51 quoting the German Lutheran theologian Hans Lietzmann in his work *A History of the Early Church* vol.4 London: Lutterworth Press 1951 p.49.

[22] ibid p.76

[23] ibid p.76

[24] ibid p.78

[25] ibid p.80

[26] ibid p.80

...may well be a model through which we can reach fellowship with
those who practice the meditative and contemplative aspects of
God such as Hinduism and Buddhism (perhaps especially those
Theravada Buddhists whose belief includes no God).[27]

However she thinks it "...more true to our Quaker experience to speak of God in
terms of transitive verbs of action, as a dynamic spirit acting towards us".[28]   A
usage which refers to:

...the God who is at work in the world, in history, and in every
human being, initiating and sustaining the cosmic drama, creating
and saving.[29]

Scott recognises that these three linguistic models of God are inadequate,
both when considered invidiually and when taken together.   Nevertheless, using
them to balance one another:

...we may hope to be brought closer to the truth in holding the
tension of simultaneous models, the transcendent, the immanent and
the active;   the greatness and the closeness, the beyond and the
within, the dynamic and the resting.[30]

Finally, and reflecting the Liberal Quaker emphasis on religious experience,
she contends that the truth to which her models point is one that cannot be reached
through words but only through a living relationship with the God whom we
encounter in the silence of the Quaker meeting for worship:

in the end, this is the truth not of words but of response, of the
living relationship of worship, love, trust and hope, of God in us
and we in God, caught up out of self and out of time into the
foreshadowing of what shall be and ever is.  We are called to turn
to that tenderest compassion, that inexpressible story, that most

---

[27] ibid p.80-81

[28] ibid p.81

[29] ibid p.81

[30] ibid p.82

profound humility, that deepest friendship, that truest vision, to the God who meets us, whom we know, in the silence waiting.[31]


## Christ

Scott, like the majority of British Quakers in recent years, diverges from the core of conviction and the teaching of the early Quakers in that she sees Christ as Man rather than God.

Like the Quaker Liberals Scott bases her Christology on what can be known about the man Jesus as a result of the historical investigation of the Gospels. However, unlike Rendel Harris or Grubb, she takes a pessimistic view of what such investigation can tell us, declaring that  "...the results of modern Biblical study show us that we can know for certain very little about Jesus".[32]   This scepticism concerning the amount we can know about the historical Jesus reflects the opinions of radical New Testament scholars such as the German Lutheran scholar Rudolf Bultmann,[33] which had been popularised in this country by the Anglican scholar Dennis Nineham in his Pelican Commentary on Mark's Gospel published in 1963.[34]

On the basis of what she thinks we can know about Jesus, Scott agrees with those recent British writers who have rejected the idea that Jesus can be said to have been either intellectually or morally perfect.

She rejects the idea of His intellectual perfection because:

> Such evidence as we have tells us that Jesus was a man of his time, limited by the knowledge and culture available to him.  He was not perfect in knowledge or in his interpretation of religion - there were times when he said things we regard as mistaken.[35]

---

[31] ibid p.82

[32]v ibid p.55.

[33] See Rudolph Bultmann *Jesus and the Word* London and Glasgow: Fontana 1958 p.14 and I.Howard Marshall *I believe in the Historical Jesus* London: Hodder and Stoughton 1977 ch.6.

[34] D.E.Nineham *St.Mark* Harmondsworth: Penguin 1963

[35] Scott op.cit. p.55

She likewise rejects the idea that His behaviour was perfect on the ground that "if we apply the words 'good' and 'loving' to Jesus we are using the words in unusual ways".[36] She gives two reasons for this view.

Firstly, if we look at Jesus' life we can see that He only demonstrated love in a limited way:

> There is no evidence of any family love. He is not known to have married and he quarrelled with his mother and brothers. There is no evidence of the love involved in stable community living. Much of the evidence of his compassion is in situations such as healing miracles which we cannot emulate. There is no evidence to suggest that his death was a result of love for humanity.[37]

Scott concedes that there is evidence of: "love towards friends and the outcasts of society and those who were seeking God" but argues that her point still stands because "this is not the whole meaning of the word 'love'".[38]

Secondly, she argues that it is difficult to say that Jesus was good because good behaviour is, as Kant said, that behaviour which is good at all times and everywhere and this is not true of Jesus' behaviour:

> How much of the behaviour of Jesus is this sort of example? We surely cannot suggest that the ideal behaviour for everyone is to be a celibate, jobless, miracle worker?[39]

Having agreed with those British Quakers who deny that Jesus was intellectually and morally perfect, she further agrees with those who are unwilling to grant Him any uniquely significant place in religion. She does this in three ways.

In the first place, she rejects the claim made by Macquarrie in his *Principles of Christian Theology* that Jesus can be said to be "definitive":

> 'In the sense that for Christians he defines both the nature of man _ and the nature of God'. 'In Christ there is an entire constellation of

---

[36] ibid p.55

[37] ibid pp.55-6

[38] ibid p.56

[39] ibid p.56

qualities which we recognise as constituting the essence of authentic personal being'.[40]

She argues that Jesus cannot be an adequate model for what Macquarrie calls "authentic personal being", a term which he uses to describe the adequate fulfilment of human potential. This is because although Jesus can show us how to face death He cannot:

> ...be a model for the fulness of human life. No one person can represent the authenticity which we find in community, and especially in our closest relationships such as friendship,marriage and parenthood.[41]

Furthermore, reflecting the influence on Scott of the women's movement and particularly the work of the American feminist theologian Mary Daly,[42] she says:

> ...the use of Jesus as definitive for the nature of Man means that a whole half of humanity is left out. Not only as women robbed of the authenticity of their deepest experiences, in particular the experience of childbirth, but the model of humanity and of God is robbed of the qualities which women have to offer.[43]

The second way in which Scott agrees with those unwilling to grant any unique significance to Christ is by arguing that if we consider Jesus as a historical individual there was really nothing unique about him:

> ...he was not unique in the sense that there is nothing in his teachings and actions that has not been seen in some other life. There have been other martyrs, other teachers, others who have forgiven those who harmed them, other workers of miracles, others reported as raised from the dead.[44]

---

[40] ibid p.56 quoting Macquarrie *Principles of Christian Theology* revd.ed. pp.303-5.

[41] ibid p.56

[42] Scott specifically refers to Daly's work *Beyond God the Father* Boston: Beacon Press 1977.

[43] Scott op.cit. p.57

[44] ibid pp.57-58

It is true that Scott is prepared to concede uniqueness to what she calls the "Christ-event", an expression she employs as a shorthand for the impact which Jesus' "life and death, the resurrection experience and the impetus to follow him" have continued to have in the life of the Christian Church in "a whole complex of response and interpretation based on an historical event, and still going on today".[45]  However, she nevertheless insists that in the context of the "Christ-event":

> What is important about Jesus is what we respond to in our most profound religious moments.[46]

Whereas the Christian tradition has seen Jesus as possessing unique importance in Himself, for Scott the important issue is our response to Him as part of the continuing 'Christ event' and Jesus only has significance as the historical catalyst for this response.

The third way in which Scott denies unique significance to Christ is by denying that the revelation of God given to us by Jesus through the 'Christ event' is the: "only, or the final revelation".[47]  As I have already noted, she makes this point in her treatment of the subject of Revelation, but she also makes it in her treatment of the subject of Christ.

After discussing the 'Christ event' Scott puts forward two ways of describing the importance of Jesus within it.  The first, which is influenced by the book *God as Spirit* by the Anglican theologian G.W.H.Lampe,[48] describes Jesus as "the inspired Man".[49]  He is seen as the one who enables us to recognise the universal workings of God's Spirit because "He placed his life and talents at God's disposal in such a way that the spirit of God was made manifest more clearly than ever before".[50]

---

[45] ibid p.58

[46] ibid p.58

[47] ibid p.61

[48] G.W.H.Lampe *God as Spirit* Oxford OUP 1977

[49] Scott op.cit. p.58

[50] ibid p.58

The second way of describing Jesus is as the "bearer of revelation", a description which draws on the work of Macquarrie.[51] According to Scott, Jesus can be described in this way since:

> Through the response to the spirit seen in his life and death, words and deeds, he became the vehicle through which the nature of God was disclosed to us.[52]

Both of these ways of looking at Jesus see Him as someone who reveals God to us. However, Scott rejects the uniqueness and finality of this revelation again for two reasons.

Firstly, she argues that it cannot be seen as the only revelation of God because the traditional Quaker idea that the Internal Monitor or "Inner Light" is present in everyone entails the belief that "...we must see God's self disclosure in many ways and lives and a world wide possibility of interpreting the ways of God".[53] and this belief is borne out in practice because in fact:

> God is revealed not only in well known ways,the Exodus, the Exile, through Muhammed, Buddha, Gandhi, Guru Nanak, George Fox, but in countless millions of happenings and people wherever we have eyes to see.[54]

Secondly, she contends that those who wish to say that the revelation of God given through the Christ event is "the most significant" revelation are expressing a subjective value judgment which has no absolute validity because "We cannot judge God's interactions with others - only marvel at the infinite variety and creativity of the divine spirit".[55]

---

[51] ibid p.59 referring to Macquarrie *Priniples of Christian Theology* revd.ed. p.7

[52] Scott op.cit. p.59

[53] ibid p.61

[54] ibid p.61

[55] ibid p.61

**Man**

On this subject Scott departs from the core of conviction and the teaching of the early Quakers in that, like the Quaker Liberals and most contemporary Quakers, she does not believe either that there was a historical Fall of Man or that Mankind is tainted and depraved by original sin.

She holds that the story of the Fall in Genesis 3 represents an attempt to explain the presence of suffering in the world by blaming it on ancestral sin and that this story: "can in no sense be regarded as literally true".[56]

She agrees that human beings "...can be cruel or oppressive, can have all the faults of pride, selfishness and greed which have traditionally been called sin".[57] but she finds the traditional Christian belief that human nature is so sinful as to deserve punishment from God to be unacceptable. She identifies this belief with the idea that human beings are so sinful as to be incapable of doing anything good and she dismisses this latter idea for four reasons.

Firstly, she argues that it runs contrary to Quaker tradition. In support of this contention she cites a study of George Fox's teaching by the American Quaker scholar Rachel H.King in which King notes that:

Fox could not accept any description of Man's nature that "takes away his responsibility for sin by making him incapable of doing good".[58] and also quotes Grubb's rejection of the doctrine of total human depravity which I noted in my last chapter.[59]

Secondly, she claims that both current educational theory and Quaker experience show that it is necessary to believe in the "basic goodness" of human beings because:

---

[56] ibid pp.29 and 38

[57] ibid p.38

[58] ibid p.38 citing Rachel H.King *George Fox and the Light Within* Philadelphia: Friends Book Store 1940 p.41

[59] ibid p.38 see above p.298 footnote 59

> ...if we regard people as fundamentally sinful that is what they are
> likely to become.  If we regard them as capable of love and
> goodness and trust, these are the capacities that they develop.[60]

Thirdly, she further claims that taking a pessimistic view of human nature
has had terrible consequences. The belief that people are sinful and so are hated by
God has provided the rationalisation for the persecution of: "heretics and witches
and Jews" and the belief that they need to be saved from their sinfulness "...has
supported the Inquisition and that type of paternalistic evangelism that has led
directly to colonialism and exploitation".[61]

Again revealing the influence of feminist thinking, she also observes that
the Fall story, with its record of the sin of Eve, has been used as an excuse for the
subordination of women by the Church.[62]

Fourthly, she notes that if taken to the extreme:

> ...any belief that human beings are incapable of goodness destroys
> the motivation for moral actions and makes a mockery or our
> experience that there are many people who are good, loving, caring,
> and responsible.[63]

Having for these reasons rejected the understanding of the human
predicament held by the core of conviction and the early Quakers she suggests that
what we need in its place is a description of human nature: "which will be both true
to experience and a basis for ethical interaction".[64]  As a contribution to such a
description she puts forward an inclusive interpretation of the parable of the
Prodigal Son[65]:

---

[60] ibid p.38 referring to Robert Rosenthal and Lenore Jacobson *Pygmalion in the Classroom*
Eastbourne: Holt-Saunders 1968.

[61] ibid p.39

[62] ibid p.39 giving as examples 1 Timothy 2:11-14 and Tertullian *De Cultu
Feminarum* 1.1

[63] ibid p.39

[64] ibid p.39

[65] Lk 15:11-32

The parable of the two sons may help here - it is usually known as 'The Prodigal Son', but it is in fact about two brothers, the elder of whom, who is often neglected, stayed close to the father and worked for him. And despite his annoyance at the reception given to the returning prodigal, he was reassured by the father, 'Child, you are always with me and all that is mine is yours'. Though the brothers were different in their motivations and their actions we should not stress the difference. They were brothers and there was room for both in the father's house. Any way of looking at human nature must seek the unity between us. In our goodness and our sins we are all the children ofGod.[66]

## Salvation

On the subject of Salvation, Scott, like the Quaker Liberals and many contemporary Quakers, disagrees with the core of conviction and early Quaker teaching in that she regards the traditional images used to describe the saving significance of Christ's death as both theologically and morally unsatisfactory. Specifically, she rejects the traditional pictures of Christ as: "the punished, the redeemer and the sacrifice"[67] on four grounds.

First of all, she makes the general point that while all three pictures depict Christ as saving us from something, it is difficult to see what that something might be. In her view it is not from death: "for we still die", nor is it from sin: "for we still sin", nor is it from suffering for suffering is not: "a punishment for sin sent by God from which we might seek to be saved but is something permitted by God as part of His providential purposes".[68]

Secondly, she argues that if we see Jesus: "redeeming or buying us out of the power of sin" this implies that: "there is a power as strong as God".[69]

Thirdly, she declares that if we depict Jesus as a "sacrifice" this means that we are suggesting that God: " is a wrathful vengeful deity who has to be bought off with the blood of the innocent", an idea which was rejected by the prophet

---

[66] Scott op.cit. pp.39-40

[67] ibid p.40

[68] ibid p.40. Scott has already outlined the idea of suffering as providential on pp.29-35 of her lecture.

[69] ibid p.40

Hosea and by Jesus Himself in their teaching that God requires mercy and love rather than sacrifices.[70]

Fourthly, and reflecting the idea of cultural relativism, she contends that taken metaphorically rather than literally these pictures may have had "striking force" for the early church because they were drawn from the contemporary culture, but for us they have no value even as metaphor because they do not correspond to anything in our culture and experience.[71]

Although she rejects these traditional pictures of Christ as saviour, she is willing to follow in the footsteps of Liberal Quakers such as John Wilhelm Rowntree and Edward Grubb and say that: "Jesus was saviour because he demonstrated the love of God and in so doing caused people to turn to God and seek reconciliation".[72]   However, in line with her radical rejection of the unique importance of Christ which I have already noted, she qualifies this picture of the saving work of Christ by insisting that it means that Jesus' death was not necessary for people to be saved and reconciled to God.  As she puts it:

> It implies that the death of Jesus brought about no fundamental change in God's saving will;  that is, it was always God's intention to save, so that the death of Jesus was not necessary for salvation.
> It also implies, from the very fact that the knowledge of Jesus is not worldwide, that this is not the only means of reconciliation and this is not necessary to reconciliation.[73]

In conclusion Scott declares that:

> Jesus may be called 'saviour', but only in the sense that he leads us towards the salvation which is offered by God.   Any other interpretation runs into profound difficulties.[74]

---

[70] ibid p.40 referring to Hosea 6:6 and Mk 12:32-34.

[71] ibid pp.40-41

[72] ibid p.41 compare the quotations from Rowntree and Grubb on pp.126-7 and 170 above.

[73] ibid p.41

[74] ibid p.41

Having said that Jesus leads us towards the salvation offered by God, Scott then proceeds to explain the nature of this salvation. Building on the theology put forward by the second century Father Irenaeus of Lyons and the twentieth century Anglican theologian Leonard Hodgson in their works *Adversus Omnes Haereses* and *For faith and freedom*[75], and reiterating a point she has already made, she maintains that we should not see salvation in terms of being saved from death and suffering since these are necessary conditions for our spiritual growth. Instead, she argues, we should see salvation: "not as a saving from but as a saving to".[76]

In accordance with her view that the truth about God is ultimately ineffable she declares that that to which we are saved is finally "inexpressible",[77] but she nevertheless agrees with Lampe's definition of salvation as:

> Æ that part or aspect of the divine creative activity by which man comes to be informed by God's presence, made in his image and likeness, and led to respond with trust and willing obedience to the love and graciousness of his creator.[78]

Scott agrees with the Quaker Liberal tradition and with the majority of contemporary Quakers in that, unlike the core of conviction and the teaching of the early Quakers, she does not put forward the idea that there will be a final separation between the saved and the lost. In her case this is because she accepts the contention of Hick in his book *Evil and the God of Love* that the doctrine of Hell implies either that God does not wish to save everyone and is therefore not good or cannot and therefore lacks power and must in consequence be rejected in favour of the idea that in the end all will be saved.[79]

---

[75] Iranaeus *Adversus Omnes Haereses* in A.Roberts and J.Donaldson eds. *The Ante-Nicene Fathers* vol.1 Grand Rapids: Eerdmans 1981 and Leonard Hodgson *For faith and freedom* London: SCM 1968

[76] Scott op.cit.p.44

[77] ibid p.44

[78] ibid pp.44-5 quoting Lampe op.cit.p.17

[79] ibid p.45 quoting John Hick *Evil and the God of Love* London: Macmillan 1977 2ed. p.378ff.

In summary, we can say that Scott's treatment of these five subjects reflects in two ways the divergence of contemporary British Quakerism from the core of conviction and the teaching of the early Quakers.

Firstly, the Universalist and Unitarian theology which she puts forward, with its depiction of Christ as ultimately only a flawed human being, its rejection of the fallenness and depravity of Man and of the necessity of Christ's death for salvation and its belief that in the end all will be saved, mirrors very precisely the ways in which recent British Quakerism as a whole has departed from the core of conviction and early Quaker teaching.

Secondly, Scott's theology also mirrors the reasons behind this departure in the way in which it builds on the Quaker Liberal tradition and is influenced by the writings of non-Quaker theologians and by contemporary movements of thought such as feminism and the growth of dialogue and unity between the world's religions.

## Diversity

Scott's Swarthmore Lecture also reflects the diversity of contemporary British Quakerism in two ways.

In the first place her lecture reflects this diversity by contributing to it. Her treatment of Revelation, God, Christ, Man and Salvation differs from the way in which other Quaker writers have treated them and therefore makes its own contribution to the diversity of modern British Quakerism. For example, I have found no other British Quaker writer who has either anticipated or followed her use of verbal models for God.

In the second place, and more importantly, Scott attempts in her lecture to bridge the major division which exists in contemporary British Quakerism. As we saw in Chapter Four, this division is between the radical wing, which has moved away from traditional Christian beliefs and has tended towards universalism, and the conservative wing which has remained more traditionally Christian in emphasis. Scott herself belongs to the radical wing but at four points in her lecture she seeks to take into account the views of those who are more conservative and to integrate these into her theology, so that, in her words, she can "achieve a Quaker theology for this generation ... that has room for both a Christian and a Universalist emphasis".[80]

The first of these points comes after she declares that "... there is no need in Quakerism for a doctrine of redemption through Christ or a doctrine of the Trinity".[81]    She notes that "some Friends may find this conclusion slightly shocking, not least because if Christianity is defined by these doctrines, then we cannot be Christians"[82] and responds to their concern in three ways.

Firstly, she reminds them of the non-credal tradition of Quakerism, stating that Quakers: "have never set much store by doctrines".[83]

Secondly, she declares that in any case doctrines: "cannot be a full definition of Christianity",[84] so rejecting the doctrines she has mentioned does not necessarily mean abandoning Christianity itself.

Thirdly, she claims that reluctance to give up traditional modes of thought is partly due to "fear" and partly to "nostalgia" and both of these are unjustified. We do not need to fear that God will punish us if we do not hold the right beliefs because "The love of God casts out fear. True religion consists not in right belief but in right relationship".[85]    Furthermore, we must not let a nostalgic regard for long held beliefs hold back the development of our religion, because such beliefs and the music and arts and buildings which both express and reinforce them are only symbols and:

> We must hold to our symbols lightly for as long as they are helpful but let them go gradually as we seek new interpretations. For the power lies not in the symbols themselves but in the Spirit they try to represent. It is the Spirit we seek.[86]

---

[80] ibid p.10

[81] ibid p.11

[82] ibid p.11

[83] ibid p.52

[84] ibid p.52

[85] ibid p.52

[86] ibid p.53

The second point at which she tries to accommodate more conservative views comes after she has suggested that the idea that Christ was the "bearer of revelation": "...can be held without there being any logical necessity to maintain the divinity of Jesus".[87] She concedes that this conclusion will be "unacceptable" to those Quakers whose experience of God is "closely bound to Jesus"[88] and for their sake she tries to consider what it might mean to say that Christ is divine.

Her first suggestion is that we should see the "Christ event" as a symbol of the fact that in the end all of humanity will be brought into unity with God and to back up this idea she quotes Macquarrie's statement that the person of Christ points us to:

> ...the coming into one of deity and humanity of creative Being and creaturely being ... Christ is the first- fruits but the Christian hope is that in Christ God will bring all men to God-manhood.[89]

This statement by Macquarrie is a highly orthodox one and Scott qualifies it in two ways which minimize its support for traditional views of Christ. Firstly, she suggests that this way of looking at Jesus is really an expression of faith: "...in God's ultimate redeeming purpose" and: "it is possible to believe in this purpose without faith in Jesus" so faith in Him is not necessary.[90] Secondly, she argues that this view of Jesus does not justify the traditional ideas of Christ's incarnation or pre-existence with God before the incarnation.[91]

Her second suggestion is that we can see Christ not as a symbol of the deification of Man but as: "a symbol of God, a concrete example of divine being and action".[92] In her view this is a useful symbol for God because it enables us to see God as sharing our vulnerability, and as being present in every aspect of our lives and in every human being.[93] However she qualifies this understanding of

---

[87] ibid p.60

[88] ibid p.60

[89] ibid p.60 quoting Macquarrie *Principles of Christian Theology* rev.ed. p.303.

[90] ibid p.60

[91] ibid p.60

[92] ibid p.60

[93] ibid pp.60-61

Christ also by insisting, as I have noted, that the revelation of God given through
this symbol is not a final or unique revelation of God.

The third point at which Scott endeavours to take into account the beliefs
of more conservative Quakers is at the conclusion of her discussion of revelation.
She contends, as we have seen, that part of the revelation of God given through
Christ is: "an invitation to abandon certainty and to live with risk".  Having made
this point Scott then applies it to the debate between radicals and conservatives
within British Quakerism concerning whether or not Quakers are Christians by
declaring:

> ...we may answer the question 'Are Quakers Christian?' by saying
> that it does not matter.  What matters to Quakers is not the label by
> which we are called or call ourselves, but the life.   The
> abandonment of self to God means the abandonment of labels, of
> doctrines, of cherished ways of expressing the truth.  It means the
> willingness to follow the Spirit wherever it leads and there is no
> guarantee that this is to Christianity or to any 'happy ending' except
> the love, peace and unity of God.[94]

That is to say, Scott claims that the very revelation of God in Christ which is so
important to conservative Quakers should itself lead them to see that it is not
ultimately that important whether Quakers are Christians or not.

The final point at which Scott tries to bridge the division between radical
and conservative Quakers is in a discussion of her idea that God is disclosed
through an infinitely large number of models, all of which can be held
simultaneously.  She maintains that one of the virtues of this idea is that it helps to
resolve the tension between Christ-centred and universalist views of Quakerism
because it enables us to see these as:

Known?

> ...two emphases, two ways out of many in which God is disclosed.
> Both are significant to Quakerism, but neither is the whole truth.
> The truth of God is greater than both of these models, and this
> principle is maintained by the maintenance of the tension which
> comes from holding both simultaneously.[95]

---

[94] ibid p.70

[95] ibid p.72

In other words, both Christian and Universalist Quakers are right, but neither of them are exclusively right and both are needed within Quakerism.

# Chapter Seven
# Summary and Further Questions

## Summary

In this study I have shown that in the period before the Manchester Conference British Quaker theology as a whole was Evangelical in character and fell within the mainstream Christian theological tradition, whereas contemporary British Quaker theology, exemplified by Scott's lecture, generally falls outside this tradition and is marked by extreme theological diversity. I have also examined how and why this change took place.

As I explained in Chapters Two to Six this change took place in three stages.

Firstly, from the time of the Manchester Conference the efforts of a group of Liberal Quakers, led by men such as John Wilhelm Rowntree, William Charles Braithwaite and Rufus Jones, resulted in Liberal Quakerism replacing Evangelicalism as the dominant form of theology among Quakers in this country. This process took place gradually, but was completed by the time *Christian Doctrine* was revised between 1919 and 1921.

Secondly, from then onwards until the end of the 1950's, Liberal Quakerism remained the dominant form of British Quaker theology. However, it was challenged during this period both by Evangelical Quakers who regarded it as too Liberal and by Radical Quakers who regarded it as too conservative.

Thirdly, from the beginning of the 1960's British Quaker theology ceased to be dominated by Liberal Quakerism and as a result it has become highly diverse, being divided between a radical wing and one that is more conservative, and has not been dominated by any one school of thought.

During the first two stages British Quaker theology moved away from the mainstream Christian theological tradition but it still remained on the whole an explicitly Christian form of theology in which Christ was given a central place, was seen as having a uniquely close relationship with God and was believed to be the one who brought salvation to mankind.

During the third stage British Quaker theology has moved even further away from the Christian mainstream, to the extent that an influential strand of Quaker thinking would now question whether Christ should have a central role in theology and whether Quakerism should still be viewed as an essentially Christian form of religion.

The reason for the theological change which has taken place in British Quakerism has been the outworking of two principles which were central to Quaker Liberalism.

The first principle was that Quakerism should adapt itself to the contemporary development of thought. It was the application of this principle that led the Quaker Liberals to move away from the mainstream Christian theological tradition as they followed theologians from a variety of denominations in rejecting those aspects of traditional Christian belief which seemed incompatible with the modern thought of their day. It has also been this principle that has caused Radical Quakers to move even further away from the mainstream Christian tradition since the 1960's as they have tried to develop forms of Quakerism which they think will fit in with the increasingly secularised and pluralist outlook of our day.

The second principle was intellectual tolerance. This principle has led Quakers to feel free to reject those aspects of the Christian tradition they have found unacceptable. It has resulted in ever increasing diversity as Quaker writers have felt free to utilise different aspects of contemporary thought, the works of different non-Quaker theologians and different facets of the Quaker tradition to produce their own particular versions of Quaker belief.

In this study I have also established that in the years since the Manchester Conference British Quaker theology has ceased to be in agreement with the teaching of the early Quakers. As I explained in Chapter One, although the early Quakers did not entirely agree with the mainstream Christian theological tradition they were nevertheless in general agreement with it on the five subjects of Revelation, God, Christ, Man and Salvation. Therefore in departing from this tradition in its treatment of these five subjects British Quaker theology has also departed from early Quaker teaching.

It might perhaps be argued that while the contemporary British Quaker theology which Scott represents differs from the letter of early Quaker teaching it has nevertheless retained its essential spirit. For instance Marsden argues that ".... though we do not use their language in the mode in which they used it, their spirit is preserved in us".[1] I find this difficult to accept. How can we separate the 'spirit' of early Quakerism from what the early Quakers actually said? It seems easier to accept that if modern Quakers have said something different from what the early Quakers said then this points to a real difference between modern and early Quakerism.

For example, in *Introducing Quakers* Gorman quotes the declaration of Penn:

> It is not opinion, or speculation, or notions of what is true, or assent to, or the subscription of articles or propositions, though never so soundly worded, that .... makes a man a true believer or a true Christian; but it is a conformity of mind and practice to the will of God, in all holiness of conversation, according to the dictates of this Divine principle of light and life in the soul, which denotes a person truly a child of God.[2]

and argues that this means that for early Quakers such as Penn:

> ...the quest for truth started with the awareness of values known in their personal experience, which could rightly be described as spiritual. These were not magical, supernatural qualities injected into them, but the very values that made them truly human. Yet

---

[1] Marsden *The Prepared Heart* p.18.

[2] Gorman *Introducing Quakers* p.10

while really their own, these values seemed to have a transcendent quality about them that pointed to a source beyond human life, yet never divorced from it.[3]

Gorman is equating Penn's theology with his own secularised religious beliefs. This equation seems to me to be a false one. Penn's belief in a "Divine principle of light and life in the soul" is not the same as Gorman's belief in the existence of spiritual values. These beliefs are different and it is a mistake to try to pretend that they are really the same. Similarly, it would be a mistake to pretend that British Quaker theology since 1895 has really been in agreement with the thought of the early Quakers.

## Some Further Questions

Those are my conclusions about the nature and development of British Quaker theology during the period of uncertainty and transition through which it has passed in the years since the Manchester Conference. In my judgement these conclusions raise a number of questions which contemporary Quakers might profitably consider.

### Was the development of Liberal Quakerism necessary?

In his book *The Quakers their Story and Message* Brayshaw declares that the development of Liberal Quakerism:

> ...has brought to many a firmer hold on Christian faith, a deeper understanding of the Quaker setting forth of it, and an increase both of desire and ability to make this known.[4]

However, it can be asked whether these results could have been achieved in some other way. Did meeting the challenge of 'modern thought' and commending Christianity and Quakerism to the younger generation necessarily involve the development of a theology which moved away from the core of conviction and the Quaker tradition? For example, in his Kerr lectures for 1891, *The Christian View*

---

[3] ibid p.10

[4] Brayshaw op.cit.p.263

*of God and the World*, the Scottish Presbyterian theologian James Orr gives a detailed and wide ranging defence of traditional Christian belief in the face of the challenges posed to it by contemporary thought.[5] If Quaker Evangelicals such as J. Bevan Braithwaite or Alice Hodgkin had been able to mount a similar defence of the beliefs of Evangelical Quakerism might not this have been able to meet the pastoral needs of British Quakerism just as effectively as Liberal Quakerism did?

### Was Evangelicalism as flawed as it has been portrayed?

Since Evangelical Quakerism ceased to be the dominant form of Quakerism in this country it has tended to receive a 'bad press' among British Quakers. For example, in *The Faith of a Quaker* Graham declares:

> Though modified Evangelical beliefs have always been held within the society, and are not inconsistent with it, they make its testimony rather blurred; it loses incisiveness. The plate is somewhat fogged. The modern Liberal theology is a far more congenial intellectual outfit for the Friend.[6]

The question I want to ask is whether this negative verdict needs to be accepted. Could it not be argued that Evangelical Quakerism was more authentically Quaker than subsequent British Quaker theology has been, since its theology was far more closely in line with the beliefs of the first founders of Quakerism?

### Is Liberal tolerance essential to Quakerism?

As I have explained, since Quaker Liberalism became dominant within British Quakerism it has come to be seen as axiomatic that intellectual tolerance is an essential part of Quakerism. For example, in his introduction to Damaris Parker-Rhodes' autobiography *The way out is the way in* David Blamires states:

> Quakers are theologically liberal in outlook, undogmatic as regards matters of Christian belief and insistent on the primacy of personal experience. Among them are to be found individuals at many stages on the spiritual journey, some with a firm, simple Christian

---

[5] James Orr *The Christian View of God and the World* 7ed. Edinburgh: Andrew Elliot 1904

[6] Graham *The Faith of a Quaker* p.141

commitment akin to that of mainstream Churches, while others
have an openness of approach that may seem venturesome or
foolhardy; all are held together by mutual tolerance and respect.[7]

This statement of Blamires is perfectly accurate as a description of what British
Quakerism is like today, but what he says would not have been true of British
Quakerism before 1895, and would certainly not have been true of Quakers in the
seventeenth century. Even a cursory reading of early Quaker literature such as
Fox's journal makes it abundantly obvious that the early Quakers were neither
theologically liberal, nor undogmatic, and that their dealings with those with whom
they disagreed were not normally marked by either tolerance or respect. As a
contemporary Puritan observer, Francis Higginson, put it:

> They (the Quakers) are also as horrible railers as ever any age
> brought forth, a generation whose mouths are full of bitterness,
> whose throats are open sepulchres, etc. The Billingsgate oyster-
> women are not comparable to them in the letters they write to other
> men to call them fools, sots, hypocrites, vain men, beasts,
> blasphemers, murderers of the just. It is a customary thing with this
> gang of people in their discourse with others, to tell them they are
> dogs, heathen, etc.[8]

The sort of liberal tolerance described by Blamires has only really been a
feature of Quakerism since 1895, and this raises the question of whether it is
essential to Quakerism. Could it not be argued that a form of Quakerism that was
less liberal and tolerant, because more deeply committed to the propagation of
traditional Christian and Quaker beliefs, might have just as much claim to be in the
Quaker tradition as the form of Quakerism which exists in this country at present.

### Has the move away from the core of conviction and the Quaker tradition been theologically justified?

During this century many theologians have written in defence of the sort of
beliefs which British Quakers have largely abandoned as a result of their move
away from the core of conviction and the Quaker tradition. Nor can these

---

[7] Damaris Parker-Rhodes *The way out is the way in* London: Quaker Home Service 1985 p.3

[8] Francis Higginson *The Irreligion of the Northern Quakers* 1653 quoted in Barbour and Roberts op.cit. p.75

theologians be dismissed as simply ignorant 'fundamentalists'.  Jurgen Moltmann, Karl Barth, and Emil Brunner are arguably three of the greatest Protestant theologians of this century.  Yet Moltmann expounds the doctrine of the Trinity in *The Trinity and the Kingdom of God*,[9] Barth defends the doctrine that Christ is true God and true Man in *Church Dogmatics* 1:2,[10] and Emil Brunner describes the Cross in penal and sacrificial terms in his book *The Mediator*.[11]  Given that such eminent theologians have been prepared to accept beliefs which British Quakers this century have largely abandoned, the question arises as to whether these British Quakers have been right to reject them.  Might it not be the case that they have been too precipitate in their abandonment of these beliefs, and that there is more to be said for them than they have allowed?

### What are the proper criteria for judging whether any theological belief is compatible with Quakerism?

Given that they have largely rejected the beliefs of the early Quakers, what alternative criteria have contemporary Quakers now got for deciding whether any given belief is or is not compatible with Quakerism?

For example, in a document entitled *The Road to Damascus - Kairos and Conversion*,[12] a group of Third World Christians identify a phenomenon which they call 'Right Wing Christianity',[13] which they describe as:

> ...a way of believing that rejects or ignores parts of God's revelation and selects or distorts other parts in order to support the ideology of the national security state.[14]

If someone wished to put forward this form of Christianity as a part of Quakerism why would they be wrong to do so?  Given the enormous variety of theologies

---

[9] Jurgen Moltmann *The Trinity and the Kingdom of God*  Tr. Margaret Kohl London: SCM 1981

[10] Barth op.cit. pp. 120-202

[11] Emil Brunner *The Mediator*  Tr. Olive Wyon  London: Lutterworth Press 1934  Bk. 3 Section 2.

[12] *The Road to Damascus - Kairos and Conversion*  London and Washington: Catholic Institute for International Relations, Center of Concern, and Christian Aid.

[13] ibid p.19

[14] ibid p.19

which exist within Quakerism at the moment why should an extreme right wing theology not be added to the list? The Christians who produced *The Road to Damascus* reject 'Right Wing Christianity' because their faith in Jesus Christ has led them to believe that: "God is on the side of the poor, the oppressed, and the persecuted".[15] On what specifically Quaker grounds could it be rejected? If it were argued, for instance, that the support given by 'Right Wing Christianity' to the national security state was incompatible with the traditional Quaker belief in peace and social justice, why should it not be counter-argued that Quakers should abandon their belief in these, in the same way as they have abandoned other traditional Quaker beliefs?

To put the question simply, where are the limits of Quaker diversity, and how could these limits be justified? Should the limits of Quakerism simply be what the Quaker consensus is willing to accept at any given time, or is some more fundamental standard of assessment required? If so, what should this be?

**What is the identity of Quakerism?**

The final question which I think is raised by my study of the development of British Quaker Theology since 1895 is that of the theological identity of Quakerism.

Prior to 1895 Quakers in this country were in general agreement that Quakerism stood for a form of Christian belief that was close to the theology of the core of conviction. Since that date this consensus has gradually ceased to exist, with the result that there are today a great diversity of opinions among British Quakers about what Quakerism stands for, and there is a fundamental division over whether or not it should be understood as a specifically Christian form of religion.

This means that British Quakerism as a whole is now unsure of its theological identity. As a body, the Society of Friends in this country is not sure what it believes.

---

[15] ibid p.13

If the man in the street mentioned at the beginning of this thesis was to ask about the meaning of contemporary British Quakerism he would not get a very clear answer.

For instance, the book *Quakers in the Eighties - What its like to be a Friend*,[16] is designed to introduce Quakerism to non-Quakers. It gives eighteen interpretations of Quakerism by contemporary British Quakers, and these are all different.

The issue which British Quakers might want to consider is whether this lack of clarity is a sign of a healthy open-minded pluralism, or simply of theological confusion?

---

[16] Anne Hoskins and Alison Sharman (eds.) *Quakers in the Eighties - What its like to be a Friend* London: Quaker Home Service 1980

# Bibliography

1.PRIMARY SOURCES - QUAKER

## Seventeenth Century

Barclay, Robert *Apology for the true Christian Divinity* London: 1676
    *Catechism* London: 1673
Bathurst, Elizabeth *Truth Vindicated* London: 1691
Burrough, Edward *Declaration to all the World of Our Faith* London: 1657 *The Memorable Works of a son of Thunder and Consolation* London: 1672
Dewsbury, William *A True Prophecy of the Mighty Day of the Lord* London: 1654
Fox, George
    *A collection of many select and Christian Principles* London: 1698
    *A line of righteousness stretched forth* London: 1661
    *George Fox's Book of Miracles*; Henry J. Cadbury (ed) Cambridge: CUP 1948
    *Paper to Friends to Keep out of Wars and Fights* Swarthmore Manuscript 7:47 N.D. Text in H. Barbour and A.O. Roberts (eds) *Early Quaker Writings* Grand Rapids: Eerdmans 1973 pp.406-7
    *The Journal of George Fox* John W. Nickalls (ed) London: Religious Society of Friends 1975
Howgill, Francis *The Glory of the True Church discovered* London:1661
Nayler, James *The Lamb's war against the Man of Sin* London: 1657
Penn, William
    *A key opening the way to every common understanding* London: 1694
    *One Project for the good of England* London: 1679; *Primitive Christianity revived* London: 1696
    *The rise and progress of the people called Quakers* London: 1694
    *The Sandy Foundation Shaken* London: 1668
Penington, Isaac
    *An examination of the Grounds and causes etc.* London: 1660
    *Collected Works* Vols 1-4 London: James Phillips 1784
    *Some positions concerning the Apostacy from the Christian spirit and life* London: 1680
    *The Works* London 1681

## Eighteenth Century

Anon *The True Quakers' Principles defended from Scripture* Lewes: 1786

Besse, Joseph *An abstract of the sufferings of the people called Quakers* 3 vols London: J.Sowle 1735-1738

Bownas, Samuel *An account of the life and travels and Christian Experiences of Samuel Bownas* London: Luke Hinde 1756

Grubb, Sarah *Some account of the Life and Religious Labours of Sarah Grubb* Dublin: R. Jackson 1792

Holmes, Benjamin *A serious call in Christian love to all people to turn to the Spirit of Christ in themselves* London: J.Sowle 1725

London Yearly Meeting
> *Extracts from the Minutes and advices of Yearly Meeting* London: James Phillips 1783
> *Yearly Meeting Epistle 1770 Epistles from Yearly Meeting of Friends* London: Edward Marsh 1858 pp.1-5

Turford, Hugh *The Grounds of a Holy Life* 16th ed London: James Phillips and Sons 1797

## Nineteenth Century

Ash, Edward *The Christian Profession of the Society of Friends* London: John and Arthur Ash 1837

Bevan, John *A Defence of the Christian Doctrines of the Society of Friends against the charge of Socinianism* London: William Phillips 1810

Bevan, Joseph Gurney *Thoughts on Reason and Revelation* London: Phillips and Fardon 1805

*The British Friend* Volumes I-XLIX 1843-1891

Cadbury, Richard *What is my Faith?* Carlisle 1888

Crewdson, Isaac *A beacon to the Society of Friends* Manchester: Henry Smith 1835

Dudley, Elizabeth *The Life of Mary Dudley* London: Elizabeth Dudley 1825

Duncan, David
> *Can an outward revelation be perfect?* 2ed London: F. Bowyer Kitto 1863
> *Essays and Reviews* Manchester: Edward Slater 1861

Foster, J.B. *On Liberty* London: F. Bowyer Kitto 1867: *The Society of Friends and Freedom of thought in 1871* London: F. Bowyer Kitto 1871

*The Friend*
> Old Series vols I-XVIII and New Series vols I-XXXV 1843-1895 'Biblical Criticism' *The Friend* vol XXXVII No. 35, 27th August 1897 pp. 559-60
> 'A Quaker Summer School of Theology' *The Friend* vol XXXVII No. 36 3rd September 1897 p.586

Grubb, Edward *First Lessons on the Hebrew Prophets* London: Headley Bros. 1897

Gurney, Joseph John *A Peculiar People* Richmond Indiana: Friends United Press 1979

Harris, J. Rendel Letter published in *The Friend* vol XXXV No. 48 29th November 1895 pp.784-5

Hodgkin, Howard Letter published in *The Friend* vol XXXV No. 50 13th December 1895 p.825

London Yearly Meeting

*Book of Christian Discipline of the Religious Society of Friends in Great Britain* London: Samuel Harris and Co 1883

*Extracts from the Minutes and advices of Yearly Meeting* London: William Phillips 1803

*Extracts from the Minutes and Proceedings of the Yearly Meeting* London: Edward Marsh 1882

*Extracts from the Minutes and Proceedings of the Yearly Meeting of Friends 1895* London: Office of the Society of Friends 1895

'General Epistle 1836' Text in *Christian Doctrine Practice and Discipline* London: Friends Book Depository 1864 pp.14-17

Manchester Conference *Proceedings of the Manchester Conference* London: Headley Bros. 1896

Pickard, Daniel *An Expostulation on behalf of the Truth* London: A W Bennett 1864

Richmond Conference *Proceedings, including Declaration Christian Doctrine, of the General Conference of Friends held in Richmond , Indiana* Richmond Indiana: Nichols and Bros. 1887

Rowntree, John Stephenson *Quakerism, Past and Present* London: Smith Elder & Co 1859

Rowntree, John Wilhelm 'The Problems of a Free Ministry' in J.W.Rowntree and H.B.Binns (eds) *Present Day Papers* vol II Sept 1899

Rowntree, John Wilhelm and Binns, H.B. (eds) *Present Day Papers* vols I-II 1898-1899

Scarborough Summer School

*Echoes from Scarborough* London: Headley Bros. 1898

*Scarborough Summer School for Religious Study* supplement to *The Friend* 30th April 1897

Shillitoe, Thomas *Journal of the Life and Labours of Thomas Shillitoe* London: Harvey and Darton 1839

Stephen, Caroline E. *Quaker Strongholds* 3ed London: Edward Hicks 1891

Summer School Continuation Committee *First Annual Report 1898*

Tuke, Henry *Principles of Religion* London: Phillips and Fardon 1805

Turner, William, Frith, Francis, Pollard, William *A reasonable Faith - by three Friends* London: Macmillan & Co 1884

Wordsell, Edward *The Gospel of Divine Help* London: Samuel Harris and Co 1886

## Twentieth Century

Allen, Richard 'The Open Letter Movement' et al. *Quaker Monthly* vol 60:10
    October 1981 pp.200-1

Anon 'A statement of Faith' *Friends Quarterly Examiner* vol 62 1928 pp.229-38

Anon 'Diversity of Belief United in Worship *Quaker Monthly* vol 54:1 January
    1975 pp.9-10

Arnold, Godwin 'The New Foundation Fellowship' *Quaker Monthly* vol 61:4 April
    1982 pp.69-71

Bell, Robert 'Jesus as the Universal Self' *The Friend* vol 138 No. 36
    September 5th 1980 pp.1111-2

Benson, Lewis
    *Catholic Quakerism* Philadelphia: Book and Publications Committee
    Philadelphia Yearly Meeting 1977
    *The Quaker Vision* New Foundation Publications No. 4 Gloucester: George
    Fox Fund 1979

Blake, Joyce 'I Believe' *The Friend* vol 125 No. 43 October 27th 1967 pp.1134-5

Boobyer, George 'Bible, Creeds, and Quakerism' *The Friend* vol 144 No. 17 April
    25th 1986 pp.517-8

Bowman, Eric F. 'Humanism and Quakerism: 'co-existence or conflict?'*The Friend*
    vol 126 No. 1 January 5th 1968 pp.21-2

Braithwaite, Charles William *Spiritual Guidance in Quaker Experience* London:
    Headley Bros 1909; *What does the Society of Friends stand for?* Bannisdale
    Malton: Yorkshire 1905 Committee N.D.

*The British Friend* New Series vols 10-22 1901-1913

Canter, Bernard 'Life and Eternal Life' *The Friend* vol 122 No. 46 November
    13th 1964 p.1354

Chapman, Frances L.and Chapman. John B. Letter published in *The Friend* vol
    132 No. 1 January 4th 1974 p.17

Committee on Christian Relationship *To Lima with love* London: Quaker Home
    Service 1987

Court, Donald 'A Scientific age and a declining Church what has a Friend to Say?'
    *The Friend* vol 123 No. 39 September 24th 1965 pp.1141-4

Creasey, Maurice
    *A Christian Affirmation* London: Friends Home Service Committee 1969
    *Bearings or Friends and the New Reformation* London: Friends Home
    Service Committee 1969

Curle, Adam 'What do Friends Really Mean?' *The Friend* vol 140 No. 38
    September 17th 1982 p.1167

Doncaster, Hugh
    *That of God in every Man* London: George Allen and Unwin 1963
    *The Quaker Message: Personal Affirmation* Wallingford Pennsylvania:
    Pendle Hill Publications 1972

Dunstan, Edgar G. *Quakers and the Religious Quest* London: George Allen and Unwin 1956

Elliot, Annie M.C. 'Thinking of Salvation' *The Friend* vol 139 No. 46 August 14th 1981 p.1027

Fairn, R. Duncan *Quakerism: A Faith for Ordinary Men* London: George Allen & Unwin 1951

Foat, Richard 'Unless one is Born Anew' *The Friend* vol 126 No. 10 March 8th 1968 pp.269-70

Friends Home Service Committee *Studies in Christian Fundamentals* London: Friends Home Service Committee 1943

Friends' Witness to Scriptural Truth
'Editorial' *Friends' Witness to Scriptural Truth* vol I No. 1 First Month 1908 p.1
'The authority of Holy Scripture' *Friends' Witness to Scriptural Truth* vol I No. 8 Eighth Month 1908 pp.85-6
'The Sin of Unbelief' *Friends' Witness to Scriptural Truth* vol 27 No. 10 Tenth Month 1934 pp.109-10

The Friend 'The Adjourned Yearly Meeting-Revising the Book of Christian Practice' *The Friend* vol L1 No. 46 November 17th 1911 pp.741-50

Fry, Joan M. *The Communion of Life* London: The Swarthmore Press 2ed 1925

Gillman, Harvey *A minority of one* London: Quaker Home Service 1988

Gorman, George *Introducing Quakers* London: Friends Home Service Committee 1974; *The Amazing Fact of Quaker Worship* London: Friends Home Service Committee 1973

Graham, John W.
*The Faith of a Quaker* Cambridge: CUP 1920
*The Quaker Ministry* London: The Swarthmore Press 1925

Green, Thomas
'The Holy Spirit' *Quaker Monthly* vol 43 No. 7 July 1964 p.101
'Studies in Christian Belief 4 - Eternal Life' *Quaker Monthly* vol 43 No. 8 August 1964 pp.121-122

Grubb, Edward
*Authority and the Light Within* London: James Clarke 1908
*Christianity as Life* London: The Swarthmore Press 1927
*Christianity as Truth* London: The Swarthmore Press 1928
'Some Personal Experiences' *Friends Quarterly Examiner* vol 72 October 1938 p.301
*The Historic and Inward Christ* London: Headley Bros. 1914
'The Society of Friends' in W B Selbie (ed) *Evangelical Christianity its W.history and witness* London: Hodder and Stoughton 1911

Hall, Arnold Letter published in *The Friend* vol 128 No. 17 April 24th 1970 p.493

Harris, J. Rendel  *The Origin of the Prologue to John's Gospel*  Cambridge: CUP 1917

Harrison, Cyril
'Love Immeasurable' *The Friend* vol 129 No. 18 April 30th 1971 pp.493-4
'Propagating Quakerism 1' *The Friend* vol 132 No. 7 February 15th 1974 pp.158-9

Harvey, Donald  Letter published in *The Friend*  vol 135 No. 2 January 14th 1977 p.39

Hendley, Sheila  'It's time to Quake' *The Friend* vol 134 No. 51 December 17th 1976  pp.1469-70

Hetherington, Ralph  'Finding a name for it'*The Friend* vol 127 No. 50 December 12th 1969 p.1525

Hobling, Margaret B.  *The Concrete and the Universal* London: George Allen and Unwin 1958

Hodgkin, Alice  'The Fourfold Vision of the Cross' *Friends' Witness to Scriptural Truth* vol XXVII No 6 Sixth Month 1924

Hodgkin, Henry T.  *The Missionary Spirit and the Present Opportunity* London: Headley Bros 1916

Hogan, Gwen  'Miserable Sinners' *The Friend* vol 135 No. 15 April 22nd 1977 pp.445-6

Holtumm, Eric
'Agents of God' *The Friend* vol 139 No. 8 February 20th 1981 pp.205-6
Letter published in *The Friend*  vol 126 No. 4 January 26th 1968 p.110

Hoskins, Anne and Sharman, Alison (eds)  *Quakers in the Eighties* London: Quaker Home Service 1980

Hubbard, Geoffrey  *Quaker by Convincement*  London: Quaker Home Service 1974

Hughes, John A  'Quakerism and Christianity' *The Friend* vol XCIII No. 5 February 1st 1935 pp.89-92

James, Edward  'The Personality of God' *The Friend* vol 125 No. 2 January 13th 1967  pp.37-8

Jones, Rufus M.
*A dynamic faith* London: Headley Bros 1901
*Quakerism a religion of life* London: Headley Bros. 1908
*The Double Search*  London: Headley Bros 1906
*The trail of life in college* London: Macmillan & Co. 1929

Lampen, John  *Twenty Questions about Jesus* London: Quaker Home Service 1985

Lawton, John C.  Letter published in *The Friend*  vol 134 No. 47 November 19th 1976 p 1360

Lea, Alec
'An immense salvation purpose' *Quaker Monthly* vol 64 No. 8 August 1985 pp.158-9

'Through the Cobweb Curtain' *The Friend* vol 143 No. 1 January 4th 1985 pp.5-6

Linton, John *Quakerism as Forerunner* Quaker Universalist Group Pamphlet No. 1 1984.

LondonYearlyMeeting

*Christian Discipline of the Religious Society of Friends in Great Britain and Australia - Part III Church Government* London: Headley Bros 1906

*Christian Discipline of London Yearly Meeting of the Religious Society of Friends - Part II Christian Practice* London: Headley Bros 1911

*Christian Discipline of London Yearly Meeting of the Religious Society of Friends - Part III Church Government* London: Friends' Bookshop 1917

*Christian Faith and Practice in the experience of the Society of Friends* London: London Yearly Meeting 1959

*Christian Life Faith and Thought in the Society of Friends* London: The Friends Bookshop 1922

*Extracts from the Minutes and Proceedings of London Yearly Meeting of Friends* London: Office of the Society of Friends 1917

*London Yearly Meeting of the Society of Friends 1932* London: Friends House 1932

Loukes, Harold *The Quaker Contribution* London: SCM Press 1965

Marsden, Lorna M.

'Fox's Word of Life' *Friends Quarterly* vol 19 No.7 July 1976 p.296

*The Prepared Heart* London: Quaker Home Service 1988

Miles, T.R.

*Religion and the Scientific Outlook* London: Allen and Unwin 1959

*Towards Universalism* Leicester: Quaker Universalist Group N.D.

Mitchelson, Mary 'The Fall - History and Myth' *The Friend* vol 134 No. 18 April 30th 1976 pp.485-7

Neill, Joyce *Credo* London: Quaker Home Service 1986

North, Peter 'Walking in the light' *Quaker Monthly* vol 54 No. 6 June 1975 pp.117-8

Payne, Jesse 'I Believe' *Quaker Monthly* vol 129 No. 18 April 30th 1981 pp.171-8

Peacock, Arthur

Letter published in *The Friend* vol 134 No. 14 April 2nd 1976 pp.374-5

'The Christhood of all Mankind' *The Friend* July 11th 1975 pp.783-4

'The Quaker Universalist Group' *Quaker Monthly* vol 61:5 May 1982 pp.95-6

Petrie, Gerald Letter published in *The Friend* vol 109 No. 8 February 23rd 1951 p.160

Pickard, Bertram and Irene Letter published in *The Friend* vol XCIII No.7 February 15th 1935 pp.150-1

Priestland, Gerald  *Reasonable Uncertainty - a Quaker approach to doctrine*
    London: Quaker Home Service 1982

✗ Punshon, John

    ✗ *Encounter with Silence* Richmond Indiana and London: Friends United Press
        and Quaker Home Service 1987

    Letter published in *The Friend* vol 133 No. 10 March 7th 1975 p 246

Quaker Women's Group  *Bringing the invisible into light* London: Quaker Home
    Service 1984

Rhodes, Damaris Parker  'Our Corporate Commitment to Christ' *The Friend* vol
    128 No.46 November 13th 1970 pp.1349-51; *The way out is the way in*
    London: Quaker Home Service 1985

Richards, Gerald  Letter published in *The Friend*  vol 135 No. 9 March 4th 1977
    pp.255-6

Richardson, Lawrence  'Newcastle Upon Tyne Friends and Scientific thought'
    *Journal of The Friends' Historical Society* vol XLV 1953  pp.40-44

Rowntree, John Wilhelm and Binns, H.B. (eds)  *Present Day Papers*  vols III-V
    1900-1902

Sandy, Joseph R.  Letter published in *The Friend*  vol 128 No. 45 November 6th
    1970  p.1338

Scott, Janet  *What canst thou say?*  London: Quaker Home Service 1980

Scott, Richenda C.

    *Rejections and Discoveries* London: Friends Home Service Committee 1965
    *Tradition and Experience* London: George Allen and Unwin 1964

Snell, Beatrice Saxon

    'Atonement and Redemption' *Quaker Monthly* vol 44 No. 5 May 1965  p.68
    'Humble learners in the School of Christ' *The Friend* vol 123 No. 4 June 11th
        1965  pp.693-4

    Letter published in *The Friend* vol 134 No. 14 April 2nd 1976 p.375

Soper, Betty  Letter published in *The Friend* vol 133 No. 42 October 17th 1975
    p.1179

Stephen, Caroline E.  *The Vision of Faith* Cambridge: Heffers 1911

Summer School ContinuationCommittee  *Third Annual Report 1900; Sixth Annual
    Report 1903; Tenth Annual Report 1907*

Thompson, Silvanus P.

    *A not impossible Religion*  London: The Bodley Head 1918
    *The Quest for Truth* London: Headley Bros 1917

Vincent, Ben  Letter published in *The Friend*  vol LXVIII No. 31 August 3rd 1928
    pp.708-9

Wilsher, Barry  *Quaker Organisation*  London: Quaker Home Service 1986

Wood, Herbert G.

    *Quakerism and the Future of the Church*  London: The Swarthmore Press
        1920
    *Why did Christ die?*  London: Epworth Press 1953

*The Quaker Understanding of the Christian Faith* London: Friends' Home
    Service Committee 1955
Woodbrooke College *Woodbrooke Settlement for Religious and Social Study*
    *Programme of Lectures* Spring Term 1905
York, Alan 'The Allegory of God' *Quaker Monthly* vol 65  December 1986 p.239


2. PRIMARY SOURCES - NON QUAKER

**Creeds Confessions and Statements of Faith**

*Apostles'Creed*  Text in John H Leith (ed) *Creeds of the Churches*  Richmond Va:
    John Knox Press  revd ed. 1973  pp.22-26
*AugsburgConfession*  Text in ibid pp.63-107
*Chalcedonian Definition*  Text in Henry Bettenson (ed) *Documents of the*
    *Christian Church* 2ed Oxford: OUP 1979  pp.51-2
*Council of Orange*  Text in Leith op.cit. pp.37-45
*Decrees of the Council of Trent*  Text in ibid pp.399-439
*Dordrecht Confession*  Text in ibid pp.292-308
*Edwardian Homilies*  Text in ibid pp.230-66
*Nicene Creed*  Text in Bettenson  op.cit. pp.25-6
*The Road to Damascus- Kairos and Conversion* London and Washington:
    Catholic institute for international relations, Center of Concern and Christian
    Aid
*Westminster Confession*  Text in Leith op.cit. pp.192-230


**Works by individual writers**

**Patristic**

Athanasius
    *On the Incarnation of the Word* Text in Edward R Hardy (ed)
    *Christology of the Later Fathers* Philadelphia and London: Westminster
    Press and SCM 1954 pp.41-110
Augustine of Hippo
    *Enchiridion on Faith Hope and Love* Tr.J F Shaw Chicago: Regnery
    Gateway 1961
    *The City of God* Tr. Henry Bettenson  Harmondsworth: Penguin 1972
*Epistle to Diognetus*  Text in *Early Christian Writings* Tr. Maxwell Staniforth
    Harmondsworth: Penguin 1978 pp.169-85
Gregory of Nyssa *Address on Religious Instruction* Text in Hardy op cit  pp.268-
    325 and 300

Irenaeus of Lyons
    *Adversus Omnes Haereses* text in A Roberts and J Donaldson (eds)
    *The Ante Nicene Fathers vol 1* Grand Rapids: Eerdmans 1981
Justin Martyr *Apology* text in Justin Martyr *The Works* Oxford: Parker 1861

### Reformation and Puritan

Bullinger, Heinrich *The Fourth Decade* Parker Society edition Cambridge: CUP
    1851
Calvin,John *Institutes of the Christian Religion* Tr. Henry Beveridge Grand
    Rapids: Eerdmans 1975
Luther, Martin *A Commentary on St. Paul's Epistle to the Galatians* Philip S.
    Watson (ed) Cambridge: James Clarke 1978
Luther, Martin *Lectures on Romans* Tr. Wilhelm Pauck Philadelphia and London
    Westminster Press and SCM 1961
Vincent, T *The Shorter Catechism Explained from Scripture* London 1679

### Nineteenth Century

Dale, R.W.
    *The Atonement* London: Congregational Union 1894
    *The Living Christ and the Four Gospels* London: Hodder and Stoughton
    1891
Denison, G A *A Letter to the Rev C. Gore* London: Longman Green and co 1890
Driver, S.R. *An Introduction to the Literature of the Old Testament* 7ed
    Edinburgh: T and T Clark 1898
Fairbairn, A. M.
    *Christ in Modern Theology* London: Hodder and Stoughton 1893
    *The City of God* London: Hodder and Stoughton 1883
Feuerbach, L.A. *The Essence of Christianity* Tr. Mary Ann Evans London: J
    Chapman 1853
Gore, Charles (ed) *Lux Mundi* London: John Murray 1889
Horton, R.F. *Inspiration and the Bible* London: T. Fisher Unwin 1888
Spurgeon, C.H. *The Sword and the Trowel* vol. XXIII No.72 August 1887
Temple, F.W. *The relations between religion and science* London: Macmillan
    1884
Temple, F.W. et al *Essays and Reviews* London: J W Parker 1860
Westcott, B.F. *The Gospel of the Resurrection* 4ed London: Macmillan 1889

### Twentieth Century

Adam, Karl *The Christ of Faith* New York: New American Library 1957
Baillie, John *Our Knowledge of God* Oxford: OUP 1939

Barr, James *The Bible in the Modern World* London: SCM 1973

Barth, Karl *Church Dogmatics* 1:2 Tr. G.T. Thomson and Harold Knight
    Edinburgh: T and T Clark 1956

Bentley, G.B. *The Resurrection of the Bible* Westminster: Dacre Press 1940

Bowden, John *Jesus - the unanswered questions* London: SCM 1988

Brunner, Emil
    *The Divine Human Encounter* Tr. Amadus W. Loos London: SCM 1944
    *The Mediator* Tr. Olive Wyon London: Lutterworth Press 1934

Bultmann, Rudolph *Jesus and the Word* Tr. L.P.Smith and E.H. Lantero London
    and Glasgow: Fontana 1958

Cuppitt, Don *Taking Leave of God* London: SCM 1980

Daly, Mary *Beyond God the Father* Boston: Beacon Press 1973

Fackre, Gabriel *The Christian Story* Grand Rapids: Eerdmans 1978

Hick, John,
    *Evil and the God of Love* 2ed London: Macmillan 1977
    *God has many names* London: SCM 1980
    'Towards a philosophy of religious pluralism' in *Faith and Freedom* 34:3:102
    1981

Hick, John (ed) *The Myth of God Incarnate* London: SCM 1977

Hodgson, Leonard *For faith and freedom* London: SCM 1968

Hodgson, Peter and King, Robert (eds) *Christian Theology* London: SPCK 1983

Jung, C.G. *Psychology and Religion* Yale: Yale University Press 1938

Kee, Alistair *The way of Transcendence* Harmondsworth: Penguin 1971

Lake, K. *The Resurrection of Christ* London: Williams and Norgate 1907

Lampe, G.W.H. *God as Spirit* Oxford: OUP 1977

Lewis, C.S.
    *Mere Christianity* London: Geoffrey Bles 1952
    *Miracles* Glasgow: Collins 1985
    *The Problem of Pain* Glasgow: Collins 1978

Liddon, H.P. *The Divinity of Our Lord and Saviour Jesus Christ* 14th ed
    London: Longmans Green and Co 1900

Lossky, Vladimir *The Mystical Theology of the Eastern Church* London and
    Cambridge: James Clarke 1957

Macquarrie, John
    *Principles of Christian theology* 1st ed London: SCM 1966
    *Principles of Christian theology* revd ed London: SCM 1977

Mascall, E.L. *Man: His origin and Destiny* Westminster: Dacre Press 1940

Moltmann, Jurgen *The Trinity and the Kingdom of God* Tr. Margaret Kohl
    London: SCM 1981

Nicolai, G.F. *The biology of War* London: J.M. Dent 1919

Nineham, D.E.
    *St. Mark* Harmondsworth Penguin 1963
    *The use and abuse of the Bible* London: SPCK 1976

Orr, James
    *Sin as a problem of Today* London: Hodder and Stoughton 1912
    *The Christian view of God and the world* Edinburgh: Andrew Elliot 7ed
    1904
Robinson, J.A.T.  *Honest to God* London: SCM 1963
Robinson, J.A.T. and Edwards, D.L.  *The Honest to God Debate* London: SCM
    1963
Rosenthal, Robert and Jackson, Lenore  *Pygmalion in the Classroom* Eastbourne:
    Holt-Saunders 1968
Sanday, W.R.
    *Christologies Ancient and Modern* Oxford: Clarendon Press 1910
    *Inspiration* Oxford: OUP 1893
Streeter, B.H.  *The Four Gospels* London: Macmillan 1924
Torrance, T.F.  *Reality and Scientific Theology* Edinburgh: Scottish Academic
    Press 1985
van Buren, Paul  *The Secular Meaning of the Gospel* London: SCM 1963
Vermes, Geza
    *Jesus and the World of Judaism* London: SCM 1983
    *Jesus the Jew* London: SCM 1983
    *The Dead Sea Scrolls* London: SCM 1982
Vidler, A.R. (ed)
    *Objections to Christian Belief* London: Constable 1963
    *Soundings* Cambridge: CUP 1962
Ware, Kallistos  *The Orthodox Way* London: Mowbrays 1979
Williams, H.A.  *The true wilderness* Harmondsworth: Penguin 1968

## 3. SECONDARY SOURCES - QUAKER

Baker, W.K.  *John T Dorland* London: Headley Bros 1898
Barbour, Hugh  *The Quakers in Puritan England* New Haven and London:  Yale
    University Press 1964
Barbour, Hugh  and Roberts, Arthur (eds) *Early Quaker Writings* Grand Rapids:
    Eerdmans 1973
Barclay, Robert  *The inner life of the Religious Societies of the Commonwealth*
    London: Hodder and Stoughton 1879
Besse, Joseph  *An abstract of the sufferings people called Quakers* vols 1-3
    London: J. Sowle 1735-38
Braithwaite, William Charles
    *The beginnings of Quakerism* London: Macmillan 1912
    *The Second Period of Quakerism* London: Macmillan 1919
Brayshaw, A. Neave  *The Quakers their story and message* London: The
    Swarthmore Press rev ed 1927

Brinton, Howard *Friends for 300 years* London: George Allen and Unwin 1953

Creasey, Maurice *Early Quaker Christology* Manasquan N J: Catholic and Quaker Studies 2 1973

Davis, Robert (ed) *Woodbrooke 1903-1953* London: Bannisdale Press 1953

Doncaster, L. Hugh 'Rufus Jones 1863-1948 1 His Life' *The Friend* vol 121 No. 4 Jan 25th 1963 p.92

Dudley, James *The life of Edward Grubb* London: James Clarke and Co 1946

Grubb, Edward *The Evangelical Movement and its impact on the Society of Friends* Leominster: Orphans Printing Press 1924

Hodgson, William *The Society of Friends in the Nineteenth Century* Philadelphia: Smith Elder and Co 1875

Jones, Rufus M.
  *Studies in Mystical Religion* London: Macmillan 1909
  *Spiritual Reformers in the 16th and 17th centuries* London: Macmillan 1914
  *The later periods of Quakerism* 2 vols London: Macmillan 1921

Jones, Rufus, Sharpless, Isaac and Gummere, Amelia *The Quakers in the American Colonies* London: Macmillan 1911

King, Rachel H. *George Fox and the Light Within* Philadelphia: Friends' Book Store 1940

Milligan, E.H. 'How we got our book of Discipline' *The Friends' Quarterly* vol 23 no 3 July 1988 pp.110-17

Punshon, John *Portrait in Grey* London: Quaker Home Service 1984

Scott, Richenda C. 'Authority or experience, John Wilhelm Rowntree and the dilemma of 19th century British Quakerism' *Journal of the Friends Historical Society* vol XLIX Spring 1960 pp.75-95

Sewel, William *History of the rise increase and progress of the Society of Friends* Lindfield: Friends' Library vol 5 1833

Thomas, A.C.B. and Emmott, E.B. *William Charles Braithwaite –memoir and papers* London: Longmans Green and Co 1931

Vining, E.G. *Friend of Life - The biography of Rufus Jones* London: Michael Joseph 1959

Wood, H G *Belief and Unbelief since 1850* Cambridge: CUP 1955


4. SECONDARY SOURCES - NON QUAKER

Atkinson, James *Martin Luther Prophet to the Church Catholic* Exeter: Paternoster Press 1983

Baker, Frank *The relations between the Society of Friends and Early Methodism* London: Epworth Press 1948

Bevan, Edwyn *Christianity* London: OUP 1963

Cave, Sidney *The Doctrine of the Work of Christ* London: Hodder and Stoughton 1947

Chadwick, Owen  *The Victorian Church* vol 2 2ed London: A&C Black 1972

Clarkson,Thomas  *A portraiture of Quakerism* London: Longman 1806

Clements, Keith W.  *Lovers of Discord* London: SPCK 1988

Creighton, Louise  *Life and letters of Thomas Hodgkin* London: Longmans Green and Co 1917

Cross, F L  and Livingstone, E A (eds)  *The Oxford Dictionary of the Christian Church* 2ed Oxford: OUP 1974

Davies, Horton  *Worship and Theology in England from Newman to Martineau 1850-1900* London: OUP 1962

Glover, W.B.  *Evangelical Nonconformists and Higher Criticism in the 19th Century*  London: Independent Press 1954

Harrison, T.  *The Durham Phenomenon* London: Darton, Longman and Todd 1985

Hastings, Adrian  *A History of English Christianity 1920-1985* London: William Collins 1986

Hatch, E.  *The organisation of the Early Christian Churches* 3ed London: Rivingtons 1888

Hebblethwaite, Brian  *The Christian Hope*  Basingstoke: Marshall Morgan & Scott 1984

Hordern, William  'Man, Doctrine of' in Alan Richardson (ed) *A Dictionary of Christian Theology* London: SCM 1969

Isichei, Elizabeth  *Victorian Quakers* Oxford: OUP 1970

Jones, Hubert Cunliffe and Drewery, Benjamin (eds) *A History of Christian Doctrine* Edinburgh: T and T Clark 1980

Kaiser, Christopher B  *The Doctrine of God* London: Marshall Morgan and Scott 1982

Knox, R A  *Enthusiasm* Oxford: OUP 1950

Kung, Hans, Barth, Karl and Cullmann, Oscar et al. *Christianity Divided* London and New York: Sheed and Ward 1962

Lietzmann, Hans  *A History of the Early Church*  vol 4  London: Lutterworth Press 1951

Mackintosh, H.R.  *The Doctrine of the Person of Christ* Edinburgh: T and T Clark 1912

Marshall, I. Howard  *I believe in the Historical Jesus* London: Hodder and Stoughton 1977

McGrath, A E  *Iustitia Dei* vol 1 Cambridge: CUP 1986

Moore, J.R.  *The Post Darwinian Controversies* Cambridge: CUP 1979

Mozley, J.K.  *The Doctrine of the Atonement* London: Duckworth and Co 1915

Murray, I.H.  *The Forgotten Spurgeon* London: Banner of Truth 1966

Neill, Stephen
 *The Christian Society* London: Collins 1964
 *The interpretation of the New Testament 1861-1961* Oxford: OUP 1966

Nesti, Donald S. *Grace and Faith the means to Salvation* Pittsburgh: Catholic and
    Quaker Studies No 3 1975
Pelikan, Jaroslav *The Christian Tradition* vols 1-5  Chicago: Chicago University
    Press 1971-89
Prestige, G.L. *The Life of Charles Gore* London: Heinemann 1935
Reardon, B.M.G. *Religious thought in the Victorian Age* London: Longman 1980
Richardson, Alan *Christian Apologetics* London: SCM 1949
Robinson, H W *The Christian Doctrine of Man* 3 ed Edinburgh: T&T Clark
    1934
Rogerson, J *Old Testament Criticism in the Nineteenth Century: England and
    Germany* London: SPCK 1984
Rowell, G *Hell and the Victorians* Oxford: OUP 1974
Runia, Klaus *The present-day Christological Debate* Leicester: IVP 1984
Schweitzer, A. *The Quest of the Historical Jesus* London: SCM 1954
Selbie, W.B. *The Life of Andrew Martin Fairbairn* London: Hodder and
    Stoughton 1914
Sellers, R.V. *The Council of Chalcedon* London: SPCK 1952
Stephenson, A.M.G. *The rise and decline of English Modernism* London: SPCK
    1984
Sykes, Stephen *The identity of Christianity* London: SPCK 1984
Vidler, A.R.
    *The Church in an Age of Revolution* Harmondsworth: Penguin 1961
    *Twentieth Century Defenders of the Faith* London: SCM 1965
Walsh, J.D.'Origins of the Evangelical Revival' in G.V. Bennett and J.D. Walsh
    (eds) *Essays in Modern English Church History*  London: A&C Black 1966
    pp. 132-62
Watts, Michael *The Dissenters* Oxford: OUP 1978
Young, Frances *Sacrifice and the Death of Christ*  London: SPCK 1975

# Index

Universal Salvation, 239-240, 242,
    261, 262


Van Buren, Paul, 178
Vermes, Geza, 243
Vidler, Alec, 70, 151-4, 155
Vincent, Ben, 145-7
Vincent, Thomas, 27n
Virgin Birth, 115, 137, 166, 222, 241


Walsh, John, 37
Ware, Kallistos, 8, 21n, 136n
Watts, Michael, 10n, 11, 18n
Wellhausen, Julius, 66
Westcott, B.F., 66, 122
Westminster Assembly, 8
Westminster Confession 25n
Whiting, J.R., 85, 92
Williams, Charles, 150
Williams, H.A., 153-4, 162, 203,
    209, 234
Wood, H.G., 47n, 85, 139-140, 183-
    4, 239
Woodbrooke, 84-88
Woodbrooke Extension Committee,
    85
Worsdell, William, 49, 239
York, Alan, 216, 241
Yorkshire 1905 Committee, 87
Young, Frances, 27n